India's New
Middle Class

India's New Middle Class

✳

Democratic Politics in an Era of Economic Reform

Leela Fernandes

University of Minnesota Press

Minneapolis · London

Portions of chapter 2 were published as "Nationalizing 'the Global': Media Images, Cultural Politics, and the Middle Class in India," *Media, Culture, and Society* (2000): 611–28; reprinted with permission of Sage Publications. Parts of chapter 3 were published in "Restructuring the New Middle Class in Liberalizing India," *Comparative Studies of South Asia, Africa, and the Middle East* 20, nos. 1 and 2 (2000): 88–104; reprinted by permission of Duke University Press. Parts of chapter 4 were published in "The Politics of Forgetting: Class Politics, State Power, and the Restructuring of Urban Space in India," *Urban Studies* 41, no. 12 (2004); reprinted with permission by Taylor and Francis.

Published by the University of Minnesota Press
111 Third Avenue South, Suite 290
Minneapolis, MN 55401-2520
http://www.upress.umn.edu

Library of Congress Cataloging-in-Publication Data

Fernandes, Leela.
  India's new middle class : democratic politics in an era of
economic reform / Leela Fernandes.
     p. cm.
  Includes bibliographical references and index.
  ISBN-13: 978-0-8166-4927-3 (hc : alk. paper)
  ISBN-10: 0-8166-4927-8 (hc : alk. paper)
  ISBN-13: 978-0-8166-4928-0 (pb : alk. paper)
  ISBN-10: 0-8166-4928-6 (pb : alk. paper)
  1. Middle class—India. 2. India—Economic conditions—21st century. 3. India—Social conditions—21st century. 4. Democratization—India. I. Title.
  HT690.I4F47 2006
  305.5'50954—dc22

                                                         2006021627

Printed in the United States of America on acid-free paper

The University of Minnesota is an equal-opportunity educator and employer.

12 11 10 09 08 07 06   10 9 8 7 6 5 4 3 2 1

For Ellie

Contents

———※———

Acknowledgments

———————————— ✳ ————————————

During the long period I spent researching and writing this book, I benefited from a number of individual and institutional sources of support and feedback. An early period of field research funded by the American Institute for Indian Studies in 1996 first sparked my interest in the middle class. An American Council for Learned Societies/ Social Science Research Council fellowship enabled me to conduct a longer period of uninterrupted fieldwork in 1998–99. Rutgers University provided crucial support through a Research Council grant, sabbatical leaves, and additional time off through fellowships from the Institute for Research on Women.

During my field research in Mumbai, I benefited from the support, hospitality, and logistical help of a number of people. Ongoing intellectual conversations and support from Sharit Bhowmick were extremely helpful; I am particularly grateful to him for sharing his insights on Mumbai's politics, his help in setting up interviews with union officials, and for introducing me to many interesting faculty members at the University of Mumbai. Andre Ferns provided logistical assistance and helped me set up interviews in the advertising industry. Michele Fernandes provided tireless help and became my de facto research assistant. Finally, I am grateful to Rian and Anu D'Costa for their constant kindness and for generously opening their home to me during all of my visits to Mumbai.

The arguments put forth here have benefited from suggestions, comments, and responses from many people. Miduk Kim, Gaurav Sood, and Anil Jacob offered helpful research assistance. Various chapters benefited from presentations at the Center for Race and

Gender, University of California at Berkeley; the University of California, Irvine's workshop "Race, Labor, and Empire," organized by Gilbert Gonzalez and his colleagues in labor studies; the National University of Singapore's workshop "Forgotten Spaces," organized by Yong-Sook Lee and Brenda Yeoh; the Association for Asian Studies meetings; and a fruitful discussion at the Netsappe meeting in Paris helped shape the introductory chapter.

The manuscript is improved as a result of specific comments, suggestions, and critiques made by many people. Thanks in particular go to Itty Abraham, Karen Barad, Sharit Bhowmick, Tim Bunnell, John Echeverri-Gent, Ruthie Gilmore, Sumit Guha, Christophe Jaffrelot, David Ludden, Leslie McCall, Mustapha Pasha, Peter Reeves, Lloyd Rudolph, Susanne Rudolph, Yong-Sook Lee, E. Sridharan, and Yogendra Yadav. I am also grateful to Patrick Heller for a review of the entire manuscript and for constructive comments that substantially contributed to the shaping of the arguments.

I have been lucky to have had a number of colleagues who provided important support over the years. Amrita Basu, David Laitin, and Susanne Rudolph provided invaluable and ongoing professional support. At Rutgers, several colleagues have been important sources of support. My thanks go to Mike Aronoff, Sue Carroll, Drucilla Cornell, Cyndi Daniels, Nancy Hewitt, Jan Kubik, Dan Tichenor, and my former colleagues who are still missed, Linda Zerilli and Dorothy Ko. I have also benefited from conversations with my comparative politics colleagues Barbara Callaway, Eric Davis, Bob Kaufman, and Michael Shafer.

I am grateful to Jason Weidemann for his help throughout the publication process and to the University of Minnesota Press for support of this project.

At various points, many individuals provided invaluable personal support, distractions, and fun. I am grateful to Caridad, Prema, Brinda, Joan, Karen, Ruthie, Laura, Michelle, Valerie, Carmen, Pearl, Milbhor, Karl, Natalie, and Christopher.

My biggest debt, of course, is owed to the many unnamed individuals who took time away from their hectic schedules in order to share their knowledge and views through interviews and conversations. My hope is that their insights and contributions will surface through-out this book in ways that permanently move us away from stereo-typical views that seek to either condemn or romanticize the Indian middle class, especially from the privileged vantage point of the United States.

Introduction

----- ❋ -----

The most striking feature of contemporary India is the rise of a confident new middle class . . . whether India can deliver the goods depends a great deal on it.

—*Das (2000)*

Harsh Gahlaut's three-month-old Hyundai Accent still smells new. But the 27-year-old is already thinking about his next car. . . . Gahlaut works up to fifteen hours a day—often seven days a week—to earn his living. It is just that he is uninhibited when it comes to spending his earnings—current or future. Consumers like Gahlaut may have existed before too but only as exceptions. Today he is [one of] a new breed of consumers sprouting across cities and among income classes.

—*Goyal (2003)*

A cadre of ambitious government officials, pricey consultants, and local high technology entrepreneurs is trying to accomplish something almost as ambitious—transforming this sleepy farm state capital into the "technology hub of northern India." . . . As tens of thousands of service jobs continue to flow to India from the United States and Europe, small cities like Chandigarh offer even lower labor costs than India's "first tier" technology hubs like Hyderabad, Bombay, and Gurgaon, outside New Delhi.

—*Rohde (2003)*

In recent years, rapid socioeconomic changes in cities and small towns in India have sparked the local, national, and transnational imaginations of writers and political analysts. Small towns are increasingly marked by mushrooming institutes for computer training, Internet booths, and satellite dishes—symbols of India's high-tech globalizing economy. Comfortable middle class housing colonies have sprouted up across the country and new models of cars have displaced the Ambassador, which was once an iconic signifier of middle class status. India's larger metropolises like Mumbai (formerly known as Bombay) and Bangalore now aggressively seek the status of global cities, and their urban middle classes assertively claim a national visible role as the agents of globalization in India.

This new middle class has been represented in film, theater, and the media both by traditional "Bollywood" films and by new genres of films such as Mira Nair's *Monsoon Wedding*, which brought the image of India's upwardly mobile middle class to global audiences. Meanwhile, transnational views of India's new economy have also begun to turn from celebrations of a burgeoning 250-million-strong middle class consumer market to anxieties over an educated workforce that now threatens the U.S. and European middle classes through the outsourcing of service-sector jobs.

Such changing perceptions point to the growing significance of the urban Indian middle class in local, national, and transnational imaginations of globalization in the twenty-first century. The rise of this new middle class identity has begun to shape contemporary politics in India in distinctive ways. Explaining the political dynamics of transnational processes such as globalization and answering questions about how groups resist or consent to policies of economic reforms require an analytical lens that can address the political emergence of groups such as the new middle class. A study of the rise of the new Indian middle class provides us with such a lens, one that demonstrates the ways in which an analysis of the processes, practices, and identities involved in the politics of group formation provides a deeper understanding of the sources of democratic contestation both over policies of economic reforms and over the broader trajectories of globalization such policies embody.

Consider the links between the implementation of economic reforms and the rise of a new middle class in contemporary India. Policies of economic liberalization initiated since the 1990s have been accompanied by an array of visual images and public discourses that have centered on a shifting role of the middle class and their attitudes, lifestyles, and consumption practices. For example, popular stories, advertising images, and news reports that detail the spread of consumer items such as cell phones, rising wage levels for the managerial staff of multinational companies, and expanding consumer choice for goods such as cars, washing machines, and color televisions have produced an image of the rise of an emerging middle class culture in India. These representations have identified the rise of this new middle class with the success of economic reform.

The growing visibility of this new Indian middle class embodies the emergence of a wider national political culture, one that has shifted from older ideologies of a state-managed economy to a middle class–based culture of consumption. While in the early years of independence,[1] large dams and mass-based factories were the national symbols of progress and development, cell phones, washing machines, and color televisions—goods that were not easily available during earlier decades of state-controlled markets—now seem to serve as the symbols of the liberalizing Indian nation. While earlier state socialist ideologies tended to depict workers or rural villagers as the archetypical objects of development,[2] such ideologies now compete with mainstream national political discourses that increasingly portray urban middle class consumers as the representative citizens of liberalizing India.

Preliminary evidence of the public impact of such shifts can be seen in public debates on the social and political implications of the rise of this new Indian middle class. Proponents of economic liberalization portray the middle class as a group that is fundamentally tied to the success of economic reforms and assert that the middle class is a sizeable market—one of India's major selling points in attracting foreign investment. Furthermore, supporters of reform have adopted consumer-based understandings of the middle class and have argued that the middle class has benefited from economic reforms through the availability of new commodities and increasing opportunities for consumer choice.

Critics of liberalization, on the other hand, often point to the negative social and cultural effects of consumerism and have condemned the middle class for its vulnerability to the excesses of consumerism. A classic example of such a reaction is the public debate sparked by the publication of Pavan Varma's *The Great Indian Middle Class* (1998).[3] The book launched a sharp attack on the declining social responsibility of the Indian middle class and its gradual abdication of a broader ethical and moral responsibility to the poor and to the nation as a whole. Varma argued that in the early years of Indian independence,

> Material pursuits were thus subsumed in a larger framework that did not give them the aggressive primacy that they have acquired today. There was less of the feeling that one must have it all in the shortest time possible. Even the more well-to-do families felt that to flaunt their assets was in bad taste. Indeed there was a sense of slight disdain for those who lived only at the level of their material acquisitions. There were other countervailing concepts such as status and respect which had a higher priority in the scale of social values. Status, and the respect it earned, was not so directly linked to what one owned; it still had more to do with what one did or what one had achieved. Keeping up with the Joneses was somehow a less compulsive pursuit than keeping up with the image of refinement associated with a restraint on materialistic exhibitionism in a poor country——an ideal directly imbibed from Gandhi, Nehru and the freedom movement. (40)

Aside from his idealized image of earlier historical periods, Varma's commentary echoes a wider form of public moralism that has focused on the negative effects of middle class consumerism and what Rajni Kothari has termed a "growing amnesia" (1993) toward poverty. While such public critics of liberalization have tended to focus on middle class consumerism, proponents of liberalization have projected this new middle class as an idealized standard for an Indian nation that is finally competing in a global economy. Both views, while located on oppositional poles of the ideological spectrum, converge in their conception of the urban middle class as a self-evident force of consumption and as the prime recipients of the benefits of liberalization.

In contrast to the public visibility of the urban middle class, academic scholarship has been marked by a relative lack of sustained research on this social segment.[4] Existing academic research that has addressed the middle class in relation to economic liberalization has largely tended to echo the two variants of public discourses that I have outlined above. On the one hand, existing analyses have either focused on estimating the size of the middle class or have pointed to the growth of such intermediate classes as a potential base of support for liberalization.[5] On the other hand, culturally oriented research has tended to analyze the middle class through the lens of consumption, an approach that has rested on an underlying conception of the middle class as a consumerist class.[6]

I analyze the political processes that result in such associations between the middle class, consumption, and a pro-liberalization orientation and then move beyond these connections and examine the internal differentiations and political practices of this new middle class. I specifically argue that an analysis of the rise of the new Indian middle class deepens our understanding of the political dynamics of economic reform in contemporary India.

Such an analysis specifically entails a shift away from the assumption that the middle class is a self-evident beneficiary or proponent of economic liberalization. Scholars writing about economic reforms and globalization have for the most part tended to assume that the middle class benefits uniformly from policies of economic liberalization. This assumption has tended to ignore important internal differentiations within the middle class.[7] For instance, Satish Deshpande's (2003) assertion that "if there is one class for whom the benefits of globalization seem to clearly outweigh the costs, it is the middle class, particularly its upper (managerial-professional) segment" (150) rests on a slippage between a particular segment of the urban (metropolitan) middle class and the middle class in general, which is a much wider group that includes the rural middle class and urban middle class in small towns.[8]

The middle class is differentiated in terms of its economic standing in ways that make generalizations about the effects of liberalization at best premature without systematic research. For instance, the restructuring and privatization of public-sector units yield short-term costs to some segments of these middle class workforces (Sridharan 1999, 124–25)[9] and we cannot assume that all of these segments will transition smoothly to new-economy jobs. Furthermore, various internal social hierarchies such as caste, region, religion, and language shape the middle class. The emerging liberalizing or "new" middle class is not identical with a generalized sociological description of the middle class.

My central argument is that the rise of the new Indian middle class represents the political construction of a social group that operates as a proponent of economic liberalization.[10] This middle class is not "new" in terms of its structural or social basis. In other words, its "newness" does not refer to upwardly mobile segments of the population entering the middle class.[11] Rather, its newness refers to a process of production of a distinctive social and political identity that represents and lays claim to the benefits of liberalization. At a structural level, this group largely encompasses English-speaking urban white-collar segments of the middle class who are benefiting from new employment opportunities (particularly in private-sector employment).[12] However, the heart of the construction of this social group rests on the assumption that other segments of the middle class and upwardly mobile working class can potentially join it. For example, the privileged lifestyles and patterns of consumption depicted in media images are associated with individuals who can afford English-based higher education and credentials such as MBAs. Youth in the lower middle classes in small towns and rural areas may attempt to adopt credentialing strategies by refining their public speaking skills or accumulating marketing diplomas through unaccredited institutes. Individuals in the middle or working classes also may use the purchase of particular kinds of commodities and brands as symbolic strategies of upward mobility.

This potential access to membership makes the boundaries of this interest group both fluid and political in nature. As I noted earlier, estimates of the size and nature of the Indian middle class vary greatly.[13] In the face of such diversity, the identity of the new Indian middle class provides a kind of normative standard to which this larger group can aspire.[14] The boundaries of this emerging group are fluid precisely because they hold the promise of entry for other social segments.[15]

The underlying claim is that individuals from varying social segments can acquire the kinds of capital (such as education, credentials, skills, and cultural resources) that can provide them with access to membership in this distinctive middle class. The result, as I will argue, is that the emerging politics of the new middle class have broader national political and material implications both for the Indian middle class and for more marginalized socioeconomic groups.

My argument is not that the effect of this rising social group is all encompassing, or that its political ascendancy is predetermined. For instance, the rise of such aspirations can have diverging political implications. On the one hand, the belief in the promise of access to socioeconomic mobility and future benefits can lead to support for reforms. For example, segments of the middle class employed in both the private and public sectors have been faced with retrenchment, job insecurity, and increased workloads. However, this is not necessarily transformed into resistance to economic restructuring if individuals believe they can still benefit from a globalizing economy through future job prospects or through the consumption of new commodities.

On the other hand, discrepancies between lived realities of the middle class or upwardly mobile social groups and the idealized representations of the new middle class can lead to frustration and opposition to reforms. Moreover, as I will argue in later chapters, the rise of this group can also exacerbate existing conflict between the new middle class and subordinated social groups. Thus, my concern is not just with the rise of this social group but also with the fissures between hegemonic representations of new middle class identity and the contradictory socioeconomic realities of those who both constitute and aspire to this group. As I demonstrate, it is precisely such fissures that produce the anxieties, responses, and practices that constitute the daily substance of contemporary democratic politics.

Elites and the Politics of Economic Reform

The argument that I will make builds on and intervenes in a long-standing debate in political science about the relationship between the consolidation of economic reforms and political processes of democratization.[16] Political scientists intervening in these debates have demonstrated that economic reforms can be undertaken in the context of political democracies and have challenged earlier assumptions that political democratization necessarily produces opposition to reform.[17] As Przeworski (1996) and Stokes (1996a) have argued, while economic reforms create at minimum a transitional economic decline for some segments of the population, this decline does not necessarily lead to political opposition to the reform in democratizing societies. The political responses that stem from such a decline depend on the ways in which it is interpreted by various segments of the population. For instance, Przeworski (1996) notes that in the case of Poland, while economic conditions declined, the government was able to use the legacy of communism as an effective explanation for this decline. This process of interpretation, which Przeworski terms a form of "intertemporal interpretation," is a critical factor in shaping public opinion and political responses to the policies of economic reform. In other words, an anticipation of future benefits mediates the immediacy of political opposition to the economic disruptions or deterioration produced by reforms.

I argue that it is this sense of temporality that is at play in India, in the way in which the construction of the new middle class is mediating public responses to economic reforms. Idealized images of middle class consumption signify such future benefits, to which upwardly mobile segments of the population can aspire. This analysis builds on existing research that has demonstrated the importance of the role of elites in pushing forward reform processes and in mediating the relationship between state policies and mass political responses (Chhibber and Eldersveld 2000, 354).[18] The rise of the new Indian middle class represents an emerging political elite that is shaping responses to economic reform.

An understanding of such processes, requires a departure from two central conceptual assumptions that underlie existing studies of elites, public opinion, and the politics of economic reform. First, existing studies have tended to focus primarily on political elites, whether at the national or local levels[19]—an approach that has led to a neglect of the impact of the new middle class. Second, studies that have attempted to assess mass public responses to economic reform have either focused mainly on formal voting behavior (that is, how attitudes to reform shape electoral politics) or have sought to measure public opinion through survey research data on attitudes to reform (Chhibber and Eldersveld 2000; Przeworski 1996; Stokes 1996a). My approach calls for both a shift from an analysis of political to socioeconomic elites[20] and, more significantly, for an examination of the political processes involved in the creation of new groups and identities that mediate consent to reform.[21]

What traditional studies of economic transitions often miss is that public responses to reforms may be culturally coded in ways that do not correspond to more formal kinds of knowledge or opinions either about specific policies or about the question of economic reforms in general. For instance, existing research findings suggest that (1) knowledge about economic reforms in India is relatively low, and (2) despite evidence of negative views on its effects, the question of economic reforms has not been a major mass electoral issue.[22] However, conflict and consent over policies of economic reform do not play out only in the formal domain of electoral politics. Moreover, perceptions of reforms are often shaped by local cultural and social meanings and practices that may fall outside survey codings of formal forms of knowledge.[23] For instance, as I will argue, consent and conflict over reforms often unfold through a range of middle class contestations over issues such as the restructuring of urban space, competing definitions of national culture, and identity-based conflicts.

An understanding of these forms of politics of the rising new middle class requires an in-depth interpretative approach. In other words, if we are serious about understanding the ways in which "intertemporal interpretation" shapes the political dynamics of reforms, we must understand the politics of this group in terms of a project of interpretation rather than one of pure measurement.[24] As we will see, the emergence of a middle class consumer identity has significant political implications not because the middle class is a consumerist class or is following the teleological pattern of modernization of advanced industrialized countries, but because emerging consumption practices represent an important set of everyday signs and symbols through which people make sense of the more abstract term "economic reforms."[25]

The most visible cultural coding of economic reforms is the emergence of consumption patterns and lifestyles associated with newly available commodities. Contestation over shifts in economic policy therefore often unfolds in the space of public culture and involves conflicts over cultural globalization (such as the threat of Westernization). Certain strands of cultural nationalism often represent negotiations over changes associated with shifts in economic policy. For example, I will demonstrate that processes of economic restructuring also unfold through the spatial reorganization of neighborhoods within cities and small towns. In this reorganization, the middle class develops new suburban aesthetic identities and lifestyles that seek to displace visual signs of poverty from public spaces. Such middle class practices provoke conflicts with the urban poor over the control of public space. For example, spatial practices produce conflicts over whether street vendors should be able to sell their wares in middle class neighborhoods in a city like Mumbai. While on the surface this might appear to simply represent a local political issue, I demonstrate that it is fundamentally linked to the rise of an assertive new middle class identity in the context of liberalization. Furthermore, street vendors represent a burgeoning working class service sector that has been absorbing workers from manufacturing sectors such as the textile industry that have experienced economic decline in the face of global competition. Such local conflicts between street vendors and middle class civic practices then are structurally, culturally, and politically linked to broader processes of economic restructuring.

Conflicts like these, which constitute the substance of daily democratic politics, usually fall under the radar of studies whose analyses of the political dynamics of reforms are based on narrower definitions of democratic politics or associational life. Chhibber and Eldersveld (2000), for instance, argue that "India, despite its democratic lineage, has not developed strong independent interest groups. Few

Indians belong to associations" (356). Such an assumption only holds up if associational life is strictly defined in terms of formal organizations—a definition that excludes an array of activities, practices, and discourses in civil society. Everyday examples of associational activity are also often overlooked because they do not appear as self-evident or explicit cases of political responses to economic *policy*.[26] For example, the rise of a new middle class identity begins to take the form of organized associational activity as segments of this social group form civic and neighborhood organizations in order to reclaim public space and consolidate a style of living that can adequately embody its self-image as the primary agent of the globalizing city and nation.

Such examples demonstrate that an understanding of the rise of this social group necessitates a move away from a focus that is restricted to formal electoral politics. How then do we begin to conceptualize the politics of this emerging group? This project requires an adaptation of James Scott's (1985) reconceptualization of social movements and his call for a move away from the grand narratives of organized large-scale movements and revolutions to a focus on the everyday, informal forms of politics; or, as he puts it, "a social movement with no formal organization, no formal leaders, no manifestos, no dues, no name, and no banner" (35). However, in contrast to the peasant protests that Scott analyzes, the everyday politics of such "elite revolts" (Corbridge and Harriss 2000) unfold in distinctive ways. For instance, while Scott argues that for everyday peasant resistance, "By virtue of their institutional invisibility, activities on anything less than a massive scale are, if they are noticed at all, rarely accorded any social significance" (1985, 35), the politics of the new middle class are somewhat more contradictory. The new middle class is marked by its social and cultural visibility, yet its political role is often invisible. Meanwhile, its claims tend to be coded in terms of representative citizenship yet in practice are often defined by exclusionary social and political boundaries. Consider the example of the politics of urban space that I have outlined above. In such cases, emerging middle class civic organizations make political claims on public space by invoking discourses of citizens' rights and public interest. In the process, middle class practices transform citizenship into a category that is marked by exclusions based on the social markers (such as caste and class) that delineate the identities of the urban poor. The result is that the rise of this social group has broader implications for our understanding of the links between economic policies and processes of democratization.

The New Middle Class in Comparative Perspective

The rise of the new middle class is not a political process that is distinctive to India. The significance of the new middle class in the context of economic globalization[27] can be demonstrated in comparative contexts in the cases of other newly industrializing countries. Various case studies in Asia, Latin America, and Africa have begun to examine the rise of the new middle class in those areas (Pinches 1999; Robison and Goodman 1996).[28] Such studies have drawn on two dominant approaches in their conceptualization of the new middle class. On the one hand, a central trend in such studies is the adoption of a consumption-based definition of the new middle class (Beng-Huat 2000). On the other hand, the new middle class is defined through occupational-based definitions corresponding to white-collar, professional–managerial workers (Embong 2002; Pinches 1999). Michael Pinches (1999), for example, has identified the growth of the new middle class in terms of "highly educated salaried professionals, technical specialists, managers and administrators who assume powerful positions in the running of large corporations and state agencies" (25). It is this occupational grouping, Pinches argues, that is fundamentally linked to the rise of consumer cultures in cross-national contexts.

While both elements of these approaches are important, a limitation in these conceptualizations is the association of the new middle class both with the upper echelons of white-collar work and with consumerist behavior. A comparative perspective demonstrates that the new middle class has a much greater degree of differentiation both within and across various national contexts. For instance, the expansion of white-collar work is not limited to the upper tiers of the professional–managerial workforce but also includes a much broader set of white-collar jobs (for example, secretarial–administrative jobs and wide range of occupations within the service sector).

Meanwhile, less-privileged segments of the middle class may participate in consumption practices based on emerging trends of consumer cultures simply as a strategy of upward mobility that leads to access to membership in the new middle class. For example, Solvay Gerke (2000) has argued that in Indonesia, members of the middle class have deployed a form of "virtual consumption," a set of strategies designed to display standards of living that they in fact could not necessarily afford.[29]

Processes of differentiation intensified in Asian countries affected by the Asian economic crisis.[30] The crisis had uneven effects for the middle classes. While processes of retrenchment affected some segments, others with financial resources were able to take advantage of the scarcity in credit.[31] While there were variations in the effects of the crisis in East and Southeast Asia (Pempel 1999), such examples are significant because they serve as a corrective to generalizations regarding the assumed homogeneity of the socioeconomic position of the new middle class.[32] The effects of the Asian economic crisis have served as a cautionary note to earlier idealized representations of the "new rich in Asia" (Robison and Goodman 1996), representations that have led to conceptual slippages between the new middle class and the rise of the "new rich," the uppermost tier of the new middle class that has traditionally benefited from economic globalization in comparative contexts. While Robison and Goodman (1996) do address internal differences within the middle class, they present a broad definition of the new rich in which they argue that the social basis and power of the "new rich" is derived from "capital, credentials and expertise" (5) rather than from their position in the state apparatus.[33] Their definition encompasses members of various segments of the middle class (ranging from wealthy entrepreneurs to managerial employees with MBAs to secretarial staff and employees working in call centers) who attempt to negotiate the labor market through access to education and credentials. The definition also tends to treat them as a homogeneous category, "the new rich."

This problem of homogenization has also tended to characterize recent trends in studies of globalization and diasporic elites. Such studies have tended to overlook internal and cross-national differences and have produced an image of the new middle class as a transnational set of circulating elites. For instance, in the Indian context, Salim Lakha (1999) has argued that in the definition of the middle class, "a rigid distinction between diasporic Indians and locally based Indians is not particularly meaningful" (252).[34] Such an assumption too easily glosses over the ways in which the socioeconomic circumstances of particular nation-states and their levels of economic development shape the lives of the middle class in general, and the emergence of the new middle class in particular.

Problems of definition and differentiation stem, in part, from the fact that the categories are derived from older conceptions of the emergence of the new middle class in advanced industrialized contexts. In his classic formulation, C. Wright Mills (1951) defined the new middle class in the United States in terms of the rise of salaried white-collar professionals with a distinctive lifestyle. However, the specific conditions of late-developing nations distinguish the politics of the new middle class in significant ways. For instance, the new middle class in late-developing countries may be smaller in terms of size (in proportion to the national population), may lack access to similar levels of infrastructure (such as roads and electricity), and may represent an emerging rather than a stable socioeconomic group.[35] In late-developing nations, the new middle class is still in an emerging relationship with traditional segments of the middle class that are still largely dependent on state employment. Furthermore, the national role of the new middle class (and its implicit claim that it can be representative of the goals of national development) is one that is still in the making. For instance, in the Indian case, the identity of the new middle class continues to compete with other national political forces such as the rise of caste-based movements and politics. Moreover, the making of this identity is often pulled between its secular-modernist orientations and a growing identification with the Hindu nationalist movement.[36]

These factors point to the cultural and political dynamics of the role that the new middle class plays in shaping national development. In her study of the rise of the new Malaysian middle class, for instance, Maila Stivens (1998) argued, "what really stands out in all the present commentary about the future of Malay society is the way that the development of these new [middle] classes is seen as a *cultural* phenomenon, a cultural project" (92). The rise of the new middle class is a cultural and, I would add, a *normative* political project because it helps shape the terms of development and national identity. The new middle class is marked by a set of interests that are identified with India's embrace of a free-market-oriented approach to development. In other words, the new middle class in late-developing countries such as Malaysia or India serves as a group that represents the promise of a new national model of development, one with a global outlook that will allow such nations to successfully compete with the advanced industrialized countries.

The distinction between late-developing and advanced industrialized (and particularly American) ideas about the new middle class is important because Western categories have historically provided an ideal type with which the non-Western middle classes have been measured. Brian Owensby (1999) notes that the Brazilian middle class has historically been judged in terms of a "standard to be met" (9) through a kind of "invidious comparison, so that the existence of the Brazilian middle class was always unsettled in relation to what were assumed to be proper European and American middle classes" (9–10).[37] These invidious comparisons have tended to transform the middle class in non-Western countries into an overladen (though understudied) sociological category. Comparative scholarship has historically pinned hopes for successful modernization and democratization on the role and leadership of the middle class.

Consider the way in which political science literature, in particular, has grappled with the role of the middle class within political and economic transitions. With the emergence of modernization theory in the 1950s and 1960s, studies that argued that economic development would further political democratization were based on an underlying assumption that the emergence of the urbanized middle class would play a central role in the development of civil society and the resulting democratic transition (Lipset 1963).[38] When the middle class has behaved in more contradictory ways and political events have not measured up to such assumptions, scholars have often responded by resorting to more static notions of cultural difference (for instance, by arguing that non-Western middle class culture is antithetical to liberal democratic values), or by turning away from the study of the middle class altogether.[39]

A central challenge in studying the rise of the new middle class is to circumvent the limitations of such invidious forms of comparison with the American or European middle classes. Certainly, any urge to assume that the politics and contradictions of the new Indian middle class are simply hurdles as the new Indian middle class matures into an American model of the middle class is ironic in light of current debates on the politics of outsourcing. Significant public and political debate in the United States has begun to focus on the rising Indian middle class as a threat to the security of the American middle class. Images of middle class Indians working at computers now routinely flash on American television as the symbol of white-collar and service-sector job losses in the United States.[40] Furthermore, these examples serve as an important reminder that the politics of the new middle class is as much about labor (the global competition over jobs) as it is about predefined images of consumerism (the global competition over consumer markets), and that the new middle class does not constitute a singular transnational elite.

My study of the new Indian middle class contributes in a number of ways to the questions and debates that I have outlined above. The study seeks to move debates on globalization away from a simplified opposition between global elites and subaltern groups. Aside from the literature on transnational elites discussed earlier, interdisciplinary political economy literature, which has generally been critical of the effects of reforms, has tended to focus primarily on subaltern social groups such as urban and rural workers.[41] This research has produced important insights about the impact of globalization on labor, and on the reworking of identities of class and gender (Bishop and Robinson 1998; Chang 2000; Ong 1988; Parrenas 2001). However, such scholarship has often been restricted to an analysis of the politics of reforms and of economic globalization in terms of an interplay between multinational companies and international organizations such as the World Bank and IMF on the one hand and marginalized social groups on the other.[42] Meanwhile, analyses of the politics of class and gender have tended to focus almost exclusively on patterns of employment within export-oriented processing zones.[43] Furthermore, by focusing on the rise of the new middle class as a pro-reforms group, I contribute to existing political science scholarship that has tended to focus primarily on interest groups that are opposed to reforms (for instance, organized labor, state bureaucracies, political parties, and organizations that espouse economic nationalism).

Finally, this study contributes to the comparative literature on the rise of the new middle class by addressing three central areas that have been understudied in the existing literature on the new middle class. First, I examine the rise of the new middle class as an ongoing political project—one that results in the creation of a unified political identity that coexists with the internal socioeconomic differentiation within the middle classes. Second, I examine the restructured relationship between the new middle class and the state, and demonstrate that the state continues to play a significant role in shaping the politics of the new middle class.[44] Third, I examine the implications that the rise of the new middle class has for processes of democratization. Rather than assuming that this group has an essentially democratic or antidemocratic character, I argue for an approach that examines the ways in which this emerging group engages in everyday practices that shape the substantive content of democracy and citizenship.[45]

Conceptualizing the Middle Class: Boundaries, Practices, and the Mechanisms of Group Formation

The rise of the new Indian middle class can be understood in terms of a political process of group formation that has unfolded in the context policies of economic liberalization—a process that involves questions of culture and discourse, socioeconomic factors, and the role of the state. The question that arises, then, is: How does one specify the theoretical and empirical boundaries of this social group? That is, what are the mechanisms that shape this process of group formation? The answer, I argue, rests in the ways in which a range of practices produces the boundaries of social groups. Such practices are not merely individualized or subjective forms of behavior that rest solely on the contingency of daily life; rather, they are the outcome of a dynamic set of processes that are both symbolic and material, and that are shaped both by longer historical processes as well as by the temporality of the everyday. These mechanisms, as Pierre Bourdieu (1984) has argued, are "classificatory practices" that are developed as individuals and segments of social groups use strategies of conversion of different forms of capital (sets of cultural, political, and economic resources) to preserve their relative social standing and capacities for upward mobility.[46]

The ability of individuals and social segments to accumulate capital and engage in strategies of conversion, moreover, are both shaped and constrained by their interaction with existing structures of inequality. Such strategies of conversion, as we shall see, are shaped by the reworking of longstanding social inequalities such as the symbolic and material structures of caste, class, and gender inequality.[47] Finally, the particular field or site under analysis shapes this process of interaction.

I examine the ways in which individuals who either identify with or aspire to middle class status attempt to deploy various forms of capital in four primary fields: (1) the media and public sphere, (2) the labor market, (3) urban neighborhoods, and (4) democratic politics. This occurs through a dynamic and interactive process in which individuals and groups accumulate resources, seek to convert these resources into strategies designed to further their social standing, and respond to and draw on historically produced inequalities. The outcome is a set of classificatory practices (civic, discursive, and consumption) that begin to fix the boundaries of this social group (Bourdieu 1984, 56 and 101). The dynamic nature of the mechanisms and practices involved in this process make the boundaries fluid and open to contestation even as resources and historical inequalities *structure* the boundaries.[48] The paradoxical quality of this process— that it is both fluid and structured—allows for the coexistence of the rise of a singular hegemonic representation of "the new Indian middle class" that begins to act with a dominant set of interests, on the one hand, and a range of internal forms of social differentiations that exist within this group, on the other hand.

Consider specific examples of the kinds of classificatory practices that have begun to constitute the new middle class in India. Within the labor market, middle class individuals' access to "new economy" jobs may rest both on the individual's ability to access particular forms of cultural and social capital (for example, English education, credentials of higher education), as well as on durable structural inequalities and identities such as gender or caste that track individuals into particular segments of the labor market. For example, middle class women with a bachelor's degree and an English education increasingly comprise a segment of lower-tier service-sector work in the new economy. Access to the lifestyle of the middle class is also shaped by the media images and the interaction between various forms of capital (income-based economic capital and individuals' cultural capital, such as the aesthetic knowledge of what brands or commodities to purchase) and forms of identity (for example, discursive images of gendered and class-based models of family and work identity).

Consumption practices of the new middle class are not merely determined by shifts in income levels or as a result of individuals responding to advertising images; rather, they are a result of the complex interaction between such subjective and objective dimensions of group formation. This structural dimension to the mechanisms of group formation has been neglected by recent research, which has reduced practices such as consumption to purely subjective or symbolic processes.[49]

In contrast to assumptions sometimes made in culturalist approaches, "structure" is not a deterministic, prediscursive realm but is reproduced both diachronically through historical processes and synchronically (see Figure 1) as various forms of capital are converted into classificatory practices.[50] Consider, for instance, the role of middle class civic organizations noted earlier. Middle class neighborhood organizations increasingly have begun to mobilize in an effort to regain their control over public space and reproduce a clear sociospatial separation from groups such as street vendors and squatters. In such cases, these organizations deploy particular forms of capital such as leverage with the state (political capital) and models of beautification (cultural capital) in their activity. Such organizations stem from longer historical patterns in which the colonial urban

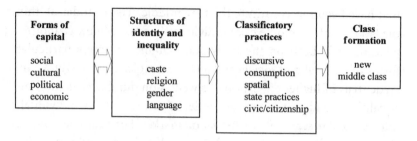

FIGURE 1. Synchronic mechanisms of new middle class formation.

middle classes deployed such civic strategies as a means of political self-assertion in opposition to the lower castes and urban poor. The result is a set of aesthetic, spatial, and civic practices that create cultural and social boundaries that differentiate the new middle class from subaltern groups.

Such historical trajectories that shape the rise and decline of social groups also point to the ways in which the postcolonial specificities of non-Western nation-states such as India depart from the European empirical research that Bourdieu drew on in his theoretical formulations. Bourdieu's theory of group formation, which I have been reworking in my conceptualization of the formation of the new middle class, rests on an analysis of internal processes within the national context of France. However, a significant dimension that shapes group formation in postcolonial contexts is the ways in which such processes are always simultaneously marked both by internal forms of differentiation as well as by external differentiation.[51] The rise of the new Indian middle class is distinguished by national narratives that seek to manage India's relationship with external forces such as "Westernization" and "globalization." The nation is not simply a neutral territorial container of class formation but a central force in the historical (diachronic) creation of the new middle class, which represents a national political project that unfolds in relationship to economic policies of reforms and that in large part signifies a form of interaction with and response to external globalizing forces.

The mechanisms involved in the creation of the new middle class represent layered and mutually constitutive processes that cannot be

reduced to a set of linear or teleological relationships between variables. The politics of the new middle class is fundamentally shaped by
the dynamics that arise through the interaction between these sets of
resources, identities, and practices. The formation of the new middle
class does not result in a homogeneous cultural or socioeconomic
group. The creation of this group is shaped by the internal differences
that are in turn created through unequal distributions of capital and
structured, identity-based inequalities. For instance, the identity of
the new middle class is forged through specific kinds of intersections
between class and gender, caste, and religion.[52] Thus, throughout my
analysis I point to the ways in which such intersections shape new
middle class practices, identities, and politics.

Such an analysis does not rest on an assumption that class is a foundational category that subsumes all other social identities. On the contrary, my analysis demonstrates the ways in which middle class identity
is constructed through identities such as caste, gender, or religion. As
I demonstrate in chapter 1, historical processes constructed middle
class identity through a politics of gender, caste, and religion. Caste
has continued to provide segments of the middle class with an important source of capital, which has shaped the upper-caste character of
the emerging identity of a new liberalizing middle class.

The interplay of intersecting identities does not, however, unfold
in a formulaic manner; it is contingent on historical legacies, on the
strategies that individuals and social groups deploy, and on context.
Thus, while discussions of the intersection between new middle class
identity and the politics of gender, caste, and religion are continually
woven into my analysis, such dynamics do not surface mechanisti-
cally or in a predictably uniform manner in each chapter.

The dynamics of intersecting identities and inequalities also point
to the ways in which the political significance of the new middle class
lies in the tension between the emerging hegemonic identity of this
group and the differentiation and disparities that characterize the social composition of the middle classes.[53] The identity formation of
the new middle class is also shaped by the often unsuccessful attempts of broader social segments (such as the rural and traditional
middle classes and upwardly mobile working classes) to gain access
to membership. As Loic Wacquant (1991) has argued, the middle

class "must be constituted through material and symbolic struggles waged simultaneously over class and between classes; it is a historically variable and reversible effect of these struggles . . . the middle class is necessarily an ill-defined entity. This does not reflect a lack of theoretical penetration but rather the character of reality" (57). In fact it is this dynamic struggle that fundamentally characterizes the politics of the new middle class as it emerges as a significant historical and political actor.

My conceptual approach takes up Wacquant's (1991) call for theories of the middle class to "consciously strive to capture this essential ambiguity of their object rather than dispose of it" (57). This requires a move away from more traditional theoretical and empirical approaches to the study of the middle classes that I have outlined in earlier sections. Consider, for instance, traditional approaches to the study of the Indian middle classes, which tend to rest on four central definitions of the middle classes as: (1) an income-based group (Sridharan 1999, 2004), (2) a structurally defined group (Bardhan 1993, 1998; Rudra 1989), (3) an aspirational–cultural class (Mankekar 1999; Rajagopal 2001b), and (4) a product of discourse and the social imagination (Appadurai 1996).[54] These approaches, in effect, seize on a specific layer of the interactive processes that I have outlined. However, an analysis that limits itself to one definition misses the ways in which an understanding of the politics of the middle class rests precisely on the slippages, fractures, and tensions that arise through the interaction between these layers. Narrower definitions miss the ways in which the politics of the new middle class are fundamentally shaped by this underlying politics of classification. In my analysis, I therefore draw on elements of all four of these approaches without resorting to a fixed sociological or anthropological definition or description of middle class identity in order to provide a more dynamic understanding of the making of the new Indian middle class.

Methodology

My analysis of the rise of the new Indian middle class draws on a set of interpretive methodologies that can grasp the various sets of classificatory practices that create the boundaries of this group. The epistemological assumption underlying this methodological approach is that a genealogical approach to the study of categories can contribute to our understandings and explanations of broader political outcomes. In other words, my objective is not to treat class as a variable that can explain responses to reform but to argue that an analysis of the political process involved in the construction of the new middle class broadens our understanding of the political responses to reforms.[55] This approach requires a return to Weberian approaches to social sciences based on a connection between the realms of understanding (the construction of categories and meanings) and explanation.

A genealogical approach is not simply a descriptive project that traces existing political processes; it is an approach that allows us to use an analysis of the construction of categories to rethink explanations of particular outcomes.[56] On the other hand, my objective is not to reduce my discussion of the formation of this social group to a contestation over competing meanings, representations, or discourses. Interdisciplinary approaches in fields such as postcolonial studies and cultural studies have often too easily rejected the significance of specifying and analyzing nondiscursive realms such as structure.[57] Yet as I demonstrate in this book, a reliance on purely discursive or representational analysis has also led to erroneous images of a burgeoning consuming middle class in contrast to highly differentiated patterns of consumption that exist within the middle class.

The theoretical premise that shapes the methodology of this book is thus twofold. On the one hand, my premise is that the traditional study of political economy in a discipline like political science has much to gain from a genealogical theoretical approach that analyzes the social construction of a group such as the new middle class.[58] On the other hand, my premise is that interdisciplinary fields such as postcolonial studies will benefit from a return to a more systematic discussion of the relationship between cultural/symbolic politics and economic/structural realms.[59] My approach thus draws on a variety of methodologies and sources of data that are aimed at both capturing the representational, discursive, and dynamic elements of group formation on the one hand and assessing the empirical parameters through measures of income and consumption on the other hand.

I draw on three types of data in the analysis that follows. First, I use published quantitative data to assess the parameters of the rise of the new middle class, particularly in relation to changing income and consumption patterns. Second, I use archival and secondary source research both to trace some of the historical precedents of contemporary debates on the new middle class, as well as to analyze contemporary political discourses and practices. Finally, I draw on qualitative interviews and ethnographic research based in Mumbai that I conducted between 1996 and 2003.[60] While the field research was based in Mumbai, I have not defined this book solely as a study of the politics of cities.[61]

My research and analysis focus on the creation of an elite group with claims of national representativeness. The norms associated with such claims shape the political economy of India in larger ways—for instance by shaping cultural norms and practices in small towns and by creating resistance from segments of the middle class that fail to get access to the benefits claimed by this group.[62] Furthermore, throughout my analysis I draw on comparative regional cases and processes outside of Mumbai and Maharashtra.

The qualitative field research in Mumbai draws on two sets of data—formal interviews and ethnographic research.[63] Formal interviews were used to obtain data on two dimensions: (1) the political/cultural production of dominant discourses on the new middle class, and (2) data on new middle class employment and labor market restructuring that have occurred in the context of liberalization. The first dimension consists of twenty-five qualitative interviews conducted with representatives in leading advertising firms (both Indian and multinational), as well as journalists and editors of new publications established in the context of liberalization that consciously target (and therefore construct) the new middle class. Such representatives are explicitly engaged in attempting to determine the size, nature, and aspirations of the middle class and provide a rich source of data on changing patterns of middle class behavior. During these interviews, I examined the ways in which creative teams conceptualized and produced images of the middle class. Such interviews also shed light on the problems of defining the middle class and the ways in which the middle class has in fact often not lived up to hegemonic assumptions that it is primarily a consumerist class. The advertising firms provide insights on national trends as their campaigns are not Mumbai-specific.

I also used formal interviews to obtain data on the effects of liberalization on middle class employment in new economy segments of the labor market. This section of the research provides in-depth qualitative work histories of individuals who are attempting to negotiate the restructured labor market in the private sector. Such qualitative methods are a critical part of the research design as existing census and survey data do not provide information on these areas of inquiry. In addition, existing scholarly research on the employment-related effects of liberalization have focused primarily on the rural poor and working classes.

I obtained general employment patterns of new-economy sectors through interviews with placement agencies that cater to middle class employees ranging from secretarial workers to upper-level management representatives.

My fieldwork demonstrates that a sizeable section of the middle class is engaged in a process of obtaining new skills and credentials in order to gain entry into a restructured labor market. While upper layers of the middle class concentrate on credentialing through MBA programs, a majority of individuals attempt to draw on a range of educational institutions that provide diploma courses (such as in computer training, public speaking, and marketing). Such institutions provide a critical entry point into an analysis of middle class strategies as they cater to the vast proportion of the middle classes that cannot afford to enter MBA programs. Therefore, I conducted interviews with individuals running some of these institutes. In addition, I conducted in-depth interviews with a cross-section of graduates of one such diploma program to make an in-depth analysis of individual work histories and attitudes about shifts in the labor market. I used social networks developed by graduates of this program to make a qualitative analysis of the range of their occupational experiences.

Finally, in addition to formal interviews, the book draws on ethnographic research that includes informal interviews at sites such as working women's hostels where white-collar women from different segments of the labor market reside, media discourses (including both the print media and visual images), and a range of other everyday conversations and interviews with individuals who could provide insights on the political dynamics of the new middle class and economic reforms (e.g., with white-collar union leaders in the banking and insurance industries, small business owners, and other white-collar workers).

The study, as I have noted, is not attempting or claiming to serve as a general sociological study of the middle classes—research that would include a wide range of dimensions such as descriptions of personal attitudes, religious identity, and family life. Rather, my methodology has sought to capture the fluid symbolic, structural, and fundamentally political boundaries of the new middle class that speak to shifts in economic policy and the broader processes of globalization unleashed by such shifts.

Overview of the Argument

I begin my analysis in chapter 1 with an examination of the historical roots that shape the contemporary politics of the new middle class. In particular, the chapter examines debates on the new Indian middle class in the colonial period, the effects of partition (particularly in terms of the impact on the Muslim middle class), and the relationship between the middle class and the developmental state in the early decades of the postindependence period. This perspective serves to foreground both the historical continuities and discontinuities with the contemporary politics of the new middle class.

Chapter 2 analyzes the rise of the new middle class in the contemporary period of liberalization. The chapter begins by analyzing the way in which the representation of this group begins to take shape during Rajiv Gandhi's experimentation with reforms and extends into the contemporary period of reforms in the 1990s. The chapter also examines the representational practices (in the media, advertising industry, public sphere, and survey research projects on the middle class) that create a hegemonic consumer-based identity of the new middle class.

Chapter 3 moves beyond the lens of consumption through an analysis of employment patterns and the new middle class. In particular, the chapter addresses labor market restructuring and the implications of global outsourcing. I argue that such processes of restructuring are contingent on the acquisition and distribution of various forms of social capital (English education, aesthetic knowledge, credentials). Representational practices that define new middle class lifestyles are transformed into forms of stratification within the labor market.

Chapter 4 examines the ways in which the identity of the new middle class becomes an arena for the negotiation of uncertainties and anxieties sparked by liberalization. This negotiation involves local state practices, and formal and informal associational activities of the new middle class. The chapter examines the ways in which this identity is based on a reworking of distinctions of religion, gender, and class. It also examines the ways in which this identity is expressed in a range of formal and informal associational activity. For instance, new middle class identity unfolds through conflicts over public space and the expansion of middle class civic organizations that reinforce conflicts and distinctions from subaltern groups.

Chapter 5 analyzes the ways in which the emerging political identity of the new middle class has been reconstituting meanings of citizenship in ways that accentuate intersecting forms of social exclusion. The chapter looks at some of the broader implications that the rise of the new middle class and its claims on citizenship and national representativeness have for contemporary democratic politics in India.

Finally, the conclusion discusses some of the broader comparative and theoretical implications of the Indian case and the theoretical framework developed in this study.

1

The Historical Roots
of the New Middle Class

·※·

In the nineteenth and early twentieth centuries, a diverse range of public discourses debated the identity and practices of a new middle class that emerged in colonial India. Such discourses unfolded in arenas such as social reform legislation, theater and literature, political rhetoric, and the emerging narratives of Indian nationalism. Debates on the character and effects of the rise of this new middle class sought to manage the distinctive position of this social group, one that rested in a liminal[1] area between the colonial state on the one hand and traditional elites on the other.

These past debates resonate in significant ways with contemporary discourses on the new middle class in liberalizing India and underline the importance of placing current trends in historical perspective. As I will demonstrate in this chapter, the rise of the new Indian middle class is marked by a long historical trajectory. Far from being an outgrowth that is simply defined by contemporary globalization, the emergence of this social group can be traced back to earlier periods in India's colonial past.

An analysis of the historical roots of the new middle class demonstrates the continuities between earlier periods and trends in the postindependence period, and allows us to specify the particular characteristics of the new middle class that are associated with the contemporary politics of economic liberalization. Three central characteristics stand out with regard to the rise of the new middle class in the colonial period. First, the distinctiveness of this social group is marked by specific kinds of socioeconomic resources such as access to English education and modern forms of professional employment. These resources came to distinguish this social group from traditional elites, and led to specific forms of connection with and dependence on the colonial state. Second, the newness of this middle class rested on an emerging set of political claims of public representativeness that this group made within the realm of democratic civic life. The political assertiveness of the new middle class rested on its claim to represent the general interests of the public, often against colonial state power. Finally, this claim of representation was continually accompanied by a project of self-identification that was marked by a politics of distinction from both the colonial state and more marginalized social groups. This distinction, along with the internal forms of differentiation within the new middle class, accentuated a sense of uncertainty and contradiction within this group. The management of these contradictions has historically constituted the politics of the new Indian middle class.

The objective of this chapter is to provide a historical overview of the rise of the new middle class and to examine the broader implications for the middle class and contemporary Indian politics. The first part of the chapter focuses on the emergence of the new middle class in the colonial period and examines both the socioeconomic and political boundaries that defined this class as it began to assert its political leadership through various forms of associational activity. While the Indian middle class has generally been an understudied area within the social sciences, existing historical studies provide rich empirical data on this social group. I draw on the vast literature on the colonial and early nationalist periods in order to outline some of the central characteristics of the identity and politics of the colonial middle class.

The second part of the chapter extends the analysis into the early decades of independence, up to the 1980s, the period when the first public discourses on a liberalizing consumer-based middle class begin to emerge and compete with existing models of a state-managed middle class. I examine the ways in which these historical patterns are reshaped in the postindependence period, focusing on the continued centrality of the role of the state in shaping the politics of the new middle class in this period. The dependence of the middle classes on the developmentalist state in the early decades of the postindependence period served as a source of both contestations and convergences between the middle classes and state power. On the one hand, this dependence led to political tensions as the middle class tended to make claims on the state for access to benefits, in particular white-collar jobs associated with the new middle class. On the other hand, state and middle class interests often converge on a shared vision of modernity in India, as evident in civic discourses, models of urban development, and discourses of family planning.

The chapter provides an overview of the historical processes that have shaped the emergence of the new middle class in liberalizing India. On one level, these processes reveal the importance of the transnational dimensions and distinctiveness of the conditions of the postcolonial period in shaping the formation of this social group—conditions marked by the uncertainties associated with the mediation between internal forms of differentiation on the one hand, and the tensions of delineating an external form of distinction from the West on the other. On another level, as I will demonstrate, such historical processes have played a central role in structuring the distribution of various forms of social, cultural, and economic capital such as language (and the politics of English), education, employment, social status, and access to state power, all of which have shaped the new middle class in enduring ways.

Structuring the Indian Middle Class in Colonial India

The creation of the new Indian middle class is historically associated with the development of British colonial educational policy. The colonial administrator Thomas Macauley believed that this educational policy would lead to the creation of a "class, Indian in blood and colour, but English in tastes, in opinions, in morals and intellect."[2] This policy, designed to create a social group that would aid in colonial administration, in fact led to the rise of a middle class that proved to be far more complex than the nostalgic imperial vision captured by Macauley's words. This rising social group was essentially shaped by the colonial character of its invention; its newness rested on its colonial roots. However, the new middle class also drew on older social distinctions in ways that would substantively shape the nature of its political claims in both the colonial and postcolonial period.

The structural characteristics of the political economy of colonialism shaped the rise of the middle class.[3] British control blunted the kind of full-fledged industrialization that would have led to the expansion of an industrial middle class (comprised of industrial managerial and supervisory staff). The emerging colonial middle class was directed toward the limited opportunities available through colonial educational policy and most members belonged to the service and literary classes (comprised of writers and intellectuals that formed an emerging intelligentsia). In Bengal, for instance, the specificity of the new Indian middle class rested on a paradoxical position—the middle class was culturally invented through colonial-based English education yet structurally limited since it lacked a basis for economic expansion in the context of colonial economic control (Chatterjee 1992).

Such structural limits were solidified by the British system of managing agencies that organized industrial development in the colonial period. In this system, when parent British companies floated new firms they were vertically integrated under the management of the parent firm (Misra 1961, 14). The result, as B. B. Misra has noted, was that "A limited number of managing agents thus came to control the bulk of the country's economic power. This financial integration restricted the growth of the Indian industrial middle classes, while the administrative integration reduced the number of superior executives, especially directors" (14). While there were of course exceptions, the overall pattern of development pushed the emerging middle classes increasingly to rely on education as a means of achieving access to employment and economic power.

The effects of British educational policy marked the colonial middle class in specific ways. At one level, it contributed to the creation of a class through the spatial patterns of colonial rule. Colonial educational policy concentrated on Presidency towns such as Calcutta and Bombay, which intensified the strength of the middle class

in these towns.[4] English education was a distinguishing feature of the
colonial middle class that set this new social group in an uneasy relationship both with traditional elites as well as with other less privileged segments of the middle classes, particularly the vernacular,
lower middle classes.[5] The politics of language, in many cases, par-
tially overlapped with the spatialized pattern of the colonial middle
class in ways that extended into and influenced politics in the postcolonial period. This overlap created new forms of distinctions between English-educated elites dominant in the Presidency towns of
Calcutta and Bombay and various tiers of the regional elites, such as
the landed middle class and vernacular elites in other towns.

The growing institutionalization of English education in the nineteenth century began to consolidate a new urbanized elite that became
invested in the reproduction of new distinctions based on education
and language. The emergence of the new Bengali middle class represents a prime example of this development and has occupied a central
role in existing historical research (Chatterjee 1992; Sangari 2001;
Sarkar 1992; Sarkar 2001). As Kumkum Sangari (2001) states, "a well-
formed connection had evolved between the acquisition of prosperity
and the language of the rulers, giving English the emblematic character of choice on the part of an articulate section of the Bengal middle
class" (133). However, these trends were by no means limited to Bengal. Consider the rise of the colonial middle class in Lucknow where
education increasingly became a critical marketable skill and means of
access to colonial modernity (Joshi 2001, 7).

Meanwhile, in western India, the spread of educational institutions in the Bombay Presidency led to a growing intelligentsia employed in a range of service and professional occupations in law and
government service (Dobbin 1972). This intelligentsia served as a
"self-perpetuating class" (Dobbin 1972, 40) as individuals trained
through new educational institutes were then employed as teachers
or became financial supporters of the institutions that had trained
them. These rising groups became actively invested in the reproduction of the language of colonial rule because their socioeconomic position rested on the social, cultural, and economic capital associated
with colonial educational training and state employment.[6]

The structural constraints of colonialism placed this newly emerging social group in a unique position of ambivalence that rested between the privileges and points of access that education provided and restricted access to economic and political power. The history of the new middle class, as Tanika Sarkar (2001) has put it, was marked by absences and voids produced by racial discrimination and the absence of economic and political leadership within the confines of colonial rule. This uncertain position has led historians of the colonial middle class to focus instead on the cultural spheres of activity, a zone in which the middle classes could begin to define, debate, and assert their social identity. For instance, Partha Chatterjee (1993) argues that the boundaries of the new colonial middle class rested on the conscious action of a subject mediating between a relationship of subordination and "a relationship premised upon its cultural leadership of the indigenized people" (36). Similarly, Sanjay Joshi (2001), in his discussion of the colonial middle class in Lucknow, suggests that the power of the middle class did not rest on its economic position but on its abilities to act as "cultural entrepreneur." Thus, he posits that the middle class in colonial north India was constituted not by its social and economic standing but through its activity in the public sphere.

The role of middle class claims to cultural and public leadership is important in understanding the broader political implications of this emerging social group and I will return to these dynamics later in the chapter. However, culturalist arguments tend to underestimate the significance of the socioeconomic dimensions of this new elite. While the strictures inherent in the colonial production of this social group certainly constrained its power, the realm of socioeconomic practices remains critical in understanding the formation and political ascendancy of this elite. Although the new colonial middle class was numerically quite small and its opportunities for advancement were certainly limited, this small but articulate elite was able to gain prominence because of the specificities of its socioeconomic position.

The role of education in shaping the formation of this class must be understood not simply in cultural terms but in the ways in which it created new and enduring socioeconomic hierarchies both within the middle class and in relation to subordinated groups. These factors are particularly significant because it is this kind of socioeconomic differentiation that shaped the political dynamics and claims of this elite.

English education did not simply represent a means for a shift in cultural status, it also provided a central avenue for various segments of upper caste, middle class individuals to consolidate their socioeconomic position within the political economy of colonial rule.

This consolidation did not, however, produce a homogeneous social group. Rather, it produced a layered economic elite that rested on a reworking of existing caste-based inequalities. At the top tier, the professional middle class found entry into Indian Civil Service (ICS) cadres.[7] Colonial policies were specifically designed to produce a highly structured elite that would conform to British norms of respectability (Potter 1996). English-language skills were necessary but not sufficient in providing access to such jobs. Such skills had to be complemented by a "respectable" socioeconomic position and family history. Consider the following criteria used by the ICS in the process of recruitment,

> The character reference assessed whether or not the candidate was "up to the ICS socially. . . ." For example, the Bihar and Orissa Government in 1931 regarded a candidate as "not suitable" because "his father is a retired bank clerk who has no property and is reported to visit courts occasionally as a tout," and "his elder brother is a *swarajist* who used to work in a Gandhi Ashram as a master tailor;" another from the same province is unsuitable because of "his poor physique, lack of personality, and humble social status"; a candidate from Mysore in 1934 was judged by the Resident there as a "suitable candidate for the ICS" because "he comes of a very respectable . . . family who are well represented in the Mysore State Service," and he "bears a good character and has not been concerned in political movements." (Potter 1996, 113)

Such considerations clearly point to the ways in which language represents a complex field of power beyond the instrumental acquisition of skill that groups use to gain upward mobility (Anderson

1990). Aside from the clear political interests of the colonial state in discriminating against individuals associated in any way with the rising nationalist movement, the specific social criteria clearly point to a process of internal differentiation within the new middle class. Entry to this elite tier of the colonial middle class was inextricably linked to social status defined by occupation and property ownership; "culture" in this context was defined in relationship to socioeconomic location and was not simply a homogenized product of middle class self-identification.

Such processes were borne out in generalized patterns of recruitment; by the mid-twentieth century, Indian ICS recruits were from family backgrounds defined by upper-tier professional occupations such as government service, medicine, law, and teaching (Potter 1996, 116).[8] Socioeconomic criteria such as occupation and property ownership were critical in the process of demarcating this upper tier of the colonial middle class.

Such patterns point to the ways in which the distribution of cross-cutting forms of social, cultural, and economic capital begin to structure this emerging social group. For instance, the upper-tier professional middle class, whether in the ICS or in private employment, represented a fairly small elite level of the new colonial middle class. The more-encompassing group of the colonial middle class included a much larger set of individuals including lower-level clerks, and teachers.[9]

In addition to differences of occupation and landownership, the boundaries of the colonial middle class were contingent on the reworking of social identities of religion and caste. In general, the formation of this class drew on members of the upper castes. In Bengal, British norms of middle class professional respectability were not purely imposed from the outside; they intertwined with and reshaped indigenous middle class definitions of *bhadralok* respectability. In northern India, middle class membership came from upper-caste Hindus or high-born Muslims or from service communities that had served in the courts of indigenous rulers and large landlords (Joshi 2001, 7).[10]

The linkages between caste and class did not of course unfold in a mechanical manner. In western India, Dobbin (1972) has noted that the English-educated classes that emerged in the nineteenth century drew both on the Brahmin and poor literary castes, rather than the wealthier commercial classes that the British had sought to recruit for educational instruction in Elphinstone College (33–34).[11] These middle classes represented a new elite that would also begin to challenge often wealthier or traditional elites. As Douglass Haynes (1991) has noted in his study of Surat, the rise of the educated middle classes posed a growing threat to the city's notables, eventually displacing them from power in local municipal politics. However, aside from the complexities of interelite competition, this upper caste character remained one of the defining characteristics of the colonial middle class.

Religious identity also played a complex role in the formation of the colonial middle class. The formation of the upper tiers of this class was often marked by the exclusion of Muslims, in part because Muslims were slower than Hindu elites to invest in English (Sangari 2001, 140)[12] and because fewer Muslim recruits were employed in the ICS. In 1933, for example, 16 percent of ICS employees were Muslims and by 1941, 20 percent were Muslims (Potter 1996, 117). However, this did not mean that Muslims were absent from the emerging colonial middle class; the intersections between religion and class were marked by regional variations. In contrast to Bengal, Muslims in the United Provinces had more access to urban, government jobs and the socioeconomic interests of the new colonial Muslim classes were often not distinguishable from the ambitions of upper-caste Hindu middle classes (Joshi 2001; Sangari 2001). Members of the upper tiers of this class trained at institutions such as Aligarh College were focused on gaining employment in government service (Hasan 1997, 37). In the Northwest Provinces, 25 percent of Muslims were urbanized in contrast to 3 to 4 percent of Muslims in Bengal (Hardy 1972). Furthermore, as Mushirul Hasan (1997) has argued, the Muslim League's demands partly represented the fears of newly emergent professional groups in northern areas such as Uttar Pradesh and Bihar (56).

Such forms of socioeconomic competition within the professional middle classes (ironically, stemming from an overlapping set of interests) intersected with religious tensions within the complex field of colonial state intervention and a growing nationalist movement.[13]

By the beginning of the twentieth century, in the United Provinces conflicts over government jobs with the 1916 Municipalities Act's reservations for Muslims in municipal bodies provoked strong opposition from the Hindu middle classes (Joshi 2001, 102). The politicization of religion cannot be reduced to middle class competition over employment. However, religious identity and class became imbricated in the structural formation of the colonial middle class. As we will see in later chapters, such intersections resurface in distinctive ways in the constitution of the politics of the middle class in liberalizing India.[14]

In this outline of the formation of the new colonial middle class I have sought to demonstrate the significance of the socioeconomic boundaries of this emerging elite. Questions that address socioeconomic location, access to employment and the intersecting inequalities based on occupation, caste, and religion risk being too easily submerged in discussions of the cultural politics of this class. Indeed, historical work addressing the politics of the middle class has often highlighted the cultural anxieties and dislocations of this social group (Chatterjee 1992, 1993; Joshi 2001). Yet it is precisely such forms of socioeconomic differentiation that shaped the middle class identities and practices in arenas such as social reform, cultural nationalism, and public-sphere activity in the nineteenth and early twentieth centuries. These dynamics move us far beyond Macauley's ethnocentric colonial vision of a homogeneous Indian middle class.[15] They take us instead to a complex and highly contested field in which the norms of the professional middle class and the attempts of the "new" urbanized middle class to stake its claims as representative public citizens would bring them into tension with vernacular elites and the lower middle classes. The materially based distinctions, inequalities, and exclusions that I have begun to point to, significantly shaped these arenas of contestation and the emerging political identity of the new Indian middle class.

The Political Identity of the Middle Class: Cultural Politics, Civic Nationalism, and Citizenship

The colonial middle class occupied an uncertain position. While it was defined in large part by its dependence on the colonial state, its development and access to socioeconomic mobility and political power was limited by the structural constraints of the colonial political economy. This uncertainty was expressed and managed in varied and sometimes contradictory ways in the creation of the political identity of the new middle class. In particular, the identity of middle class was premised on its claim to represent both its own public interests and the interests of subordinated social groups.[16] These claims were structured through a reworking of cultural identities such as religion and gender in an expanding public sphere (Sangari 2001; Sarkar 2001).[17] However, the boundaries of this public sphere were not limited to cultural identity. Rather they converged and coexisted with new forms of identity and political mobilization within an expanding arena of urban civic politics. These civic-based associational activities began to constitute new spatialized patterns of urban middle class identity that served as a central basis for the emergence of middle class forms of civic nationalism and a corresponding class-based construction of citizenship in the public sphere.

The political identity of the middle class was expressed through a range of emerging public discourses of respectability, moral regeneration, and social reform (Chatterjee 1993; Joshi 2001; Sarkar 2001). Such discourses were shaped by significant variations that mirrored and attempted to manage the socioeconomic differentiation within the colonial middle classes. At one level, the literary and professional nature of this emerging elite significantly shaped its public identity. Sanjay Joshi (2001), for instance, has traced the emergence of a new "public" in nineteenth-century Lucknow, comprised of literate Westernized men. The identity of this social segment was produced through a range of "native" newspapers, journals, presses, associations, and societies. The new middle class staked its claims to leadership in this public sphere through the invocation of new forms of social respectability and moral regeneration. Such claims of respectability built on the models of respectability and social status associated with the educational training and occupational hierarchies of middle class professional employment and enabled the middle class to distinguish itself from traditional elites in the public arena. As Joshi (2001) states:

Countering the weight of aristocratic privilege therefore, was the better character of the middle class. As opposed to the degenerate *taluqdars* who followed the same pastimes as the erstwhile *nawabs*, Indian middle class men, represented as thrifty, industrious, learned and morally upright, were the real allies of a benevolent government, and eminently more suitable to represent native society. (53)

This self-definition, in effect, enabled the middle class to stake a public claim of leadership based on assertions of moral superiority that were connected to the cultural dimensions of modernization. The result was the creation of an underlying set of linkages between the middle class, modernity, and the ability to make claims on the colonial state. This project of moral regeneration was manifested in a wide range of social practices and public discourses that included debates on temperance, consumption, the cultural implications of education, and the appropriate roles for women in both the public and private spheres (Sangari 2001; Sarkar 2001).

Such reforms were not, however, straightforward reflections of a teleological move toward modernization. The identity of the colonial middle class was defined as much by its ambivalences as by its attachments to colonial modernity.[18] These ambivalences were in large part related to both the economic constraints on the middle class and the internal socioeconomic differentiations discussed earlier. Race-based discrimination in government employment and more generally in the structure of colonial rule (Sarkar 2001, 33) and the limited financial means of large segments of the lower middle class placed the colonial middle class in an uncertain social location. The result was that modernity was experienced as a series of deprivations (Sarkar 2001, 36) that invoked a fundamental sense of anxiety in the middle class in the nineteenth century. It is this sense of anxiety, then, that was partly managed through the culturally based projects of social reform and moral regeneration.

The politics of anxiety, as much historical literature has shown, unfolded through a set of middle class debates that centered on social distinctions such as gender and religion. Gender, for instance, became a central boundary marker that could manage the uncertain and dis-

ordered array of cultural and socioeconomic identities that constituted the middle class.[19] The household became a central material site
for these processes of political management. Socioeconomic uncertainties were, for instance, mediated through gender-based discourses
on consumption such as public anxieties about excessive spending by
middle class housewives (Joshi 2001, 72; Sarkar 2001, 35).

Meanwhile, middle class preoccupations with respectability took
on specifically gendered forms as they were coded through normative
models of female chastity and morality (Joshi 2001; Sangari 2001).
For example, the question of women's education occupied a distinctive space both in colonial discourses and in middle class responses.
As Sangari (2001) has argued, "by ballasting her [the middle class
woman's] education with a weightier morality—the confines and
contours of knowledge had to begin to mark out a middle-class private sphere" (149). Discourses in the public sphere focused on the
improvement of middle class women in a regulated fashion in ways
that were preoccupied with and would solidify distinctions of caste
and class while preserving patriarchal structures both within and
outside the household.[20]

This production of an appropriate private sphere was central to
the creation of the public identity of the new middle class. Furthermore, such dynamics were not limited to questions of education and
consumption—issues that were identified in large part with the
upper tiers of the middle class. Consider the public dynamics of the
lower layers of the middle class. In a study of the Bengali middle class,
Sarkar (2001) demonstrated the ways in which social scandals were
inextricably linked to anxieties about middle class identity and autonomy. The politicization of intimate issues such as chastity, conju-
gality, and sexual transgression were widely debated in public lower
middle class vernacular sites such as popular theater, sensational local
media reports, and public rumor and gossip. Such gendered politics
of the intimate were constitutive of the emerging public sphere of the
middle class and were therefore a central factor in creating the political identity of the middle class.

The political implications of this intersection between gender and
class identity were deepened as questions of domesticity and conjugal-
ity were reworked in relationship to middle class forms of religiosity.[21]

While Hindu revivalist movements emerged in opposition to colonial interventions in the Hindu domestic sphere (Sarkar 2001), Hindu middle class concerns with disempowerment were also increasingly narrated through images of Muslim oppression (Joshi 2001, 102). The drive for middle class autonomy from colonial rule through the politicization of the domestic sphere intensified the significance of religious identity as a foundational basis for the definition of this sphere of intimacy. These overlapping middle class discourses on gender and religion were sharpened as they intersected with specific class-based conflicts and as the politicization of religious identity was sharpened in the context of colonial state policies and emerging nationalist discourses by the late nineteenth and early twentieth centuries.

The identity formation of the colonial middle class consisted of a complex set of practices and discourses involved in the management of a range of internal differences as it sought to demarcate an autonomous sphere distinct from the structures of colonial power and authority. This search for autonomy and identity underlies Partha Chatterjee's interpretation of the roots of middle class nationalism in terms of the creation of a private "inner" cultural sphere.

Chatterjee has further argued both that the specificities of colonial rule were such that the intellectual and moral leadership of the Indian bourgeoisie could never be firmly established in civil society (1986; 1990, 132) and that the middle class had to base its growing nationalist claims to power on its cultural leadership.[22] However, a reading of the historical literature provides a more complex picture than one based simply on a formulation of the cultural roots of middle class identity. As we have seen, cultural distinctions were a central part of middle class identity. These distinctions were created and contested in a differentiated public political arena and did not simply represent the attempt of the middle classes to return to a protected inner cultural sphere.[23] Furthermore, through the course of the late nineteenth and early twentieth centuries, the making of this middle class identity also centrally rested on specific claims made within civil society. Middle class self-assertions of cultural and moral leadership were inextricably linked to its claims of public representativeness through a range of civic associational activities.

During the late nineteenth and early twentieth centuries there was a proliferation of civic associations in various urban towns and centers. Such civic associations ranged from caste- and community-based associations (Joshi 2001) to informal organizations of small merchants and shopkeepers comprising the lower strata of the urban middle class and more elite voluntary associations, educational societies, and cooperative unions of the English-educated middle classes (Haynes 1991, 145; Watt 2005). As with the cultural dimensions of middle class politics, these associations reflected a disparate range of interests and factions of the colonial middle class.

A significant pattern of political activity that emerged out of this web of associational life was the growing assertion of the English-educated middle class' claims to represent the public's civic interests. Such claims unfolded primarily through increasing political contestation at the local municipal level. In an important study of Surat, Douglass Haynes (1991) demonstrated the ways in which English-educated professionals used the local electoral politics of municipal councils to gradually displace the notables, the traditional elites that had dominated local politics and used the language of civic politics to cultivate ties with the colonial state. By 1914, English-educated elites had captured significant positions in the municipality and as advisors to the British.[24]

The significance of these shifts at the local level is not limited to a question of electoral representation. Rather, the rise to power of this elite reflected a deeper transition in the nature of public civic power in urban centers. As Haynes has convincingly argued, the English-educated middle class was in effect able to use its resources of language and education to gain a growing monopoly on civic discourses and on the implicit identification between civic order and the definition of "public" interests. Thus,

In Surat, beginning about 1880, a handful of people who sought to influence colonial policy began to fashion a collective identity as public leaders—that is, as ones who cared about the welfare of the entire urban citizenry, who represented the interests of the people, and who identified with India as a nation. As public leaders, they became involved not only in pursuing the concerns of their patrons in the municipality and other colonial institutions but also in expanding civic life to include more schools for the city's boys and girls, cooperative credit societies to provide loans to farmers of the surrounding countryside, and public associations that could pressure the government in the name of the urban citizenry. One might say they created a broker culture distinct from that of their indigenous patrons, a culture that in effect became their own preserve. The larger population, unable to capture the nuances of expression key to participation in the civic arena, was essentially denied access to it. (Haynes 1991, 151)

This analysis contains a number of issues that are central to an understanding of the politics of the new middle class. First, the emerging politics of this class claimed to represent a broader set of public interests that had implications beyond the limited sphere of local urban politics. This urban-based social group, in effect, was engaged in the creation of a generalized conception of citizenship, a process that claimed to transcend differences both within urban centers like Surat as well as between rural and urban areas (Dobbin 1972; Joshi 2001). This universalized claim of citizenship was simultaneously constructed through the intensification of inequalities based on these very differences. In other words, local civic politics led to the emergence of a model of citizenship that was simultaneously defined by universalistic conceptions of public interest and differences based on cultural and socioeconomic hierarchies. Thus, meanings and practices of citizenship were constructed through such differences and inequalities, in contrast to idealized assumptions that democratic civic life rests on an opposition between formal inclusive citizenship criteria on the one hand and ascriptive identities and hierarchies on the other (Smith 1997).

Consider for example the rise of middle class associational activity in local municipal politics in Bombay. By 1870, a local ratepayers' movement of lower middle class shopkeepers and small merchants had emerged in opposition to taxes such as rates charged on shop premises and godowns (Dobbin 1972, 137). This opposition movement gained support from the professional English-educated middle classes. However, as Christine Dobbin (1972) has noted, "the professional middle class had supported the ratepayers' movement for fiscal relief and had managed to change it into a demand for representative government, because it was only through the elective principle that this class could begin its journey toward power" (147). The specific socioeconomic interests of the lower middle classes, in this case, were appropriated within the language of elective rights and political representation. While property qualifications continued to disenfranchise the majority of this class, these debates on municipal reform nevertheless point to the implicit linkages between claims for a representative civic sphere and the interests of the educated/professional middle classes.

Such middle class claims for representation rested on an intrinsically exclusionary vision of civic order, one that was centered on a spatialized politics of caste and class hierarchies. A central concern of middle class representatives on town councils was to shape models of town planning that would introduce clear forms of sociospatial control over the urban poor.[25] These forms of control were exercised both through more traditional forms of coercive regulation such as policing and political repression, as well as by new discursive forms of regulatory power embodied in middle class projects of social reformism.[26] Middle class ascendancy in cities rested on the regulation of public spaces in line with conceptions of hygiene and order that were derived from discourses of colonial modernity (Kaviraj 1997). In addition to the shared cultural vision of urban modernity between the middle class and the colonial state, middle class objectives also coincided with colonial state policies and discourses that viewed the primarily low-caste urban poor as a threat to social and political stability. The result of such practices was the emergence of models of urban development that rested on a convergence between colonial state power and middle class definitions of the "public." As Nandini Gooptu (2001) puts it in her discussion of urban politics in North India:

> Indeed, as town improvement ventures began and increasingly met with the resistance of the poor, who faced problems of scarcity or loss of housing, the local councils became even more determined and coercive in forging ahead with their policies and increasingly enlisted the help of the police to overcome resistance. Their chief concern, after all, was to reclaim the

towns for the middle classes from the threat of the poor and to ensure the universal enforcement and acceptance of the civic ideal of a planned, orderly, safe and hygienic environment. (84)

Political representation, in effect, became inextricably linked to an exclusionary middle class model of urban civic order. The project of urban development unfolded through familiar patterns of spatial politics, which included policies of slum clearance, crackdowns on hawkers, and attempts to enforce class-based forms of sociospatial segregation.[27] These policies were of course never fully successful in the face of resistance from poor and working class communities and the spatial patterning of Indian cities historically did not emerge along clearly segregated lines similar to advanced industrialized countries (Katznelson 1983). However, such spatial politics became an intrinsic component of the political identity of the new middle class, one that would continually resurface in the definition of middle class politics throughout the course of the twentieth century.

The paradoxes of the formation of the political identity of the middle class in many ways permeated the political dynamics of the growing Indian nationalist movement.[28] At a surface level, the leadership of nationalist organizations such as the Indian Nationalist Congress and the Muslim League drew in large part on the literary and professional classes that I have been discussing. At a deeper level, the substantive content of nationalist thought oscillated between both the dynamics of cultural-religious nationalism and the claims of representative citizenship that undergirded urban-based discourses of civic order. While the rise of Gandhi's influence in the nationalist movement changed its orientation, Gandhian discourses on the improvement of the social status of the poor and low castes often echoed middle class rhetoric on social reformism.[29] Moreover, despite Gandhi's success in transforming the nationalist movement into a mass-based grassroots form of mobilization, it did not significantly expand the composition of the organizational leadership base.[30] These dynamics are succinctly captured in Nehru's nostalgic ambivalence toward the role of the middle class,

The present for me, and for many others like me, was an odd mixture of medievalism, appalling poverty and misery and a somewhat superficial modernism of the middle classes. I was not an admirer of my own class or kind, and yet inevitably I looked to it for leadership in the struggle for India's salvation; that middle class felt caged and circumscribed and wanted to grow and develop itself. Unable to do so within the framework of British rule, a spirit of revolt grew against this rule, and yet this spirit was not directed against the structure that crushed us. It sought to retain it and control it by displacing the British. These middle classes were too much the product of that structure to challenge it and seek to uproot it.[31] (Nehru 1998 [1946], 57)

It is the simultaneous presumption of the "inevitably" of middle class leadership on the one hand and the identification between the elite tiers of the middle class and the structures of colonial modernity on the other that shaped the direction of middle class nationalist thought and activity.

These structures were, as we have seen, not simple derivative of Western models of modernity. Rather, they were continually created though a modernized reworking of existing social hierarchies of caste, religion, and gender.

The dawn of independence served to solidify these dynamics that based the political identity of the Indian middle class on its simultaneous reliance on secular claims of representative citizenship and the reproduction of sociocultural distinctions. The impact of partition intensified these linkages as the mass-based migrations to Pakistan substantially depleted the Muslim middle class in northern India. As Mushirul Hasan (1997) has noted, Uttar Pradesh and Bihar experienced the migration of the Muslim professional classes, leaving few Muslims in key sectors such as the defense services, police, and universities (182). Furthermore, the movement of mostly educated upper caste Hindus to Lucknow reduced Muslim influence in government, business, trade, and professions (Hasan 1997, 182).[32] Meanwhile, the implicit affinities between the middle class and the structures of colonial rule were in the process of being transformed into new sets of relationships with the newly independent Indian state. The tensions and linkages between the state, middle class models of representative citizenship, and the politics of cultural and socioeconomic differentiation would shape the patterns of middle class politics in independent India in significant ways.

The Politics of the State-Managed Middle Class in Postindependence India

The middle class in the early decades of postindependence India was shaped by a continued strong dependence on the state. Earlier colonial linkages between the state and middle class that were created through educational policies and state employment were expanded through the state-managed model of economic planning and development.[33] Recent scholarship on Indian political economy has demonstrated that the historical relationship between the state and class politics played a central role in shaping the direction of economic development.[34] In line with the direction of such scholarship, I argue that an adequate understanding of this relationship between state and class must be expanded to include an analysis of the relationship between the state and the middle class. In the early decades of independence, the state contributed both directly and indirectly to the expansion and consolidation of middle class interests in a number of ways.[35] The Nehruvian state-interventionist model of planned development consolidated the relationship between the developmentalist state and the middle class through a complex field of ideological/ discursive, institutional, and economic practices and policies.

Consider the nature and limits of Nehruvian discourses of state socialism, the primary ideological context of state-led development that has often been rhetorically contrasted with contemporary moves toward a liberalized economy oriented around middle class consumption.[36] In practice, the middle class represented a central social group that served as an agent that both shaped and was a primary target of nationalist discourses of development as well as of specific state policies. As I have noted above, historians of colonialism and the Indian nationalist movement have demonstrated the central role of the Indian middle class in shaping the model of modernist national development that would become consolidated in the initial decades of postindependence India.[37]

While Nehruvian socialist rhetoric addressed the poor, developmental practices and policies reflected a modernist outlook that tapped into urban middle class visions and desires for rapid technological and industrial growth. The centrality of the middle class as primary agents directing state socialist growth had important ramifications in the Indian case. Such dynamics underlined and expanded the ways in which the relationship between the state and the middle class had been shaped by educational policies during the colonial period. For example, in the first two decades after independence, growth rates in enrollment in higher education consistently outpaced primary education. In 1955–56, the percentage increase in enrollment growth rates in higher education was 74 percent, compared to 31 percent in primary education and 42 percent in secondary education. In 1970–71 the percentage increase in higher education was 67 percent, compared to 12 percent in primary education and 19 percent in secondary education (see Rudolph and Rudolph 1987, 298). State-subsidized higher education continued to play a central role in shaping middle class formation. In contrast, as Atul Kohli (2004) notes, "Nehru's government spent little on health and primary education, underlining the superficial quality of Indian socialism" (266). Such trends continued in the early decades of independence. Higher education received a disproportionate share of the available funds in part due to political pressure from the urban middle class and rural elite. This does not mean that the middle classes benefited uniformly from state-subsidized education or that education in general was overfunded.[38] Rather, education became a central arena in which state–middle class relationships of patronage and dependence were consolidated in this period.[39] As Rudolph and Rudolph (1987) note:

[S]tate governments responded to the insistent demands of influential urban middle class and rural notable constituents for more college seats by creating intellectually and physically jerry-built institutions or underfunding expanding enrollments in existing ones. State legislators responded by demanding that government sanction both neighborhood colleges in their districts and regional state universities. Educational entrepreneurs and sect and caste benefactors took advantage of the degree boom by founding private colleges that entailed government subventions. Motives of profit, influence and political power conspired to accelerate foundings as local politicians created colleges to secure the reliable political machine a loyal staff and students could provide. Parents, who wanted their children to have the higher more secure incomes and social status that degrees sought to provide, fueled the demand for seats in increasingly malleable institutions. The number of universities multiplied from 27 in 1950 to 119 in 1975. (296)

This provides a vivid depiction of the complex networks and interactive claims between state structures and the middle classes. An analysis of this relationship between the state and middle classes does not rest on an assumption of a reductive equation between state and class interests or a theory of middle class capture of the state. Rather, such networks of patronage were produced through a dynamic set of political processes in which middle class groups actively made demands on the state and state institutions while local officials and politicians sought to consolidate power through these social groups. In this process, the state actively participated in the protection and expansion of the social basis of the middle classes (in this case, through the provision of particular forms of benefits and resources) as it sought to transform such middle class spaces into a terrain for the expansion and exercise of state power.

The example of education begins to demonstrate the forms of dependencies that were being created between the state and middle class. However, the crux of the relationship between state and class that was consolidated in the early decades of independence did not merely rest on an external relationship of patronage. Rather, it rested on the ways in which the middle class both benefited from specific forms of support from state-led development and simultaneously were incorporated into the institutional and economic apparatus of a rapidly expanding set of state structures at both the local and national levels. Consider for instance the institutional dimensions of this process in the early years of independence. Connections between the middle class and the state in the postindependence period were first consolidated through the structure of the state bureaucracy. The basic structure of the colonial authority, the Indian Civil Service, was retained and expanded into the Indian Administrative Service (IAS).[40] For most of the early decades of independence, this bureaucratic structure continued to draw on the service and professional classes that had been rising in significance through the colonial period. By the early 1980s, 71 percent of IAS recruits continued to draw on the service class (see Table 1). In particular, the IAS remained a central draw for English-educated segments of these classes given the significance of English-language skills for entry into IAS employment.[41] As Pranab Bardhan (1998) has noted, the role of professional middle class and white-collar workers in controlling networks of patronage through the distribution of economic resources and benefits transformed this section of the middle class into one of the "dominant propriety classes" that shaped the state-directed model of Indian political economy.

TABLE 1. Middle class composition of Indian administrative services.

Years	Proportion of recruits from professional and service classes (%)
1947–56	94%
1957–63	81
1980–81	71

Source: Potter 1996, 231.

This process of class formation placed the upper tiers of the middle class in a unique location within the state apparatus—one that provided them with specific socioeconomic benefits in terms of employment, as well as with specific forms of political capital.[42] My point here is not that the Indian state was "captured" by this social group but that the early decades of state-led development created specific forms of mutual dependencies between the state and middle class. The intersecting relationship between the state, political economy, and the middle class was further consolidated and expanded through the growing significance of public enterprises in the Nehruvian model of development. The model of planned development that was established led to rapid growth in public-sector employment, quadrupling from 4.1 million in 1953 to an estimated 16.2 million in

1983 (Potter 1996, 159). A significant characteristic of state-managed development was the state provision of resources and employment to various segments of the middle class.[43] Such provisions consolidated a form of middle class economic dependence on the state, one that has continued into the current period of liberalization.[44]

These dependencies have not, however, meant that the middle class has been a passive recipient of state policy agendas. Rather, such segments of the middle class would actively make claims on the state. While popular pro-reform images of India's license raj often center on undisciplined industrial workers with permanent employment and excessive demands of poor or marginalized groups on state resources, patterns of political activity in the decades of India's planned economy were shaped in significant ways by middle class demands for state support. Consider for example the nature of political mobilization of sections of the middle class through white-collar union activity. The employment-based dependence on the state led large segments of the middle class to identify as workers and to direct their political activity through economic claims on the state. Trade-union activity in India was thus often slanted toward middle class employees in sectors such as banking, insurance, and airlines (Chatterji 1980). Large segments of the middle class were organized through employment-based identities in ways that channeled their political activities through demands on the state for wages and benefits, thus consolidating their dependence on the state.[45] This heightened the political significance of socioeconomic differentiation within the middle classes as the state attempted to cater to and mediate the various economic demands on its resources.[46] In other words, the convergences between the state and the middle class did not imply a homogenized set of interests; nor was the state merely a passive entity that was being controlled by the middle class.[47] The state, in its role as political arbiter of conflict, attempted to manage both the various segments of the middle class and their relationship to other social groups.

This contradictory set of relationships unfolded in varied and often volatile ways as they intersected with the social inequalities of caste, ethnicity, and religion that shaped the political identities of the middle class. Political pressures on the state to incorporate previously marginalized groups attempting to gain access to middle class membership engendered broader forms of social and political conflicts and strained the foundations of democratic politics.

Segments of the middle class that were not able to gain access to stable employment grew increasingly dissatisfied and pressed the state for quotas for middle class jobs, often through antimigrant "sons-of-soil" movements. Nativist claims on public-sector jobs arose in a range of areas such as Karnataka, Assam, and Chota Nagpur (Katzenstein 1979, 25–26). In Assam, for example, from the 1950s to the 1970s, middle class movements focused on the scarcity of jobs (Baruah 1991; Baruah 1999).

The most politically salient of such movements was the rise of the Shiv Sena in Mumbai as this movement has had important national implications because of the role it later played in the rise of Hindu nationalism in the late twentieth century. While the Shiv Sena has now diverted its agenda more specifically toward an anti-Muslim Hindu nationalist project, its early rise was fundamentally linked to the politics of the urban middle class. One of the central causes of the Shiv Sena's rise in Mumbai was increasing unemployment and the economic frustrations of the lower and middle classes (Gupta 1982, 57). Shiv Sena leader Bal Thackeray and his party activists were able to play on such frustrations and mobilize middle class Maharashtrians who were unable to gain access to desired white collar "office jobs" (Katzenstein 1979, 63).[48] In its initial rise to power in the late 1960s and early 1970s, the Shiv Sena drew heavily on mostly educated middle class Maharashtrians employed in lower-tier white-collar occupations.[49] Thackeray was able to effectively appeal to such economic anxieties of the lower segments of the middle classes through racialized constructions of South Indians, the group that the Sena portrayed as the main economic threat to middle class Maharashtrians, and through a demand for 80 percent reservations in employment and housing for Marathi speakers.[50]

This politicization of middle class uncertainty cannot, however, be reduced simply to an instrumental struggle over jobs.[51] As recent research has shown, a large part of the Sena's success rested in its abilities to successfully build a grassroots network of activists within local neighborhoods (Heuze, 1996, 2000; Hansen 2001). Such strategies in many ways drew on older middle class anxieties about questions of civic improvement and were constructed through distinctions of class as well as caste and religion.[52] As Thomas Hansen (2001) puts it, "For decades the Shiv Sena leadership and its substantial middle-class constituency have shared a dream of a clean, orderly, civilized city free of the constant overflow of slum dwellers and migrants" (70).[53]

While I return to such questions in more depth in chapter 4, the point at hand is that this middle class quest for urban development in fact draws on broader historical trends that have constructed the political middle class identity through modernist conceptions of space and civic life. Such political dynamics are not unique either to the case of Mumbai or to the case of the Shiv Sena. In contrast to assumptions that the middle class represents an essential embodiment of democratic civic life, this social group has in fact historically been concerned with the assertion of civic order, a quest that has tended to rest on the exclusion of marginalized social groups that have threatened to disrupt this order.[54] As I have noted earlier, such concerns with civic order must be understood through their historical continuities with colonial convergences between the state and middle class modernist ideologies of civic order. In the postcolonial Indian context, the most extreme manifestation of this quest was evident in two of the central campaigns of the emergency period, slum demolition and coercive sterilization and family planning.[55] In many ways, such campaigns embodied urban middle class desires for an ordered civic–national body politic that would cleanse the Indian nation of the unruliness of the poor.

The political dynamics surrounding middle class concerns of employment, reservations, and civic order do not simply reflect the isolated economic interests of a small, urbanized section of the population. Rather, the significance of such dynamics lies in the fact that the varied ways in which the middle class has pursued its interests have shaped broader trends in contemporary Indian politics. This can be seen in a range of examples from organized middle class resistances to the Mandal Commission recommendations for caste-based reservations, growing urban middle class support for the Bharatiya Janata Party (BJP) and its Hindu nationalist agenda, and internal tensions and competition between the rising Hindi-speaking middle class and the English-educated middle class that have led to the rise of regionally based political parties.

While I examine these trends in further depth in chapter 5, at this stage such dynamics highlight the contradictions between middle class dependence on and entitlement to state support on the one hand and the strains of democratic politics that have forced the state to manage competing interests and respond to demands from subordinated social groups on the other. While the middle class was a product of India's state-managed model of development, by the mid-1980s, the political identity inherent in organized middle class activity was shaped by a sense of state failure in delivering on its promises of the benefits of modernity to the middle class. The political expression of this failure varied in ways that were contingent on intersecting structures of inequality and culturally based languages of protest. However, at a broader level they reflected the political strains of the state-managed model of development. It is this middle class frustration stemming from the overextended politics of state-management that has led to an increasingly assertive and visible middle class role—one that has specifically been manifested through the rise of a new middle class identity in liberalizing India.

Conclusion

In this chapter, I traced the rise of a new middle class in the nineteenth and early twentieth centuries. As we have seen, this new social group was shaped by the specificities of colonial rule. On one level, the structuring of the new middle class was shaped by the role of the colonial state and the restrictions of colonial political economy. On another level, this emerging social group was placed in tension with both traditional vernacular elites as well as subaltern social groups. In response to such uncertainties, the identity of the new middle class was defined by differentiation from both the externalities of colonial rule and from the internal distinctions that threatened the reproduction of this distinctive group. The identity of the new middle class was simultaneously shaped by the structures of colonial modernity and the reproduction of social inequalities such as gender, caste, and religion. The politics of distinction in effect provided the terrain for the management and negotiation of the identity of this elite group.

Public debates and anxieties that sought to make sense of cultural and economic changes associated with the rise of the new colonial middle class foreshadow current debates on the role of the new middle class in liberalizing India. The historical overview provided here serves as an important caution against the tendency of many studies of globalization to assume the "newness" of the processes of contemporary globalization. As we have seen through the rise of the new Indian middle class, "newness" is often a social and ideological category that negotiates both continuity and change.

The historical processes I have outlined are also significant because of the ways in which they continue to shape the politics of group formation in the context of contemporary globalization. For instance, historical processes have structured the distribution of cross-cutting forms of social, economic, and cultural capital in ways that continue to shape the reproduction of the new middle class in India in the late twentieth and early twenty-first centuries. Such historical continuities shape the contemporary politics of this social group in important ways.

Meanwhile, such historical trajectories also shape the contemporary politics of liberalization by posing a negative point of departure. For example, the politics of the new liberalizing middle class have been shaped by an active attempt to carve out a new political identity that distinguishes itself from the older model of the state-managed middle class, a process that has restructured but not severed the relationship with the state. The result of such dynamics, as we will see in subsequent chapters, is that the politics of the new middle class continue to be shaped by the historical processes that I have analyzed in this chapter.

2

Framing the Liberalizing
Middle Class

———————*———————

In the 1960s and '70s this whole bit of accumulation of wealth
was still suffering from a Gandhian hangover. Even though
there were a whole lot of families who were wealthy all over
India in the North and South if you noticed all their lifestyles
were very low key. They were not exhibitionist or they were not
into the whole consumer culture. Now I see that changed completely. . . . You want to spend on your lifestyle. You want your
cell phone. You want your second holiday home, which earlier
as I said people would feel that sense of guilt—that in a nation
like this a kind of vulgar exhibition of wealth is contradictory
to Indian values. I think now consumerism has become an Indian value.

—*Editor, lifestyle magazine*[1]

India's move toward economic liberalization in the 1990s did not
simply bring about changes in specific economic policies—it set into
motion a broader shift in national political culture. This shift, succinctly captured in the preceding quote from an editor of a fashion
and lifestyle magazine, can be seen in an array of highly visible images of changing trends in consumption practices, lifestyles, and aspirations. These images have centered around the proliferation of

commodities such as cell phones, washing machines, and color tele-visions (and the associated global brand names of these products). Representations in advertisements, commercial "Bollywood" films, political rhetoric, market research, and public discourse have all con-tributed in varying ways to a perception that India is being funda-mentally changed by rapidly expanding consuming classes.

While emerging opportunities for the consumption of newly available commodities represent the public face of the benefits of economic liberalization, the central figure in such representations of consumption is the urban middle class. The urban middle class, in ef-fect, represents a hegemonic sociocultural embodiment of India's transition to a committed liberalizing nation.

In public discourses, practices of consumption and the depictions of associated lifestyle changes distinguish the new Indian middle class from the older traditional middle class that was held back by the cultural strictures on consumption inherent in Nehruvian state so-cialism and Gandhian ideals of austerity. This heightened visibility has transformed the new middle class into an object for the projec-tion of political, cultural, and ideological assumptions from a range of actors. Proponents of liberalization—and market research firms—have been preoccupied with assessments of the size of the middle class and its potential as an untapped consumer market. In the early 1990s, a time of euphoria over the potential of India's consuming classes, public discourses routinely referred to "India's 200-million-strong middle class" as a resource that could automatically be mobi-lized to consume. Although subsequent events demonstrated that the middle class was more varied then this image of a sleeping consumer giant, the definition of the middle class, in terms of consumption, has nevertheless been consolidated through such discursive practices.

While proponents of liberalization and market research firms continue to grapple with measurements of the size, income, and con-sumption levels of the middle class, critics of liberalization have condemned the middle class for its lapse into materialism and con-sumerism. Nevertheless, advertising images and films continue to contribute to such consumption and lifestyle-based definitions of the middle class. For example, Mumbai's Bollywood film industry has created new genres of film that specifically target the middle class through the exploration of a range of social issues including shifting gender roles and family conflicts (including previously unaddressed themes such as divorce and sexuality), anxieties over changing lifestyles and consumption pattterns, and the links and distinctions between this new middle class and its overseas connections, particularly in the United States and Britain.[2]

In this chapter, I examine the emergence of this consumer-based identity of the new Indian middle class. The creation of this identity represents a hegemonic process that is, as we will see, often at odds with local variations in consumption practices of middle class individuals and families. The creation of the new middle class unfolds through a process of enframing in which the boundaries of this social group are delineated through a set of public discourses, cultural narratives, and economic shifts. This process of enframing does not simply represent the marking of Cartesian lines around a set of individuals with common cultural or social traits.[3] As Timothy Mitchell (2002) has argued in his discussion of the framing of the realm of "the economy" in modern political thought, "Each piece of the frame, each rule, procedure, understanding, constraint, enforcement, and sanction, involves potential exchanges of its own . . . the frame or border of the economy is not a line on a map, but a horizon that at every point opens up into other territories" (292).

Reworking this theoretical intervention in relation to the politics of group formation, the hegemonic boundaries of the new middle class are not a simple reflection of an existing socioeconomic reality; nor are they merely an ideological invention that is imposed in a uniform way on local expressions of middle class experience and identity. Rather, such boundaries are complex symbolic–material frames that intersect with and are the product of both historical processes as well as the temporality of everyday practices. For example, at one level, the hegemonic boundaries of middle class consumer identity embody both the symbolic shifts within public discursive narratives and the material shifts produced by economic policies of liberalization that have opened up consumer markets and brought about structural changes in employment and income levels (for instance in service-sector industries, private-sector employment).[4] However, at another level, such boundaries are fractured by local variations in middle class identity formation as middle class families and individuals negotiate, contest, and are shaped by such dominant frames.[5] This chapter analyzes the hegemonic representational practices that constitute this process of enframing, a process that as we will see in later chapters intercedes in and shapes contemporary social and political processes in a range of areas such as the labor market, urban neighborhoods, civic life, and democratic citizenship.

The chapter begins with an analysis of the roots of the link between the middle classes and a consumer-based identity associated with economic liberalization that first began to emerge in Rajiv Gandhi's regime in the 1980s and has expanded since the 1990s period of liberalization. As I demonstrate, the identity of the new middle class is intertwined with shifting public cultural representations of the Indian nation-state. While the image of this group is marked both by its local urban origins and by its global aspirations of economic and cultural achievement, it is fundamentally defined in terms of national narratives. In dominant public representations, the new middle class is the embodiment of the liberalizing nation-state rather than of a localized city elite or of a Westernized global aristocracy. In other words, the image of the new middle class represents an idealized national standard of living that other social groups can aspire to and potentially achieve through practices of consumption.

Through this analysis, I also intend to move beyond easy oppositions between the state and market that often permeate liberalization discourses. The emerging postliberalization "new middle class" has not severed its historical linkages with the nation-state; rather, it is the nature of the relationship between the state and the new middle class that has been shifting.

This molding of middle class identity stems both from continuities with historical processes that I analyzed in chapter 1, as well as discontinuities marked by more recent processes of globalization. The claims of national representativeness of the new middle class are part of a longer historical trajectory in which the middle class has claimed to be a central agent in the definition of Indian national identity and in the definition of the relationship between the nation and external global processes.[6] The distinctive characteristic of the middle class identity that began to emerge in the 1980s and was consolidated in the 1990s lies in a shift in the way in which the relationship between the national and global realms is expressed through various representations of middle class consumption.

Representational practices produce this consumer-based definition of the liberalizing middle class in a range of print and visual sites. For instance, I examine particular forms of advertising images and lifestyle practices that form some of the visual technologies of a liberalizing Indian public sphere. The point of this analysis is not to suggest that advertising images are a naturalized reflection of middle class practices but to provide a sense of the cultural texture of iconic representations of the new middle class and to demonstrate the national symbolic framing of commodities and middle class consumer practices.

While anthropological and cultural studies research has engaged in the interpretive textual analysis of advertising and media images, this arena has for the most part been overlooked in political science studies of political economy. My interpretive analysis seeks to fill this gap and to demonstrate the ways in which such processes of signification provide a central avenue for understanding of shifts in the terrain of political culture.[7] Narrowly defined positivist attempts at measuring middle class consumption through income miss the material implications of cultural and symbolic practices that shape the boundaries of the new middle class. However, in contrast to cultural studies and anthropological research, my objective is not to provide an exhaustive deconstructive decoding of each image or textual representation, or to analyze the relationship between such images and particular forms of subjectivity or consumer consciousness.[8] Rather my purpose is to unravel some of the central patterns of symbolic politics that shape dominant cultural narratives of national identity—a process that occurs through the reworking of existing social identities such as language, gender, religion, and caste.

My analysis also specifically seeks to move away from narrowly defined culturalist approaches that have focused exclusively on a discursive and semiotic deconstruction of visual cultural representations. To this end I use data on middle class consumption to present a set of socioeconomic parameters that can be used to assess the nature of shifting practices and patterns of consumption. Such a project is important in avoiding the risk of overestimating the nature of shifts in consumption and reifying images of middle class consumerism that arise in analyses that rely solely on deconstructive methodologies and semiotic analysis of cultural representations.

The theoretical and empirical implications of this analysis are thus twofold. First, the data provides an important check on analyses that generalize about changing consumption practices based purely on a discursive analysis of visible shifts in middle class lifestyles or on local ethnographic studies of middle class daily life. The data shows that while there have been shifts in income, such shifts have not necessarily translated into the broad-based forms of consumerism that are represented in public discourses. However, my analysis also demonstrates that projects of income measurement have themselves been part of the representational practices that I look at in this chapter. In other words, attempts to measure the middle class are themselves representational practices that have contributed to the creation of the symbolic boundaries of the new middle class. While income-based definitions of the middle class provide important parameters for assessing and qualifying purely discursive approaches to studying the middle classes, they cannot be used as a singular foundational measure for a deeper understanding of the politics of middle class identity. Such income-based definitions neglect both the dynamic and contested processes of group formation, as well as the ways in which the politics of measurement are an intrinsic part of such processes.

The production of this emerging new middle class identity, as I will demonstrate, is shaped by a layered set of symbolic practices. Such symbolic frames of identity are fundamentally shaped by the historical presence of an elite English-speaking public sphere in India. Representational practices within this sphere inextricably link the creation of a new middle class identity with the distinction and sociocultural capital associated with English linguistic identity. The linguistic dimension of new middle class identity marks it with a clear form of differentiation from vernacular elites and subordinated social groups. Gaining access to membership in the new middle class in liberalizing India, as we will see, is not merely a question of money but of linguistic and aesthetic knowledge and respectability.

Visual symbolic representations of commodities also represent a significant means for the expression of a public language of class—

one that intersects in complex ways with inequalities of gender and caste.[9] Languages of commodities and of consumption provide a potentially accessible array of cultural registers that suggest a possibility of access and participation in this new middle class model of the Indian nation. It is this paradoxical pairing of exclusion/difference and inclusion/universality that constitutes the hegemonic boundaries of the new middle class and characterizes the politics of this group with a continual sense of ambiguity.

This ambiguity marks the politics of enframing in significant ways. Fissures arise as members of the middle class negotiate these hegemonic boundaries. As I will argue, in practice, representational practices that have created a vision of a consuming liberalizing middle class have continually been disrupted and reshaped by variations in the patterns of consumption associated both with members of this group and other social segments with upwardly mobile aspirations.

Drawing on existing quantitative data and findings from my field research, the chapter begins to unpack these fissures by analyzing the varying effects on, and responses of, those who both claim to embody and aspire to membership in this group. I specifically examine the dissonances between such discursive representations and national shifts in income and consumption. My objective is not to create a simple juxtaposition between an erroneous ideological or discursive image of the new middle class on the one hand, and a true picture based on measurements of income and consumption on the other hand. Rather, I also analyze the politics of measurement of the Indian middle classes as an example of the classificatory practices that have contributed to the creation of the new Indian middle class.

Rajiv Gandhi and the Precursor of the Liberalizing Middle Class

A new Indian middle class identified with a liberalized culture of consumption first began to emerge in a distinctive way through the policies and discourses associated with Rajiv Gandhi's reign in the 1980s. In the initial period of his rule, he brought with him a vision of a modernizing Indian nation that would rest on the fruits of high technology, managerial efficiency, and global economic competitiveness.

His national vision broke from earlier cultural and ideological restraints of state socialism and embraced the consumption of goods such as cars and color televisions.

One of the most visible national symbols both of his vision of national development and his attempts at liberalization was the availability of a new brand of car, the Maruti, which for the first time gave domestic consumers an alternative to the Ambassador car, the long-standing symbol of restrictions on choice for Indian consumers. This vision resonated in particular with the urban middle class. As one media representative at the time put it, the middle class was "Rajiv Gandhi's people, at home in a new political climate, happy with the new political jargon, relieved that the Government no longer tries to tax everyone in the name of the poor, enamored of a prime minister who understands the importance of colour TV."[10] Gandhi, in fact, specifically sought middle class support by sharply cutting tax rates and encouraging middle class consumption during his first year of office (Ninan 1990, 42). This represented an important shift in the state's policies on consumer goods and middle class consumption.[11] A considerable point of middle class frustration in the early decades of India's planned economy was the state's use of policies of indirect taxation of consumer goods as the main source of public revenues (Kohli 2004, 266).

This identification between Rajiv Gandhi and the possibilities for middle class consumption was intensified by Gandhi's own youthful, modern personal style, which resonated with the lifestyles and aspirations of the urban middle classes (Rudolph 1989, 2; Weiner 1987). As one media report put it,

> The dhoti-kurta clad politician travelling in third class railway compartments is an image of the past. Today's rulers sport Gucci shoes, Cartier sunglasses and live five-star lifestyles . . . The distance between Gandhi (Mahatma) and Gandhi (Rajiv) is a vast traverse in political ethic.[12]

Consider the shift in national political culture from the early years of the Nehruvian regime in the 1950s to contemporary liberalization in India that this vision represented. The early decades of economic policy in postindependence India were focused on the development of large-scale industrial units; the emphasis of economic development was on production in heavy industries rather than on the production of consumer-oriented commodities. Such policies were linked to a specific image of a modernizing Indian nation, one in which large-scale dams and steel and power plants "were the spectacular facades, luxurious in their very austerity, upon which the nation watched expectantly as the image of its future was projected" (Khilnani 1997, 62). Meanwhile, these icons of modern industrial development were linked to a political culture that was constituted by public discourses on the need for the advancement of the rural poor. Political rhetoric ranging from politicians' speeches to popular films such as *Mother India* linked modernist ideologies of development, the reduction of poverty, and the Indian nation; the urban middle classes were relatively invisible in this political culture.[13] If the tenets of Nehruvian development could be captured by symbols of dams and factories, the markers of Rajiv Gandhi's regime shifted to commodities that would tap into the tastes and consumption practices of the urban middle class.

Such transitions were not limited to the realm of cultural representation; shifts in political culture were accompanied by corresponding changes in economic policies and a limited phase of liberalization that took place during Rajiv Gandhi's reign. For instance, import regulations were loosened in order to allow an expansion of consumer goods that could cater to middle and upper middle class tastes, resulting in sharp rise in the production levels in import-intensive industries in the automobile and electronics sectors. From 1984–89, automobile production rose from a level of 40,000 per year to 160,000 per year and the production of two-wheel vehicles rose from 300,000 in 1980 to more than 1.5 million in 1988 (Ninan 1990, 42).

Such sharp changes in production levels were symptomatic of broader changes in consumption levels and practices that began to take shape in the 1980s. At a macro level, for instance, sharp rises in consumption were linked to national economic growth. As one scholar concluded,

From 1965 to 1980 consumption grew by only 2.7 percent a year. Investment rose by 5.0 percent and government spending by 6.3 percent annually. Gross domestic product (GDP) grew at

a modest 3.7 percent. After 1980 consumption grew by 4.9 percent a year, while investment rose at a rate of only 3.7 percent;
GDP growth was 4.6 percent annually. The surge in consumption thus appears to have contributed to sustaining the nation's
rapid economic growth after 1980. (Adams 1990, 86)

These macro changes were manifested in significant alterations in
middle class consumption trends. This period witnessed sharp rises in
middle class demand for consumer durable goods such as televisions,
VCRs, and washing machines. These changes in consumption were
consolidated into more permanent lifestyle changes for sections of the
middle class as such commodities increasingly became seen as necessary components of their lifestyle. As T. N. Ninan (1990) argued at the
time, "Everything from refrigerators to watches and synthetic clothing
was once considered a luxury and taxed accordingly. But now that
these goods are viewed increasingly as necessities by the middle class
throughout India, the government has adjusted its tax policy" (42).

Such shifts in consumption reflected a transition with deeper political implications. Changes in taxation and policies on consumer
goods marked a political process in which the state began to identify the middle class as a distinctive group with its own political and
economic interests that needed to be consciously addressed through
governmental policy and rhetoric. Rajiv Gandhi's policies denoted
a significant break from earlier historical periods not because he
was the first prime minister or politician to address middle class
concerns but because his policies and vision signified a new understanding of the middle class that rested on specific linkages between
middle class aspirations, consumption practices, and policies of economic reform. In this process, if middle class identity were defined
by specific lifestyles and consumption practices, its interests could
be best represented through a model of national development that
advocated liberalization.[14] The association between liberalization and
the middle class was further underlined by a growing participation
of the middle class in the stock market.[15]

The new middle class was the public and highly visible cultural
face of the benefits and opportunities that economic liberalization
represented for the Indian nation. The role of the state in this process

was captured by elements of both recognition and of construction. At one level, Rajiv Gandhi and his governmental policies fundamentally recognized the untapped potential for consumption that had been hidden by early nationalist Nehruvian–Gandhian discourses of socialism and austerity. However, at another level, Rajiv Gandhi's political rhetoric and policies participated in the construction of this new middle class by aiding in the shift of the dominant construction of middle class identity in terms of the figure of a consumer.

While the liberalization that Gandhi undertook during his reign proved to be limited, and while middle class support was soon dampened by allegations of corruption and by domestic religious and ethnic violence, the transformation of the liberalizing middle class into a new middle class identity marked a distinctive shift in contemporary Indian politics. The next phase of economic reforms that began unfolding in India in the 1990s brought to the forefront an intensified manifestation of the image of the Indian nation that Rajiv Gandhi had begun to create through his policies and rhetoric of liberalization in the second half of the 1980s. Much as Rajiv Gandhi envisioned, newly available commodities, consumption practices, and urban lifestyles in the 1990s became linked with a national cultural standard associated with the rise of a new Indian middle class.

Framing the Liberalizing Indian Nation: Visual Technologies, National Symbols, and New Middle Class Consumption

Economic policies of liberalization in the 1990s were accompanied by a significant shift in national political culture. In many ways, this shift represented an expansion of trends that emerged in the 1980s. Businessmen, entrepreneurs, and pro-reform politicians increasingly became visible icons that were valorized in mainstream media representations.[16] In one classic case in the late 1990s, pro-reforms chief minister of Andhra Pradesh Chandrababu Naidu became a visible public figure who represented the marriage of effective local political entrepreneurship and a savvy, high-tech modernist outlook in ways that echoed Rajiv Gandhi's image.[17] This "iconization" of Chandrababu

Naidu (Rudolph and Rudolph 2001) occurred on two different levels: He was hailed for his political entrepreneurship in seeking out foreign investment in ways that circumvented the central government and charted a new activist economic role for state government leaders[18] and at a broader level, was valorized by a more complex set of symbolic politics. For instance, the English print media, a central vehicle for the discursive expression of new middle class identity, reveled in stories about Chandrababu Naidu's distinctive personal political style—symbolized in his personal use of a laptop, his "CEO" attitude and urban-professional approach to politics, and his attempt to transform the local state bureaucracy through the use of high technology. As one newspaper report put it:

> Welcome to the hi-tech world of Mr. Naidu where old notions of collectors living the leisurely lives of nawabs are passe. This scenario has been replayed in the homes of all the district collectors of the state over the last 45 days since the teleconferencing facility was installed. The Andhra Pradesh chief minister can now conference with 28 bureaucrats—including the collectors. In two months they will be videoconferencing—and life is going to get no better for the hapless bureaucrat. (Iyengar 1999)

The bulky structures of the administration, emblems of past scripts of a state-dominated economy are, in this narrative, shaken up and professionalized by a forward-looking chief minister embracing the high-tech image that Rajiv Gandhi had attempted to portray.[19] These representations signified a broader change in the national political culture associated with liberalization. Liberalization had set into motion a process of reimagination of the Indian nation through new signs and symbols.

Consider the ways in which visual representations of newly available commodities have become central symbols that depict the benefits of economic liberalization.[20] Throughout the course of my fieldwork, individuals from various segments of the middle class consistently pointed to the choice of commodities as a central indicator of the benefits of economic liberalization. Even in interviews conducted during the relative stagnation of an economic recession in

1998, individuals indicated that they at least no longer had to depend on relatives abroad to provide them with access to various foreign commodities. Prior to liberalization, goods from abroad were primarily accessible to upper class individuals who had the financial means to travel and import goods, or to individuals who migrated to, or had relatives residing in, places such as the Persian Gulf countries or other advanced industrialized nations. Lack of access to such goods represented significant limits on the material prosperity of the Indian middle class, limits that heightened a sense of middle class anxiety and undue dependence on diasporic connections for access to consumer goods. Hence, the idea that "abroad is now in India," as one advertising executive put it, signifies the potential realization of middle class aspirations of consumption, a realization that can now take place within India's borders.[21] This transition in political culture in contemporary India signifies the ways in which the Indian nation has been reimagined in the context of liberalization.

Visual representations of newly available commodities can therefore allow us to view the ways in which meanings attached to such commodities weave together narratives of nationhood and development with the creation of middle class identity. If the historical emergence of modern nationalism has been linked to the rise of what Benedict Anderson (1983) has called "print capitalism," the imagination of the nation in the more recent past is inextricably bound to emerging technologies of vision.[22]

Let us begin with examples from the advertising industry—a classic site for representational practices of middle class consumption. A measure of the increasing significance of the advertising industry can be seen in growth figures for the industry in the early period of liberalization in the 1990s, which ranged from a 49.5 percent increase in 1994–95 to a 22.4 increase in 1996–97.[23]

As the industry became increasingly prominent in the 1980s and 1990s, as William Mazzarella (2003) argues, advertising practices and images became central "ideological flashpoints" (12) for broader social issues. A reading of such practices can provide a sense of the symbolic texture of the broad shifts in political culture and the corresponding visible rise of the new middle class.[24] Consider the ways in which advertising practices have engaged in the production of national narratives.

In interviews that I conducted with leading advertising agencies in Mumbai, representatives described a clearly defined creative strategy to "Indianize" representations of newly available commodities. As the vice president of one company put it when describing initial marketing miscalculations of multinational companies:

> They [multinationals] presumed that if you said Nike it meant something. Levi's means nothing to the middle class. You've got to build value for them. After you've done your number crunching and understood how many people have the money to buy you can't just say "look folks I'm here." That's the first mistake they've all made. Now if you follow advertising you'll find they've Indianized themselves. . . . The classic example is between Coke and Pepsi. Coke came in and said "we are here." Pepsi just took Sachin Tendulkar [India's leading cricket player] and said "we've always been here. And that's without saying it. We understand you." It's fairly clear who is winning in the market.[25]

This strategy of nationalizing foreign products has become increasingly dominant within the advertising industry. Transparent examples include advertising strategies that use well-known nationalist songs, popular commercial film actors, and the sponsorship of cultural and sporting events that evoke strong national support. Some campaigns invoke nationalist narratives through more subtle signs. Such narratives borrow from older, historically specific meanings that present a fusion between national tradition and a vision of a broader global space. I turn now to an interpretive reading of specific images as a means for mapping out some of the dominant symbolic registers and patterns of signification that have been recoding a national political culture associated with liberalization and the new middle class.

Consider a series of advertisements for air-conditioning units produced by Carrier Aircon Ltd. The advertisements cover a two-page spread, representing "before" and "after." In one such advertisement (see Figure 2), the first page depicts an old sadhu lying outdoors on a bed of nails next to a wall with faded paint and torn posters of a Hindi film. The second page depicts the sadhu lying on a bed covered with a thick printed quilt in a bedroom with lemon-colored walls. The sadhu is now surrounded by a lamp, a plant, and a few well-polished pieces of wooden furniture framing the bed. The sunlight that beats down on the sadhu in the first picture is now filtered through sloping skylights.

The image presents us with a striking representation of the contrast between the modern and the traditional, a contrast that has permeated ideologies of development. By depicting a sadhu, the advertisement invokes well-established Orientalist images that associate India with holy men, exotic religious practices, and poverty.[26] The man in this image, representing backwardness and poverty, can, however, be rescued by the luxury consumer item, in this case the air conditioning unit. Moreover, this transformation of the outer material conditions can take place without displacing the inner spiritual essence of India that the sadhu represents. In both photographs the sadhu is depicted in exactly the same position, reclining with his eyes shut. The image provides a visual embodiment of the ways in which the emergence of Indian national identity rested on the preservation of a protected inner sphere of Hindu tradition that could confront and ultimately accept Western standards of progress and development (Chatterjee 1990). The core of Indian tradition, the image suggests, can be retained even as the material context of that tradition is modernized and improved. Meanwhile, a small caption in fine print below the photos reminds us, "Carrier air conditioning can also be experienced in outer space, keeping astronauts comfortably protected in space flights." This consumer technology represents the promise of continued progress and development without disrupting the stability of the stationary reclining sadhu. The image suggests that technological progress and material wealth will not disrupt the stability of a Hindu-Indian national identity.

Such representational practices are not isolated or random examples but are in fact symptomatic of an expanding use of Hindu religious imagery in advertising. Arvind Rajagopal (2001a) has noted that the rise of Hindu nationalism in India helped open up a public symbolic field for the use of religious imagery that spilled over into specific forms of textual strategies within the advertising industry (2001b, 64). These shifting patterns, and the intersecting dynamics of the rise of Hindu nationalism and the expansion of policies and discourses of liberalization, have produced and intensified the intersection of class

FIGURE 2. Reclining sadhu. This advertisement invokes a contrast between the modern and traditional. By employing well-established Orientalist images, the ad suggests that the commodity can rescue India from its backwardness and poverty without displacing Indian cultural traditions.

The world's No.1 in air conditioning
After all, we invented it.

and religion in the formation of dominant representations of the identity of the new middle class.[27] At one level, such processes represent a continuation of historical processes that, as we have seen, imbricated class and religion during the late nineteenth and early twentieth centuries. However, at another level, the kinds of symbolic politics and public images in arenas such as the advertising industry provide a lens for an analysis of the distinctive characteristics of the kind of public middle class identity that is being shaped in postliberalization India.

Specific images that I am analyzing represent broader patterns of strategies in business management theory and practices that consciously attempt to align marketing strategies with specific national and local cultural conditions. Multinational companies consistently attempt to associate their products with signifiers of the Indian nation, for instance through sponsorship of the Indian team in the 1996 Olympics or through more subtle references to specific Indian phenomena such as the monsoon season.

Businesses have also increasingly attempted to consciously address social criticisms of the negative cultural effects of multinational products. Marketing strategies that now commonly involve the sponsorship of community events and of culturally specific symbols are constitutive of systemic shifts in business practices.[28] For instance, MTV in India hired a marketing research group in Mumbai to assess the impact of MTV on youth groups and determined that there were no negative consequences for youth attitudes to "Indian and family" norms (Vasavi 1996, 25).[29] As Vamsee Juluri (2003) noted in his ethnographic study of MTV audiences in India, far from representing a teleological form of Westernization, music television and youth programming have integrated older Indian visual traditions that have emphasized expressions of sentimentality associated with families, friendship, and kinship with new programming connected with the liberalization of Indian television (188).

Such trends were also evident in responses of groups of urban youth that I interviewed at various colleges in Mumbai in 1998. Students often consciously rejected a projection of oppositional identities between India and the West and emphasized languages of synthesis and balance. As one student put it during a discussion I had with a group of students studying communications and the mass media,

"The more you get into something the further you get away from something else. So what we used to be before the foreign marker has changed now. And don't blame us for everything. Help us find our way back. I can't stand it when someone says 'foreign society is bad.'"[30]

Meanings attached to newly available commodities that circulate through nationalist narratives do not simply bring about a simple form of postnational global culture or Westernization.[31] In many instances, this nationalization of the commodity deliberately retains a mark of foreignness as a sign that the new Indian nation has moved away from the older ideologies of state protection that largely kept foreign capital and commodities outside its borders. As one advertisement for a refrigerator puts it, "Every inch of the BPL Frost-free speaks of international technology. With an Indian accent" (see Figure 3). The photograph in this advertisement is of a woman, half-Japanese, half-Indian in her appearance, clothing, and makeup. Her hair and makeup are in traditional Japanese style yet she wears a dot on her forehead and is dressed in a sari. The gendered nature of the image transforms her nationalized foreignness into a nonthreatening, and alluring, form.

Visual representations that aim to give meaning to a liberalizing Indian nation are not presented only by multinational companies deploying nationalist narratives. They are also part of the marketing strategies of Indian companies. One prominent Indian corporation, for instance, presented its sixty-year history in a twenty-five-page series of advertisements in a major news magazine. The series opens with references to its beginnings as a cotton textiles company in the 1930s, images of cotton spools which are transformed into images of jeans while the caption alludes to a potential $33-million market for clothes within India. The advertisement goes on to note: "And a fair chunk of that will come out of the pockets of middle and lower middle income groups." The series of images explicitly provides references to the Indian middle class, vividly captured in one series of photographs of a large group of men and women standing outdoors (see Figure 4). The caption begins, "There's More Wealth on This Page Than the Country's Top Corporates Put Together." The text on the next page reads, "200 million cash rich consumers make India's middle class. Their annual spending power rivals that of many western countries. They save and invest more than the people of any other nation."

4-door 350 Litre

3-door 350 Litre

2-door 300 Litre

Every inch of the BPL Frost-free speaks of internationa technology. With an Indian accen

Open a BPL Frost-free and what strikes you first is how well adapted to your special needs. Interiors built around Indian food ha To accommodate large bartans as well as small katoris. Frost- design. So no more messy defrosting, and no fear of water floodin the event of a power failure. A tropicalised compressor that

Other Features: • Different temperature zones for different foods • 4-star rating -18°C Fre • 1°C Chiller compartment* • Humidity controlled vegetable compartm

BPL REFRIGERATION LIMITED

Contact: AHMEDABAD: 7470327/7411643. BANGALORE: 5550426/5550442. BHUBANESHWAR: 416017/416260. CALCUTTA: 2453637/2453 233206. INDORE: 557235. JAIPUR: 43699/602084. JAMSHEDPUR: 431437/436079. KANPUR: 294937/294

FIGURE 3. Hybrid woman. This advertisement nationalizes the foreign brand by representing a hybrid Japanese–Indian image of a woman. The gendered nature of the image attempts to transform her nationalized foreignness into a nonthreatening and alluring form.

2-door 250 Litre

and the rigours of the Indian climate. A sleek flatback design.

more exposed coils that are difficult to clean and unsafe for

children. And a range of models. To suit every type of family.

out BPL Frost - free. You'll see how the world's best has become

best.

BPL FROST-FREE

ational Sanyo technology • Integrated PUF insulation • Rust-proof painted steel sheet body
riser* • Flexible magic shelves* And more.   * In select models only.

3-door 250 Litre

2-door 185 Litre

McCANN/BLR/BPL/86196

BPL *Believe in the Best.*

DIGARH: 690846/694358. COCHIN: 371018/374254. COIMBATORE: 396484/391552. GHAZIABAD: 751697. GUWAHATI: 510173. HYDERABAD: 231844/
AS: 4330278/801. MUMBAI: 4122976/4128362. NEW DELHI: 6469001/6219038-40. PUNE: 350326/351873. RAIPUR: 529235.

FIGURE 4. The wealth of the middle classes. This is part of a twenty-five-page advertisement celebrating a prominent Indian corporation's sixty-year history. In this image, the ad explicitly invokes the economic significance of the Indian middle class by connecting the company's success to the wealth of the middle class. The next image (not shown) speaks of the unvaried consumer power of the 200 million members of the middle class, underlining the consumer-oriented identity of the middle class.

The series of images continues with photographs that merge the cities of New York, London, and Paris with the Statue of Liberty, Big Ben, and the Eiffel Tower in the forefront of each. The merged image, with the caption "You're Looking at the View From Our Ahmedabad Office," refers to the corporate groups' overseas global activities (see Figure 5).

This extensive series of images captures the implications of a distinctive repertoire of advertising images that cast commodities produced by Indian companies into the process of globalization while asserting that it is the very Indianness of the commodity or the company that allows it to confront the global (a sign that is coded by the use of images of major Western metropolitan cities).

In the series of images I described above, the corporate group makes explicit linkages between its products, the middle class that signifies the wealth of the Indian nation, and processes of globalization. In previous examples of multinational advertising strategies discussed above, the global is incorporated within the national, an accent that serves to improve on what is still firmly Indian. However, in this case Indian capital provides the means of access to and success over the global, a process that once again is not in danger of displacing what is Indian. It is the purchasing power of Indian middle class consumers that can compete with and outdo the Western consumer; it is an office firmly rooted in Ahmedabad that can provide a panoramic view of New York, London, and Paris. Images used by various Indian companies make references to their ability to compete in the global market; as one advertisement puts it, "We have given India what it had always deserved—recognition."

The relevance of this narrative is not limited to newly available foreign commodities but even includes advertising strategies designed to market products as varied as toothbrushes and gasoline. Consider one final example of these configurations of the national and global. An advertisement for the Ambassador car depicts two policemen with guns standing high above a road where eight white Ambassador cars are parked (see Figure 6). The police, clearly a symbol of the state, represent a particular mixture of layers of state power: military force, surveillance, and security. The male officers inscribe the subtext of a masculine narrative that marks the boundaries of state power. The white Ambassadors represent the cars used by politicians and government officials.[32] The caption states: "Congratulating the enduring success of India's democracy." At the corner of the advertisement is a separate caption that reads, "HM Ambassador: It's Always There." The image links the commodity, the automobile, with the power and the endurance of the Indian nation-state, embodied by the police and the military, traditional symbols of state power. The commodity itself— the series of white Ambassadors—stands in for the tradition of Indian democracy. The policemen survey the landscape not just to protect the enduring success of democracy but to protect the association of democracy with the commodity.

In my reading of these advertisements as visual cultural texts, I have argued that the meanings that circulate through such depictions of various commodities mediate narratives of "the national" and "the global." The aesthetic of the commodity does not merely serve as a passive reflector of wider social and cultural processes but instead becomes a central site in which the Indian nation is reimagined. The result is that the language of the nation in this process begins to borrow its aesthetic expression from the world of the commodity (Haug 1986).

A striking visual example of this process can be found in a series of *Times of India* advertisements that present the success of the newspaper by measuring its genealogy against specific manifestations of transnational capital. One such advertisement depicts an elderly middle class man standing outdoors reading the *Times of India*. In the background are shops with large signs for Pepsi. The caption at the top of the image reads: "Pepsi, born 1896. *Times of India*, born 1838." Another similar ad presents a young upper class man seated near his car underneath a sign for Shell engine oils (see Figure 7). The caption above reads: "Shell, born 1897. The *Times of India*, born 1838." In both cases, the caption below the images read "The *Times of India*: One of the World's Big Ideas."

These ads demonstrate that an icon of the Indian nation-state, one of the oldest English-language newspapers in the country, begins to represent its own history in relation to the history of particular symbols of multinational corporations. The nation is thus imagined not

Figure 5. The global view from Ahmedabad. This advertisement invokes the ability of Indian companies to compete in the global economy. The new globalizing India now provides entry to the world, depicted by a local office in Ahmedabad that offers a panoramic view of New York, London, and Paris.

Congratulating the enduring success of India's democratic tradition

FIGURE 6. The Ambassador. For the new middle class, the Ambassador car has become a cultural symbol of India's state socialist legacies, when middle class consumption was restricted to a single car. This advertisement seeks to invoke this legacy more positively by linking the car's history with the success of Indian democracy. The commodity is once again depicted as a symbol of the nation-state.

HM AMBASSADOR

It's always there.

SHELL, BORN 1897. THE TIMES OF INDIA, BORN 1838.

THE TIMES OF INDIA
ONE OF THE WORLD'S BIG IDEAS.

FIGURE 7. Reimagining national symbols through the commodity. This is one of a series of advertisements that presented the success of India's best-known English newspaper, the *Times of India*, by measuring its genealogy against familiar Western commodities such as Shell and Pepsi. The national icon is represented through the aesthetics of the global commodity.

just through the conventional sites and symbols of nationalism, such as war memorials or independence-day celebrations (Anderson 1983) but through the aesthetic of the commodity form.[33]

Representations of national identity in India begin to undergo a transformation as they are aestheticized in distinctive ways through newly available commodities. The markers of the progress of the Indian nation no longer rest on the mass-based factories of the Nehruvian vision or the physical labor of grassroots self-reliance that marked Gandhi's conception of village development. There is a significant shift in the ways in which the material progress of the Indian nation must now be measured. Such progress can no longer be limited to the desire for the physical quantity of production but must confront the aesthetic quality of commodities. Hence, it is a new vision of the Indian nation-state—rather than a homogeneous Westernized model of global cultural identity—that attempts to give meaning to India's integration into the global economy.[34] This redefinition of the Indian nation is linked to the rise of the new middle class and, as I will demonstrate, the articulation of a distinctive cultural standard associated with a hegemonic lifestyle of a liberalizing middle class.

These middle class oriented narratives of national identity rest on the reproduction of gendered symbols. Gendered representations are a central part of the technologies of vision that begin to define the aesthetic and cultural standards of what counts as ideal middle class individual, family, and community-based sociocultural practices in liberalizing India. The gendered imagination of a national future in India unfolds through a set of contradictory images. The media has been characterized by images of "the new Indian woman," one who "must attend her national identity as well as her modernity; she is Indian as well as new" (Rajan 1993, 132). "The New Indian Woman" as the publicity release for a contemporary women's magazine puts it is "the tough as nails career woman who finds it easy to indulge in the occasional superstition. Her outlook is global, but her values would make her grandma proud." As the publisher of this women's magazine argued, "our values remain, they don't leave a certain framework which is still the Indian value system. . . . I think we respect that and we function and address women within that framework. Of course she's urban, she's contemporary, she travels . . . but that framework still exists."[35]

If cellular phones and pagers denote status symbols they are also cast as the tools to keep families together, or as the text of one ad reads, "If you were told that a pager ties you down, well, it does bind your family together." A central category of images that dominate the print media attempts to associate domestic commodities such as automobiles and refrigerators with gendered images of the middle class. In particular, such images often invoke ideologies of domesticity and family order.

In addition to the explicit gendered narratives of such images, representations of new middle class lifestyle are also shaped by caste-based social codes. Idealized images of middle class families are shaped both by upper caste as well as upper middle class social codes. Arvind Rajagopal (2001b) has argued, for instance, that advertising strategies have deployed a form of caste-based aesthetics in which personal and gendered relations are cast through symbolic representations of intimacy for the upper castes and representations of utilitarianism for images of lower castes (89).

Such caste-based connotations also operate in more subtle nuances and codes in representational practices. Depictions of upper-caste middle class domesticity are represented through carefully bounded spaces, sanitized from both the chaos of outdoor urban life as well as the complexities of middle class households in which there are, for instance, complex cross-caste social interactions between upper caste middle classes and lower caste domestic workers.

The nuanced social codes point to the significance of analyzing representational strategies that move beyond a focus on the visible to an analysis of symbolic spaces of the invisible. Consider the expanded array of gendered representations of the family and domesticity that have emerged in the postliberalization period. A central pattern in such images is the representation of the middle class through new structures of the nuclear family rather than images of older joint-family household structures. Such images do not simply echo a teleological process of the impact of modernization on shifting family structures, they also point to the representation of the new middle class family as a purified, self-contained space. In the case of representations of domestic consumer goods such as washing machines, such commodities can stand in as aestheticized substitutes for the labor typically performed by low-caste domestic workers in middle class households. The unmarked codes of gender and family thus lie at the intersection of caste and class.

The intersections of gender, caste, and religion that emerge within nationalized representations of the liberalizing middle class point once again to the contradictions of middle class modernity. Such historically salient identities and structures are an integral part of representations that have sought to project the new middle class as the central agent managing India's relationship with a globalizing world. While the reworking of identities such as caste within narratives of globalization might appear paradoxical, such processes are in fact consistent with the ways in which the political project of modernity has incorporated and redefined "traditional" social identities in comparative contexts.[36] Social identities in fact serve as an important source of symbolic resources that help to manage the uncertainties associated with policies of economic liberalization and the broader processes of globalization that such policies invoke.

Consider one final example of an advertising campaign that calls to mind older narratives of the relationship between the state and middle class. A series of automobile advertisements called "Man, Woman, Child, and Car" depict idealized upper caste, upper middle class images of a nuclear family with its automobile (see Figure 8). Such images implicitly invoke older messages of state family-planning rhetoric that promoted smaller nuclear families. In particular, the image makes associations with a central state advertising campaign that depicted the ideal modern Indian family with a father, mother, son, and daughter through a sparse sketch of the heads of the four family members, a visual image that has been a national symbol of family planning policies in the postindependence period. However, the austere warnings about the ills of large families that characterized earlier state-sponsored advertisements now give way to an association between an idealized tranquility of the nuclear family with status and material comfort. The four members of the state-sponsored family model (man, woman, son, and daughter) have been replaced by man, woman, child, and car. In this vision of the modern Indian

Gaurav Seth, JEWELLER. *Shown here with members of his family. Wife Gauri, son V...*

Manual and Automatic transmission Multi-point fuel injection system: 80 HP engine Power steering Power windows Side-impact bars 530-litre b...

FIGURE 8. The new nuclear middle class family. This advertisement represents an idealized vision of an upper middle class family. The image invokes an earlier state family-planning advertising campaign that depicted a man, woman, and child as the ideal modern nuclear family. Austere warnings about large families have been replaced by the tranquility and comfort associated with the new middle class nuclear family.

family, the commodity reworks older ideological narratives that have been deployed by the nation-state with the caste- and class-based aesthetics of the new middle class family.

The examples of advertisements that I have discussed represent dominant narratives that attempt to create idealized images of middle class lifestyles. In fact the advertising industry has played an important role in the cultural creation of the new middle class and the kinds of symbols that I have pointed to are a significant component of the everyday meanings of the otherwise abstract phrase "economic reforms." However, the making of the new Indian middle class cannot simply be understood as a product of particular advertising campaigns or images. Rather, such advertisements are discursive practices that are part of broader set of structural shifts in the mainstream media. For instance, financial pressures and increasing competition have led the print media to shift in more conscious ways to targeting the new middle class through increasing coverage on lifestyle issues, fashion and entertainment, what has been termed "infotainment," and "news you can use."[37]

Consider, for example, shifts in India's most prestigious English-language newspaper, the *Times of India*. During the course of the 1990s the newspaper made significant shifts, covering lifestyle and entertainment issues and adding the *Bombay Times*, a supplement specifically catering to lifestyle concerns of the new middle class. As Pradeep Guha, the executive director of the *Times of India* put it in a candid interview,

> Undoubtedly then, the advertiser is my target audience, no question about it. It's the way commercially successful publishers have managed their businesses abroad. But that does not mean that we do not respect our readers. It's just that we market our product to those readers which our advertisers want. And these readers are then packaged and sold to our advertisers. And that's where the profits lie. Today, every copy I sell, I lose money. So who's paying for this? It's the advertiser. (Thackraney 1998, 23)

This trend was echoed in interviews I conducted with younger journalists attempting to establish themselves. In an ironic comment, one journalist noted that the *Times of India* now regularly covers Miss India contests and that the "marketing person sits over reporters' shoulders making sure all the names of sponsors are explicitly printed in the articles."[38]

The implication is not, of course, that such changes mean that the quality or seriousness of Indian journalism has declined or that lifestyle-oriented features in the print media have replaced news coverage. Rather, I point to such changes to demonstrate the political significance of specific media representations of middle class lifestyles and consumption and to demonstrate the ways in which such practices spill over boundaries between the "symbolic" and "economic" dimensions in the making of this new middle class.

Language, Identity, and the Public Face of the New Middle Class

In the representational practices I have analyzed, the urban middle class is delineated as consumers not just of the newly available commodities in liberalizing India but consumers of a new India that has been produced through the meanings attached to these commodities. Emerging formations of the nationalist imagination in liberalizing India are part of a broader array of cultural narratives in the contemporary public sphere in India. Such narratives are not limited to advertising images but cut across a range of public cultural and discursive sites that have begun to depict the urban middle classes as the principal figures in India's shift to a market-led model of economic development.

Consider the following depiction of the liberalizing middle class: "'Middle Class . . . but Millionaires' . . . they usually talk of buying farm houses, retiring from jobs and spending the rest of their days with beer mugs in their hands. You look at them and see men who are just a few years on either side of 30 and dismiss them as brash young men with extravagant pipe dreams. Until you realise they aren't kidding. Meet the new millionaires. Middle class millionaires" (Rai 1997, 50). This introduction to an article on middle class professionals who have been transformed into millionaires because of company stock option schemes captures the creation of a dream to which the urban middle classes can aspire in globalizing India. The image is repeated in a wide array of public cultural forms such as advertisements, publications in the print media (including new publications such as glossy supplements to mainstream newspapers and consumer-oriented magazines), and television programming.

The urban middle classes are, in effect, the central agents in this re-visioning of the Indian nation. Images of mobility associated with automobiles and cellular phones create a standard of progress to which the urban middle classes can and should aspire. For instance, in the early 1990s, the publishers of *India Today*, one of the leading English news magazines in India launched a new publication, *India Today plus*, which mirrors this distinctive era of consumption. The magazine, printed on thick glossy paper—which distinguishes it from other popular and news magazines, presented readers with consumer information such as a buyer's guide to home gyms, cellular phones, and cars. The edition was clearly targeted at an upper class, English-speaking audience (the quarterly magazine costs Rs 75.00—a regular magazine would cost no more than Rs 15.00 for an issue) and is a vivid example of the creation of the boundaries of the cultural standard for a globalized middle class elite.

As another example, consider the success of a new English-language consumer magazine whose readership increased from approximately 29,000 to more than 93,000 readers in 1998–99, its first year of publication, despite the effects of a national economic recession. The magazine, which provides advice to middle class individuals investing in new commodities and newly available financial products, marks the new standard of the liberalizing middle class. As one writer for the magazine argued, "We are dream merchants basically . . . we are writing to a middle class that cannot easily afford these things but who'd like to."[39] Significantly, the success of the magazine lay in the fact that it moved beyond its presumed audience of an elite English-speaking metropolitan audience and made inroads into small town markets.

The effects of such representational practices are underlined by stories and satiric commentary on the proliferation of cell phones in Mumbai as the mark of urban elite culture, which cite incidents of phones ringing in movie theaters and grocery stores, upper class teenagers carrying cell phones, and status competition over models of cell phones (Chandra and Agarwal 1996). As one representative of the creative department of an advertising agency put it,

> We have two distinct groups. One is the yuppie, and the other is the puppie, the panjabi urban professional, basically the second generation businessman trader. The businessman trader whose businesses are booming. If you look across [the street] over here you see all these camera shops. The guy who sold me this lens he's not got a very large shop. He'll be making 50 times what I make. This is bought in cash. Its smuggled into the country. There's no paper tracing this. It's a cash payment. He's got more money than I can ever dream of having. This is his father's business. His father they are *goris* [caste group], they are traditional people, he is young, he's hep; coming back to the point exposure to television, exposure to western lifestyle. Where does he get his aspirations from? These people lack, let me use the word "class" [*sic*]. The people who set the trends the people who set the values are the educated middle class. They give a brand respectability. They make a brand a thing to be seen with.[40]

Consider the way in which this statement uses a consciousness of caste-based distinction based on birth ("his father they are *goris*") to demarcate social distinctions within the middle classes ("these people lack, let me use the word 'class' "). It is the educated middle class, with an upper-caste identity (one that is left unmarked) that sets the standard for the new middle class identity that is emerging. Respectability in this context becomes a symbolic marker for the intersections between caste and class in ways that echo historical conceptions such as "*bhadralok* respectability" but rework this marker through specific consumption-based distinctions associated with the liberalizing middle class.

Linkages between middle class respectability and commodity consumption were echoed in interviews I conducted with journalists and advertisers in the print media, and are reminiscent of Bourdieu's (1984) analysis of the reproduction of socioeconomic stratification through the production of cultural distinction. The conceptions of middle class respectability and symbolic politics are in many ways typical of patterns that can be discerned in comparative contexts in both advanced industrialized and late-industrializing contexts (Lamont 1992; Owensby 1999; West 2002). However, what makes the contemporary Indian case distinctive from comparative historical conceptions of middle class morality and respectability in advanced industrialized contexts such as France and the United States (Bourdieu 1984; Lamont 1992) is the way in which such internal shifts in identity and social distinction are inextricably linked to global power relations and to an ongoing negotiation with perceptions of external social relations that are coded at various points as either global or Western. I have already pointed to the mediation between nationalist narratives of "Indianness" and representations of Westernization or globalization in the symbolic politics of advertising images. This process of interaction and differentiation unfolds through complex social processes and is a distinctive part of the creation of the identity of the new middle class.

Consider the way in which the transformation of the public world of the urban middle class extends into the realm of television media.[41] The availability of satellite television, which has provided an alternative to state programming on the Doordarshan channel, has led to the proliferation of both American television shows as well as Indian versions of American shows such as game shows, talk shows, and music videos. New talk shows, for instance, specifically target a middle class audience and address a range of issues such as the cultural effects of consumerism, changing youth attitudes, problems of small investors, and changing gender roles.

As with the case of visual images in the print media, these new forums are not merely imitations of Western shows. For instance, programs targeted specifically at the middle class are often characterized by a hybridized language, termed "Hinglish" by the popular media, which combines Hindi and English.[42] The use of English words by non-English speakers is in itself, of course, not a new phenomenon since it stems from the colonial legacies of the Indian nation-state. However, the form of Hinglish used in such programs is distinctive from the practice of using a few isolated English words that characterizes widely used cross-class linguistic practices. In some programs, English words are used within sentences spoken in Hindi while in other programs, the language shifts back and forth between English and Hindi (a talk show host may begin speaking in English and then switch to Hindi or vice versa).[43] This specific form of Hinglish requires fluency in both languages and specifically targets urban middle class audiences.

Such linguistic formations represent significant practices in the creation of middle class identity.[44] The various discursive and representational practices I have analyzed form part of the English-speaking public sphere that is associated with the rising new middle class. Command over English language represents both a form of cultural capital as well as a structural marker of middle class identity since the possession of such language skills can be transformed into social and economic capital in the labor market. In other words, fluency in English marks an individual with the distinction of class culture and locates the individual within the new middle class in socioeconomic terms as such linguistic skills are a necessary component for access to the new economy and skilled jobs. Language, in this case, shapes the definition of the interior space of the identity of this social group with a sense of external differentiation—language in this context is not merely a transparent medium for the expression of a predefined class identity. Rather, the distinctiveness of this middle class identity is constituted by language.

However, this relationship between class and language is different from existing patterns in comparative contexts (Scott 1988; Sewell 1980; Stedman Jones 1984). In the Indian case, English identity intrinsically marks this hegemonic model of middle class identity with a relationship to an outside, an external world that is represented alternatively in varying contexts as Westernized, Western, or global. The association between the new middle class and English education is such that the identity of this group is intrinsically characterized by a kind of cultural dislocation—one that differentiates it from vernacular elites. In other words, English is not merely a skill that the new middle class can use for instrumental socioeconomic ends; rather it is constitutive of the identity of this group.[45] In this dominant public identity of the liberalizing middle class, linguistic identity is constitutive of class formation and is not merely an ephiphenomenal reflection of socioeconomic processes.

Linguistic self-identification as "middle class" in the English public sphere marks this identity with a distinction that simultaneously distances this group from indigenous social strata and places it in a contradictory relationship with the external world. On the one hand, this global relationship places the new middle class in a role of national leadership; that is, it is seen as the social group that can steer the Indian nation through the shifting terrains of globalization. On the other hand, the cultural-linguistic distancing between the new middle class and indigenous elites and subordinated social groups complicates the claims the middle class makes of national representativeness. This is one of the central paradoxes in the politics of middle class identification. The cultural dislocation of the English-speaking elite tiers of the middle class have historically placed it in an ambivalent space—one that has been marked by an oscillation between this sense of differentiation on the one hand and a search for a representative cultural authenticity on the other.

Such dynamics have often unfolded in middle class invocations of cultural difference, for example through various forms of religiosity as well as in more politicized forms of ethnic and religious nationalism. The cultural ambiguity of middle class identity that is linked to questions of language has heightened the significance of other forms of identification based on caste, religion, ethnicity, and gender. Meanwhile, such processes have also intensified the political significance of responses and resistances of vernacular elites to hegemonic narratives of a new middle class identity.[46] While I analyze these processes in greater length in later chapters (see chapters 4 and 5), my objective at this stage is to provide a broad framework for the kinds of representational practices that produce the hegemonic boundaries of the new middle class.

At one level, this liminality of the new middle class is representative of a generalized pattern that is characteristic of the middle class in both Western and non-Western contexts. That is, the crux of middle class politics lies in the tension between its claims of national or universal representativeness on the one hand and the fact that as a social group it distinguishes itself from both the upper class and from subaltern groups on the other. Scholars working in a range of historical and empirical contexts have sought to pin down this politics of ambiguity. However, what distinguishes non-Western contexts such as India are the specificities of postcoloniality and the associated historical imperative for the middle class to carve out a cultural-national identity that can mediate both its relationship with the West (with its implicit colonial legacies) and its relationship with a complex social structure composed of subaltern groups and vernacular elites. Thus, public discourses in India that have decried the declining social responsibility of the middle classes (Varma 1998) are as much an expression of anxieties over the ability of a consumerist Westernized middle class to fulfill this role of national representativeness as they are resistances to economic policies of liberalization and the effects of globalization.

Furthermore, I have argued that visual technologies that have linked representations of newly available commodities, middle class consumption, and national narratives are precisely a response to such anxieties and resistances. For example, the deeper political import of the advertising images discussed earlier does not lie in a simplified view of an industry manipulating images and identities in order to sell goods. Rather, the political significance of such practices for the expression of middle class identity lies in the transformation of specific advertising narratives into a potentially inclusive language of class. The symbolic politics of commodities in effect represent a kind of public language that can transcend the exclusionary connotations of the English-speaking new middle class sphere. For instance, while the advertising industry has historically had urban English-language biases, there has been a growing shift toward rural and small-town markets and toward the use of vernacular languages.[47] Commodity consumption has taken the form of a kind of public language that holds a promise of potential access to new middle class membership that may otherwise seem too easily foreclosed by the linguistic politics of English. This language of class has been coded into narratives of lifestyle that rework existing status distinctions and mediate the anxieties and tensions of social differentiation that stem from restrictions on this promise of access.

The Politics of Lifestyle and the Redefinition of Status Distinctions

Public discourses on the liberalizing middle class in the 1990s both reflected and contributed to the construction of a new consumer-based middle class identity. Discursive practices of commodity consumption point to the ways in which such consumption practices now serve to distinguish this new middle class from the traditional middle class and from other socioeconomic groups. Newly available commodities have become the symbols of modernity and status that upwardly mobile individuals and families must acquire. They represent forms of cultural and social capital that individuals obtain in an attempt to improve their social location.

Idealized discourses of the new middle class have begun to affect individual and family consumption practices in urban metropolitan areas as well as in smaller towns.[48] Consider the following example of shifting patterns of consumption in Gujarat:

> Middle-class status demands a level of consumption that is in tune with the times, and the increased expectations that upward mobility and new consumer styles have brought. When Dharmesh explained to me that one reason Jitesh wants to have a refrigerator is that guests notice it if they don't get ice in their water when they come to visit his house, he touched upon a sensitive point. The "noticing" is a matter of devaluation. An important reason goods like refrigerators have become "requirements" is the fact that the maintenance of status among peers requires them. (Van Wessel 2001, 37)

Various segments of the middle class often consciously seek to emulate the consumption practices associated with the liberalizing middle class, with individual families often overextending themselves financially in order to obtain particular commodities that are symbols of the culture of liberalization.[49] Middle class individuals engage in conscious practices designed to acquire the aesthetic and cultural knowledge necessary to adapt to shifting consumption practices. For instance, during my field research in Mumbai I found that shopping festivals and exhibitions of consumer goods were well attended by middle class individuals.

Consider one exhibit I attended at Mumbai's World Trade Center.[50] The exhibit was constructed like a maze so one had to walk through a narrow corridor flanked by booths on both sides with only one exit at the end of the corridor. With loud music blaring and large crowds passing through, the exhibit combined the atmosphere of a street bazaar, a department store, and an amusement park. Most of the commodities on sale were luxury brands of goods such as televisions and washing machines and there was little evidence of purchases being made on a significant scale. The significance of middle class participation thus had little to do with actual economic consumption. Rather, middle class participation represented a social practice in which individuals were attempting to either gain aesthetic knowledge of newly available commodities or to exhibit a sense of social status associated with new middle class consumption patterns.

Let us consider further the ways in which the rise of the new middle class has begun to rework the status criteria for membership in this social group. With the postliberalization availability of consumer goods, individuals from the upper tiers of the middle class would point to more subtle distinctions between foreign brands made and bought in India and the same foreign brands made and bought abroad. In dominant narratives, while individuals use the consumption of commodities as a strategy of upward mobility, membership in the middle class does not rest simply on the purchase of particular commodities or brands. Rather, it rests on the creation of a distinctive lifestyle associated with a broader set of social practices. Consider leisure, a critical social space for the production of such social distinctions. The leisure and entertainment industry witnessed significant growth in the 1990s. Entertainment enterprises—ranging from bowling alleys, ice skating rinks, and video parlors to restaurants, malls, and amusement parks—are promoted as the icons of the new India of the liberalizing middle class (Jetley 1998). The proliferation of leisure and other service-sector-related industries (Rao 2000, 3571) has contributed to a growing significance of lifestyle as a status marker of middle class identity.

There is perhaps no better instance of an Indian metropolitan city that appears to fit images of the new middle class than the city of Mumbai. The expansion of the services sector and the leisure industry has included a growing bar and restaurant culture. In contrast to smaller restaurants and local tea shops, which have catered to working class and lower middle class individuals, the city now boasts a wide range of upscale bars restaurants and nightclubs that specifically target upwardly mobile urban professionals.[51] As one hotelier put it, "More important than the numbers is the kind of people that come to restaurants now. It's more broadbased, much younger, much more middle-class than ever before . . . much more hip and happening" (48).[52]

There are also changing practices in food consumption. One journalist specializing in consumer trends noted the changes in the kinds of food associated with emerging status distinctions. For example, new middle class lifestyles were creating a demand for "luxury foods" such as mushrooms, broccoli, and kiwi. Along with changes in taste, consumption, and status, new middle class lifestyle shifts have also incorporated practices such as participation in gym cultures, domestic and international travel, and changes in areas such as fashion and children's entertainment.[53] Dowry standards have also shifted in accordance with changes in status criteria and it is has become increasingly customary for dowries to now include demands for commodities such as VCRs, washing machines, and color televisions (Vasudev 2003). Such shifts are not, of course, causally produced by liberalization and can be seen to predate the 1990s (Kumar 1993). However, the reconstitution of status distinctions has been intensified by the expansion of idealized images of consumption since the 1990s.

These lifestyle changes have been defined by a politics of visibility. The public display of particular kinds of social practices marks the creation of a new middle class lifestyle in distinctive ways. Such strategies of visibility in turn become part of the representational practices that help constitute the identity of the liberalizing middle class. It is this very visibility that has provoked an array of public anxieties, criticisms, and ambivalences toward such perceived shifts in middle class culture. Political discourses ranging from traditional leftist critiques of reforms and more conservative religious and cultural nationalist fears of Westernization have decried the rise of middle class consumerism.[54]

Middle class individuals also reflect ambivalences toward the cultural effects of consumerism. Such ambivalences are often coded through moral anxieties over shifting gender roles, changes in youth culture, and the fear of a potential leveling of caste and class differences—for instance through lower class/caste worker emulations of middle class practices of consumption. For example, in everyday interactions, middle class women with whom I discussed middle class lifestyle changes would often comment with unease about female domestic workers who were using "modern" beauty salons or adopting new fashion practices. These forms of social and moral anxiety have in turn tended to intensify the presumed association between the middle class, consumption, and consumerism. In this process, there is often a slippage between the narratives of the new or liberalizing middle class on the one hand and the culture and attitudes of the middle class in general.

The kinds of representational practices I have delineated represent a hegemonic construction of a particular segment of the middle class—one that represents the promise of the liberalizing Indian nation. The discursive nature of this process of creation is such that these boundaries are necessarily fluid. It is the possibility of access to membership in this group through consumption practices that underlines the significance of the rise of this class. The new middle class, in effect, signifies the promise of a new Indian dream, and it is this very promise, as we have seen, that makes this a specifically national rather than a local or globalized elite phenomenon.

However, such discursive elements provide only one dimension of the formation of this group. Scholarship that has focused solely on cultural representations in the media and advertising industries has tended to miss the political dynamics that arise out of the interactions, tensions, and discrepancies between these discursive/representational practices and the structural socioeconomic dimensions of the middle class (Mazzarella 2003). While these cultural representations of new middle class identity are reflected in discernable shifts in consumption, such discourses have also led to a politics of miscalculation with regard to the middle class in India. The result is a set of conceptual and political confusions between the new middle class and middle classes in general—confusions that have shaped political responses to reforms in India and that have inadvertently emerged as part of the array of representational practices that have contributed to the making of India's new middle class.

Consumption, Consumerism, and the Politics of Measurement

Since the early 1990s, discourses on the new middle class and public pronouncements of a potential 200-million middle class market have catalyzed an array of attempts to measure the consumption potential of the Indian middle classes. The attempt at measuring the Indian middle class itself has represented an integral part of the political project of the framing of the new Indian middle class. Consider an early attempt of the National Council for Applied Economic Research to produce an income-based model of the Indian market. In their report on Indian market demographics, which was widely cited in news reports as well as academic analyses, the NCAER created five distinct segments (see Table 2) ranging from the "very rich" to the "destitutes." The report was cited as evidence of a significant expansion at the higher end of the consumption spectrum. An earlier NCAER survey conducted in 1989–90 had, for instance, identified "middle, upper middle and high income groups to be about 20.2 million" households (Rao 1994, 8).[55]

TABLE 2. Consumption and income in India: NCAER report data, 1994–95.

Market segment	Annual income (rupees)	Number of households (millions)
Very rich	> 215,000	1
Consuming class	45,000–215,000	28.6
Climbers	22,000–45,000	48
Aspirants	16,000–22,000	48
Destitutes	< 16,000	35

Source: Sen Gupta 1998.

The first nationwide Gallup survey of consumer attitudes and lifestyles in India was conducted in 1996.[56] The report, citing a "dramatic . . . rise in consumer disposable income, which is estimated to have risen by 47% during the 3-year period 1991–1993 alone" (Gallup Organization 2000, 1), presents an extensive analysis of practices and attitudes and an assessment of the possibilities and obstacles to marketing multinational company products in India.

Such projects of quantification engaged in specific discursive strategies, which helped create the dominant consumer-based identity of the liberalizing Indian middle class. Consider the income-based categories the NCAER produced. In the process of defining an "objective" measurement of income groups in India, the survey engages in practices of social classification.[57] This social classification is built around a consumer-based identity with the "consuming class" standing in for the new middle class, one that makes no distinctions between the lower and upper middle classes. Meanwhile the lower-income rural and urban working classes are constructed as "climbers" and "aspirants" that are striving to reach the standard of this "consuming class."

These social classifications, which were immediately picked up by public discourses in the media, in effect produced a set of hegemonic national classificatory practices that rest on a system of social stratification based on a presumed consumer-based identity of the middle classes. Central to this scheme is a notion of upward mobility and the implied potential for the majority of India's population to either join or aspire to India's "consuming class."

While this classification provided a starkly optimistic redefinition of India's social strata and one that has been used as an ideal measure of the potential of India's middle classes, the reality of middle class consumption has often proved more contradictory. While the opening up of the Indian market and the availability of new consumer goods did result in a significant rise in consumption levels, this rise in consumption has not uniformly produced the radical shift in consumer practices and attitudes that discourses on the new Indian middle class seemed to promise.

Consider some of the paradoxes that surfaced in the drive toward the quantification of India's emerging consumer market in the first phase of liberalization in the 1990s. Purchases of particular consumer goods such as color televisions, cars, and cell phones—goods that have served as the public symbols of liberalizing India and of the identity of the liberalizing middle class—have been marked by tremendous growth since the liberalization policies of the 1990s. As the Gallup India survey noted, in 1994–95, domestic consumption of color televisions grew by 43 percent and automobile production grew by 30 percent (Gallup Organization 2000, 2).

However, there has in fact been an important disjuncture between such public discourses of consumption and consumerism and actual practices of consumption among the middle class. In practice, even in segments of what the NCAER would define as the "consuming class," increases in consumption of new goods such as washing machines and color televisions did not produce the same kind of widespread consumerism that is identified with consumer behavior in advanced industrialized societies. Such cracks in the discursive production of India's liberalizing middle class began to surface by the mid-1990s with newspaper articles displaying titles such as "The Mirage of the Middle Class," "Middle Class Myths," and "What Happened to the 200 Million Consumers?" (Economic Times 1997; Times of India 1997; Reddy 1997). Multinational corporations, in particular, were affected by initial miscalculations of the middle class consumer market and the appeal of foreign brand names even to the upper tiers of the middle classes (Irani and Singh 1996). The result was a significant set of national debates about the size and character of the middle class (Deb 1998c; Prasannan 1995).

This discrepancy between the discursive production of a large consuming middle class and patterns of consumer behavior and attitudes points to a deeper set of conceptual and political questions regarding the boundaries of the middle classes. First, this quandary reflects a conceptual and political confusion between practices of consumption and the phenomenon of consumerism. Initial exaggerations of the possibilities of India's middle class market implicitly rested on an assumption that the Indian middle class would engage in patterns of consumerism similar to middle class consumer behavior in the West.[58] As one media report proclaimed, "Consumerism is the hallmark of the new middle classes. They spend more on entertainment than on education, more on luxuries than on comforts, more to consume than to produce. They are motivated by a fierce egoism coupled with derision for the present order and a strange lack of national pride" (Prasannan 1995, 64). Second, such miscalculations were in part a result of the problems of assuming that the definition of the middle class was merely a matter of income measurement and that quantitative assessments of income were sufficient in understanding (and predicting) the behavior of the middle classes. Finally, at a deeper level, the paradoxes of middle class consumption fundamentally rested on a conceptual and political confusion between the emerging new middle class identity and the middle classes in general.

The slippage between consumption and consumerism inherent in the discourses of both proponents and critics of liberalization who variously saw the rise of a consumerist Indian middle class as either a sign of economic progress or cultural decline was succinctly summed up by sociologist Dipankar Gupta (1998):

The fact is that consumption items like cars or televisions are "one-off purchases." Indian consumers simply do not have the financial power to sustain a higher level of turnover. For instance, Indian roads are littered with cars that should have been put to sleep years ago. Consuming is not the same as consumerism and the Indian middle class is still too weak to make that transition. (Times of India 1998)

It is this confusion between consumerism and consumption that has led analysts to misinterpret the impact of the identity of India's new middle class.[59] As one journalist and consumer trend analyst at a personal finance magazine humorously describes,

My belief is that they [consumer goods] don't die in one birth they have 20 births . . . they [middle class individuals] just don't give up things in one birth . . . you start 20 *janams* [lives] before and continue twenty *janams* later. How would you want me to dispose of my washing machine? I would rather repair it. That kind of attitude cannot change overnight. This use and throw attitude is very difficult.[60]

New consumption practices in India do not yet embody the ideology of disposability that permeates consumerism in advanced industrialized economies like the United States. In fact, the implications of liberalization for consumption patterns both for the middle class as well as on a broader national basis have been contradictory and are contingent on a number of variables. On the one hand, there have been significant changes in levels and trends of consumption as both new commodities and a new vision of a liberalizing India have been aggressively marketed since the early 1990s. Moreover, such effects have not merely been limited to India's new middle class. For instance, 75 percent of Indian and multinational companies have been using rural marketing organizations to develop their presence in rural markets.[61] As S. L. Rao (2000) notes:

> Indian consumer markets are growing rapidly, are changing in nature and composition, and many manufacturers and service providers are adapting themselves to these changes. There will be huge niche markets of the very rich, aged, working women, the developed states and of course the mass markets, especially in rural markets. Even lifestyle products have potential in rural markets. (3572)

However, despite such significant changes in the nature of consumer markets, broad patterns of consumption practices have often proved to be more contradictory. As the Gallup Organization (2000) survey noted, despite significant rises in the consumption of goods such as cars and televisions, "Indian households report spending 40% of their income on housing, medical care and education—categories which in China only absorb about 20% of all income due to subsidies" (2). The relevance of this qualification of the extent of the "newness" of consumption practices in liberalizing India includes large segments of the middle class that do not have the kind of disposable incomes associated with the upper middle class and upper classes.

Despite widespread national anxieties around the spread of Western-style consumerism in India, there is economic uncertainty in the Indian middle class that has not yet allowed the kind of consumerism associated with advanced industrialized societies. As one advertising executive at one of Mumbai's leading advertising firms put it:

> Actually it is very tough for the middle classes. Housing in Bombay is so expensive. No one can afford to live South of [in] Bombay. That means there's a two hour commute to work. The middle classes have to save to invest in a fridge, a television. These things are not taken for granted like in the West. They are still luxury items. Purchasing these kinds of things is a very serious decision. It involves the whole family. Family members are consulted. The middle classes can't afford luxury items like the Opal cars.[62]

Such distinctions between patterns of consumption in India and in advanced industrialized countries have been underlined by 2001 census data that showed that only 2.5 percent of the general population and 5.6 percent of the urban population owned cars (see Table 3) leading one analyst to conclude that "Judging by the proportion of households with bank accounts, cars, scooters, and telephones, the middle class in India fares badly in comparison to developed countries. The so-called large middle class is just not there" (Bose 2003, 4087).

TABLE 3. Ownership of household assets, 2001 (in percentages).

Assets	Urban households	Rural households	Total
Radio	44.5%	31.5%	35.1%
Television	64.3	18.9	31.6
Bicycle	46.0	42.8	43.7
Scooter, motorcycle, or moped	24.7	6.7	11.7
Car, jeep, or van	5.6	1.3	2.5
None of the assets	19.0	40.5	34.5
Bank accounts	49.5	30.1	35.5

Source: Government of India 2001, Table H-13.

The confusion between changing consumption practices and levels and the rise of widespread consumerism has rested on a deeper problem regarding the politics of the measurement of the middle class in India.[63] As I have noted, early attempts by the NCAER to measure consumption helped create the new middle class identity; such consumption-based definitions of social groups were in effect themselves a product of the emerging political culture of liberalization. Implicit in this project of measurement was the notion that the behavior and patterns of consumption of various social groups including the middle "consuming" class (that is, "the new middle class") could be measured purely by changing income levels. However, while household income levels provide a useful set of parameters by which to gauge some shifts in the size of the middle class, income-based definitions fall short in providing reliable markers of the conceptual and socioeconomic boundaries of the middle classes. For instance, NCAER data has shown that between 1985 and 2000, based on income, there was a steady increase in the number of lower middle class, middle class, and upper middle class households, particularly from the prereform period in the 1980s to the postreform period in the 1990s. The percentage of middle class households more than doubled from 6.9 percent in 1985 to 15.44 percent in 1999–2000 (see Table 4).

TABLE 4. Distribution of households by income in India, 1985–2000 (in percentages).

Class segment*	1985–86	1989–90	1992–93	1995–96	1998–99	1999–2000
Lower (<= 35,000)	65.2%	58.8%	58.2%	48.9%	39.7%	36.37%
Lower middle (35,001–70,000)	25.2	26.9	25.4	30.7	34.5	34.20
Middle (70,001–105,000)	6.9	10.1	10.4	11.9	13.9	15.44
Upper middle (105,001–140,000)	1.5	2.7	3.7	5.0	6.2	7.10
High (> 140,000)	1.1	1.4	2.3	3.5	5.7	6.89

*Defined by income (rupees).

Source: NCAER 2002. Data for periods between 1985–86 and 1998–99 are at 1998–99 prices, with income cut-off points adjusted for inflation.

A second measure used by the NCAER to show the sizeable base of a consuming middle class is the distribution of households by occupation of the head of household (see Table 5). The NCAER data suggests that a substantial proportion of the lower middle, middle, and upper middle classes are classified as salaried earners (monthly and annual salary earners) and professionals, and that this proportion increases with an increase in income bracket (see Table 6). While the category "salaried workers" also includes working class individuals (for instance in the manufacturing sector) that would constitute a significant portion of the lower middle and middle class salary categories, the data provides a set of parameters for assessing the size of salaried and professional middle class individuals that either fall within or would be potential aspirants to an emerging new middle class identity. Consider the income segment defined as "middle class" (within the income range of Rs 70,000–150,000). Of households headed by a salary earner, 24.12 percent are from this middle class income segment (see Table 5). The NCAER report (2002) specifically associates these segments with the expansion of the services sector in the 1990s noting that "With respect to the expected future growth in the services sector, the salaried class of consumers stands out owing

TABLE 5. Distribution of households in class segments by household head's occupation in India, 1999–2000 (in percentages)

Head of household's occupation	Lower	Lower middle	Middle	Upper middle	High
Housewife	29.99%	35.88%	19.62%	9.08%	5.42%
Cultivator	38.31	36.48	13.32	6.19	5.69
Wage earner	56.25	33.81	8.41	1.08	0.46
Salary earner	14.91	33.29	24.12	13.22	14.47
Professional	6.23	16.72	23.62	25.32	28.11
Artisan	32.51	39.56	20.87	10.11	9.64
Petty shopkeeper	23.50	36.00	20.74	10.11	9.64
Businessperson	0.42	4.48	23.35	33.07	38.68
Others	26.41	30.59	21.39	11.99	9.63

Source: NCAER 2002. See Table 4 for income brackets that define class segments.

to its constancy and regularity of income flow" (23). According to the NCAER survey, 30.98 percent of the income group defined as middle class is comprised of salary earners (see Table 6).[64]

TABLE 6. Proportion of salary earners in each class segment (all India).

Class segment	Percentage of salary earners
Lower	8.13%
Lower middle	19.30
Middle	30.98
Upper middle	36.97
High	41.65
All	19.84

Source: NCAER 2002. See Table 4 for income brackets that define class segments.

The broader implications of increases in household income level and patterns of occupational distribution must be qualified by a number of variables. The NCAER consumer survey, "Market Information Survey of Households" (MISH) relies on respondents' reporting and respondents' perceptions of their income (NCAER 2002, 4). While the data still can provide a frame for trends and changes in income distribution, such measures can be influenced by a number of factors. For example, liberalization has intensified the shift from single-wage-earner to dual-wage-earner households (with both husband and wife working) particularly in urban areas, leading to increases in household income levels. Some trends indicating shifts from a joint family structure to nuclear family households can also explain some increases in the numbers of middle class households. A new trend in the context of liberalization is the growth of younger and part-time workers (for example, college students) in urban areas.

Beyond such factors that seek to break down household structures and sources of income, the link between income and consumption practices is also contingent on a range of factors. As economist and former director general of the NCAER himself argues, "For business and marketing decisions, it is the pattern of consumption that is relevant and not a classification based merely on income" (Rao 1994, 5). For instance, sharp rises in consumption for some social segments are linked to the new identities of lifestyle that I have discussed, as well as to changing spending practices with the growth of credit card industries[65] and the availability of credit and purchasing schemes developed to encourage middle class consumption.[66] Moreover income measures themselves do not serve as an adequate predictor of consumer practices and behavior.

Ironically, individuals working in the advertising industry in Mumbai expressed some of the most nuanced understandings of the problems of defining and measuring the middle class. As an executive vice president of one of India's leading advertising firms put it:

> We classify them according to what in advertising is known as a psycho-profile which [means] you might have a few lakhs [1 lakh is Rs 100,000] income businessman in Bombay but you might find any number of farmers in Panjab earning as much money with vast properties but talking to them, their aspirations will be two different worlds. Yes the income group is the first basic demarcation but more importantly for an advertising group would be the psychotypic profile, the education, their perspective and their views on culture are equally important, at least from our creative perspective.[67]

Initial miscalculations of the middle class consumer market have led to new projects of measurement and social classification that have begun to more consciously factor in the role of the identity of a liberalizing middle class. Consider the following example of a recent set of classifications by KSA Technopak, a well-known management consultancy and market research firm. Drawing on a survey of 10,000 upper and middle class households in twenty cities, the survey attempts to move away from income-based definitions to create a new classification that factors in age and consumption (and implicitly, attitudes to liberalization) (Goyal 2004). The survey presents four groups defined by age, consumption, and attitudes: "Technology Babies," born between 1985 and 1996; "Impatient Aspirers," born between 1980 and 1984; "Balance Seekers," born between 1954 and 1983; and "Arrived Veterans," born between 1943 and 1953. As evidenced by the titles, the two younger groups are presented as stronger, bolder consumers who

have been born into or socialized into the new culture of liberalization, whereas the two latter groups have more conservative attitudes
to money, consumption, and financial planning.

As with the earlier NCAER classifications, the survey implicitly
creates an idealized standard of middle class behavior through its
quantification of the different segments and in the process contributes to the construction of the identity of the new Indian middle
class. In this case, it is age and specifically youth that embodies the
promise of this new class and its ability to shape the future trends. As
one interpretation of the survey results put it, the youngest segments
of these groups, "Born almost entirely in the post-liberalised economy and raised almost completely around modern technology (computers, Internet and other gadgets) [indicate that] this consumer
class is not only redefining its own consumption but is also beginning
to dictate the spending patterns of its elders" (Goyala 2004, 19).

The new Indian middle class dream, this representation seems to
suggest, can be safeguarded by the new generation that has identified
itself with India's postliberalization national culture; the new middle
class in this conception is "new" in a literal sense of age and generation. The politics of measurement of the middle class in such surveys
in effect serve as part of the classificatory practices that have framed
the Indian new middle class.

Conclusion

In this chapter, I analyzed the rise of a new middle class identity associated with an emerging national political culture of liberalization.
Dominant narratives of this identity in the media and public sphere
have emphasized shifting patterns of consumption and the emergence of new lifestyles. The visibility of this new middle class identity
has, as we have seen, continually produced confusions as analysts and
scholars have often overestimated the significance of the lifestyle
shifts and misinterpreted its emergence as a self-evident reflection of
the middle classes in general.

Perhaps the most striking political dynamics associated with this
slippage between the new middle class, the "old" middle class, and the
nation as a whole was captured in the BJP's miscalculated election

campaign, "India Shining." As with many of the early overestimations of India's "200-million-strong" middle class, the BJP's campaign in effect mistakenly cast the shine of the new Indian middle class dream as a national reality. If the 1990s saw the valorization of Chandrababu Naidu as an icon of the new liberalizing India following in the tracks of Rajiv Gandhi, by 2004 his electoral defeat was the source of much public satire with political cartoons of a high-tech-looking Chandrababu Naidu being erased by a computer "delete" key.[68] Such dynamics demonstrate the political significance of understanding both the distinctive nature and political implications of this emerging group, a point I will explore in greater depth in chapter 5.

The political perils involved in the slippages between the liberalizing middle class and the middle class in general also provide an important cautionary note for the ways in which we conceptualize the boundaries of social groups. Academic research and public analysts have too easily reverted to naturalized income or consumption-based definitions of the middle class. Even in this realm, as we have seen, income does not translate in self-evident ways into consumerism and the middle class is not simply an inert mass responding automatically to advertising images. The framing of the new middle class is significant not because it reflects or produces the reality of middle class lives and identities in a deterministic or linear way. Culturalist approaches that too easily reduce or identify the middle classes with advertising images and case studies of consumption risk overestimating the significance of discursive practices in shaping the contours of middle class identity.

The dominant frames that I have analyzed are complex symbolic–material products of interactions within the middle classes and between the middle classes and subaltern social groups. The representational practices I have examined are only one set of a range of classificatory practices that shape this broader process. It is thus only by moving beyond a focus on discourses and practices of consumption that the political and conceptual significance of the rise of the new Indian middle class can be fully grasped.

3

Social Capital, Labor Market Restructuring, and India's New Economy

———————✳———————

> The services sector dominates the Indian economy today, con-
> tributing more than half of our national income. It's the fastest
> growing sector, with an average annual growth rate of 8 percent
> in the 1990s. One in every two Indians earns his livelihood by
> providing services. An INDIA TODAY-ORG-MARG poll shows
> that the majority of middle class families want their children to
> work in the services sector.
>
> —*Saran (2001)*

The rapid expansion of the service sector has received much public
attention and has often been credited as being a central component
in India's accelerated economic growth since the 1990s. High-tech
workers have become a potent symbol of India's success in the global
economy. According to the National Association of Software and Service Companies (NASSCOM) estimates, revenues from information-
technology-related services increased from $565 million in 1999–2000
to $1,475 million in 2001–2 with projected estimates of continued
robust growth.[1] There has been an increase in new jobs in information technology (for example, from 522,250 in 2002 to 650,000 in
2003—a growth of 24.4 percent) (Chandrasekha 2003, 129). Salaries

for white-collar employment have also risen significantly. NASSCOM estimates that the increase has been 11 to 15 percent for entry-level positions and 30 percent for senior managerial positions, with much higher increases for information technology jobs (Srivastava, 2006).

A tour of Bangalore's internationally renowned software firm Infosys reveals a luxurious corporate campus with idyllic scenes of employees taking breaks to play basketball or swim in a plush swimming pool. Corporate success stories embody the pinnacle of what the new middle class can achieve in liberalizing India. Meanwhile, the growing outsourcing of jobs from advanced industrialized countries such as the United States and the United Kingdom to India has added a new narrative of India's high-tech workers—images of young urban Indians sitting in front of computer screens routinely circulate in both the Indian and Western media.

The service sector has, according to one estimate, accounted for 52 percent of the Indian GDP and has constituted the major growth of employment as agriculture has stagnated and industry and manufacturing have been characterized by declining rates in the growth of employment.[2]

The expansion of the service sector of the economy and of professional, white-collar private-sector employment has been fundamentally linked with the rise of the new Indian middle class. At a structural level, the new middle class is not comprised of new entrants to middle class status. Rather, it is defined by a change in the status of jobs, which now signify the upper tiers of middle class employment. The socioeconomic boundaries of the new middle class are shaped by this shift in the direction of new middle class employment aspirations. In symbolic terms, the cultural and economic standard for the "old" middle class would have been represented by a job in a state bank or the Indian civil service.[3] Members of the new middle class aspire to jobs in multinational corporations or foreign banks.[4] According to a journalist I interviewed, the distinction lies in the way in which liberalization has

redefined middle class ambition. . . . If you're a Citibanker or if you're with Am Ex [American Express], if you're with Bank Am

[Bank of America] then you're hot. You're not considered hot property if you're with SBI [State Bank of India]. You won't go to one [a state bank to look for employment]. Look at the profile of the brighter students and the kinds of jobs they will seek, where they are going. Where will the IIM [Indian Institute of Management] students go? Where will the IIT [Indian Institute of Technology] students go? Just look at that and you'll know.[5]

The new Indian middle class has thus been associated in structural terms with the expanded "new economy" service sectors and private-sector professional workforces.[6] These sectors are central areas that have been affected by liberalization and associated processes of economic restructuring.

Despite the growing interest in India's high-tech workers, there has been relatively little research on the structural effects that liberalization has had for new middle class employment in the service sectors in general. Assessments of such effects have for the most part been limited to public discourses and generally focus on the question of outsourcing. Such discourses have either celebrated high-tech workers as the embodiment of the success of the new middle class or unilaterally condemned outsourcing as a new kind of international division of labor.

The effects of liberalization on the middle class in general have varied as different groups have been marginalized, incorporated, and excluded from a restructured labor market. Such effects have unfolded through the processes of: (1) inclusion as the "new rich" (Robison and Goodman 1996) benefit from new employment opportunities and rising salaries at private-sector firms, (2) marginalization as traditional public-sector employees in industries such as banking and insurance contest processes of retrenchment and restructuring, and (3) adaptation and survival as a vast segment of the middle class draws on varying strategies to obtain the skills necessary to negotiate a restructured labor market and gain entry to new middle class employment. Drawing on an analysis of various layers of the middle class ranging from clerical workers to upper level managerial workers I demonstrate that the effects lie in between these stories of success and exploitation as liberalization has produced a set of contradictory effects for different segments of the urban middle class that aspire to membership within the new middle class.

The new middle class labor market is characterized by increasing job insecurity, a trend toward the employment of contract workers (ranging from secretarial to upper managerial positions), and sharp distinctions in income between different segments. Outsourcing has lent a new dimension to the labor market as such jobs have provided an employment boom particularly for urban youth.

Such contradictory structural dimensions of new-economy employment provide a deeper understanding of the politics of new middle class formation. Individuals from different social strata within the middle class attempt to use a range of strategies in order to gain entry to the new middle class. The acquisition of particular kinds of social and cultural capital (including particular kinds of credentials, skills, lifestyle distinctions, and aesthetic/cultural knowledge) is a central way middle class individuals negotiate new-economy segments of the labor market.

Segments of the middle class convert income (financial capital) into the kinds of social and symbolic capital necessary for upward mobility in a liberalizing economy. Conversion between these different kinds of capital shape the strategies that individuals from various socioeconomic segments within the middle class use to achieve access to, and status mobility within, the new middle class labor market. These capital conversions underline the importance of moving beyond income-based measurements that are conventionally used to assess the socioeconomic position of the middle classes.

As I will demonstrate, the labor market represents a field that crosses traditional analytical boundaries between cultural and structural variables. The politics of sociocultural distinction play a central role in producing stratification within the new middle class labor market.

The new middle class is characterized by a broad range of internal differentiations and uncertainties that have been understudied by scholars concerned with the relationship between the middle classes and liberalization in India.[7] Sizeable growth in household income and the visibility of changing consumer practices have led most scholars to assume that the middle class has uniformly benefited from liberalization.[8] Such analyses have in fact rested largely on an assessment of the "new rich," the section of the middle class that has increasingly served as the symbol of the benefits of liberalization in comparative contexts (Pinches 1999; Robison and Goodman 1996). While recent studies on the effects of liberalization in India in the 1990s have debated the effects of liberalization on social groups such as the industrial working class and rural social groups, less attention has been paid to the socioeconomic effects of liberalization on the middle class.[9]

Studies have assumed that the new middle class or the middle class in general serve as a base of political support for liberalization because these groups benefit economically from liberalization (Corbridge and Harriss 2000; Deshpande 2003). Such an assumption stems from a conceptualization of the middle class as a traditional interest group; that is, that the middle class supports reforms because it is in their economic interest to do so. In a similar fashion, research that has addressed the negative impact of reforms on employment has tended to focus on public-sector enterprises and unions that have opposed the restructuring of public-sector enterprises.[10]

Both sets of analyses assume a straightforward linkage between economic interests and attitudes toward reforms. However, the significance of the new middle class as a group that serves as a base of support for liberalization does not lie in a transparent expression of the economic interests of this group. In practice, liberalization has had uneven and contradictory socioeconomic effects on middle class employment. As I will demonstrate in this chapter, private-sector employment has been shaped by processes of restructuring that are similar to patterns in public-sector enterprises. Such contradictory economic effects have not, however, translated into political opposition to restructuring. In this context, the power of the new middle class stems from the ways in which the identity of this social group mediates and manages uncertainties and differentiations within the middle class. It is only by first analyzing such contradictory socioeconomic dimensions that we can fully understand the political significance of the process of construction of new middle class identity and the centrality of the management of differentiation that I will address in later chapters.

The objective of this chapter is to map out the socioeconomic patterns and distinctions that shape the restructuring of the middle class labor market and define the structural boundaries of the new middle class. I begin by analyzing the ways in which the structuring of the new middle class within the labor market is contingent on the acquisition and distribution of various forms of social capital. Representational practices that have defined dominant practices of new middle class lifestyle and consumption move beyond the discursive realm and are transformed into forms of stratification marked by internal socioeconomic, gendered, and caste-based hierarchies within the new economy segments of the labor market in liberalizing India. Such forms of stratification are symptomatic of a form of restructuring of middle class employment in India, as they are part of the shift from traditional state-based employment to new-economy-sector jobs. I analyze the patterns of this form of restructuring and demonstrate the ways in which they have become transnationalized through global processes of outsourcing. Such transnational processes have, as I demonstrate, built on existing intersections between labor market stratification and the distribution of social capital. The acquisition of social capital has enabled segments of the Indian middle class to take advantage of shifting patterns in the outsourcing industry. Finally, drawing on a series of oral histories, I demonstrate the ways in which such complex connections between the distribution of social capital and a hegemonic new middle class identity have led middle class individuals to respond to processes of economic restructuring through privatized strategies rather than through political opposition.

Social Capital and the New Indian Middle Class

The new Indian middle class is characterized by a form of socioeconomic differentiation that belies stereotypical notions of a homogeneous consumerist class. In line with structuralist theories of the middle class that have mapped out distinctive segments within the middle class in comparative contexts (Urry 1971; Wright 1978, 1997), the new middle class in India is composed of a varied set of occupational groups. A structural map of the middle classes working in new economy jobs would encompass an array of employees ranging from the upper tiers of the managerial-professional classes to clerical and

secretarial workers from the lower middle class. This stratified structural map confirms Erik Olin Wright's conception of the middle class
in terms of a set of "contradictory locations" (Wright 1978). However,
my aim is not to provide a fixed structural map of the social locations
that exist within the middle class but to analyze the dynamic processes
that shape the structural formation of the new middle class. As I will
demonstrate, this process of class formation is linked to the distribution of social and cultural capital and the ways in which individuals
and groups attempt to attain and convert such capital in order to gain
a foothold in new economy employment sectors.

There are vast social disparities between various segments of the
middle class employed in new economy jobs. Images of the prosperous urban middle class consumer associated with liberalization correspond to the rise of the new rich, particularly young urban professionals
who have been able to benefit from sharp rises in salaries of multinational companies and subsequently of Indian companies.[11] New ca-
reers and jobs are themselves symbols of the lifestyle markers of the
liberalizing middle class.[12] This has placed new value on business education and the achievement of MBA degrees.[13]

In addition to high salaries, a central component of the new rich is
the high level of perks multinational companies provide to their
managerial staff. These perks include the provision of cars, housing,
entertainment allowances, and clothing allowances. Such perks—in
addition to constituting a nontaxable source of income—also form
the basis for the reproduction of status distinctions. For instance,
companies may provide memberships in exclusive social clubs, a
source of cultural capital that transcends mere monetary value as
leading social clubs in Mumbai often have long waiting lists that ex-
clude even people who can afford exorbitant membership fees.

Although perks were historically provided by public-sector
enterprises—for instance in the form of housing provided by public-
sector banks—new private and multinational enterprises have transformed the status implications of these benefits by linking nonwage
provisions to new patterns of consumption. Moreover, sharp rises in
salaries and perks in private-sector employment have pushed white-
collar wages for employees in such jobs far above sectors such as education or the lower rungs of the bureaucracy.

While cars and club memberships serve as significant status symbols at the higher managerial rungs, cell phones represent status markers for lower level executives. These status signifiers increasingly shape the aspirations and job market strategies particularly of urban youth and have greatly increased the status of corporate employment.

The attainment of an MBA requires a substantial financial investment that is out of the reach of a substantial section of the middle class and this form of credentialing itself is linked to the acquisition of social capital. As an employee at a recruitment agency argued,

[F]or a typically middle class person . . . by 25 your dad has retired, you need to after your graduation start earning. You need to because that additional 6000 or 5000 you're going to contribute home is going to make a big difference. So it's not that easy for such a person to leave his job and go into further studies. At times there would be people who've got a father who maybe is not well so he's absolutely not earning so there's a requirement for you to go on earning. There are others where the father is still earning and he's going to earn for another couple of years but you know you have to . . . because your dad doesn't have enough to set you up. You're also going to look at marriage around 25, 26 . . . so its not that simple for you to go into a management school to study for 2 years. That's one. Secondly where do you get the money? A management course costs. It could be 40,000 a year. . . . Now an MBA school like Bajaj . . . would have an expectation that you need to have bought books. You need to take on projects, you need to prepare the projects, you need to have a computer to prepare a report. . . . So do you have that kind of money to invest when you're not even working for those 2 years?[14]

In practice, middle class individuals without financial capital to invest in the acquisition of MBA credentials rely on a vast field of institutes that grant diplomas and certificates to provide credentials in an attempt to gain a foothold in the new middle class dream of liberalization. Such institutes, which have mushroomed in both metropolitan areas and small towns, provide a wide array of services including the provision of computer training, English classes, various managerial diplomas, and public speaking training. Individuals who avail themselves of these services range from new college graduates unsure of their career choice to individuals employed in companies searching for credentials in order to gain a promotion or "add value" that can make them more marketable in a liberalizing labor market.[15]

This strategic credentialing represents a significant middle class strategy of skill acquisition that can allow individuals to survive in a restructured labor market. For instance, it enables individuals to develop abilities in new fields such as information technology. Such strategies are not limited to the attainment of skills such as computer literacy but also in many instances involve the acquisition of new forms of symbolic capital necessary in a liberalizing labor market as individuals attempt to respond to the image of the new middle class.

Consider the example of a private institute that grants noncertified diplomas in fields ranging from hotel catering to sales and marketing to dressmaking. This institute, which has operated in India since 1935, has developed a new course on "Personality Development and Communication Skills." The course has approximately 450 to 500 students a year, meets once a week, runs over a period of five weeks and costs approximately Rs 2,000. The objective of the course is to prepare students to engage with a distinctive class culture that characterizes corporate settings. In addition to training in basic areas such as interviewing skills and résumé preparation, a substantial portion of the course focuses on the acquisition of manners, taste, and style—"the symbolic capital" (Bourdieu 1984) that is necessary for an upwardly mobile middle class individual.

In one representative sample of students in a course that I observed, there were seventeen men and six women, representing a broad spectrum of educational and professional backgrounds. Almost all of the students were college graduates. Close to half were currently employed in a wide range of jobs including engineering, computer programming, and management. About half of the students had recently graduated from a range of colleges at the University of Mumbai, or were close to graduation. Three students had master's degrees and there were three unemployed individuals (see Figure 9).

Education	Number of students
No higher education	1
Bachelor's degree	19
Master's degree	3
Total	23

Employment	Number of students
Employed	10
Unemployed	3
Students and recent graduates	10
Total	23

FIGURE 9. Characteristics of students of educational institute training course.

A significant portion of the course that I observed emphasized the acquisition of manners and communication skills appropriate for the new corporate cultural environment. The course begins with the instructor making each student practice a personal introduction and a "proper" handshake—one that the instructor says is "not a heavy slap. Don't just hold out your hand stiffly, don't just catch the tip of the hand. Don't hold on to the hand. You smile and shake hands. That's how you become a trend setter rather than a follower."[16] Substantial portions of the first session are devoted to stylistic training that includes advice on the type of deodorants (including affordable brand names) that should be worn and how to apply them, the types of clothes appropriate for office wear, and advice that men never keep anything in their shirt pocket. While these portions of the session are presented with humor, students taken them seriously, taking careful notes and asking follow-up questions.

The individuals enrolled in this course attempt to gain the symbolic capital necessary to conform to the cultural standard of the new liberalizing middle class. Such trends point to the ways in which the representational practices that define new middle class lifestyles interact with and influence the micropractices of a broad range of individuals within the middle class. The acquisition of such symbolic capital is an example of the credentialing strategies that middle class individuals attempt to use in order to negotiate the uncertainties of a restructured labor market.

The institute described above is part of a larger trend of the rapid growth of a range of institutes offering an array of diplomas and degrees. For instance, by the late 1990s, business schools mushroomed as a demand for MBAs increasingly became a marker for entry into new middle class jobs. One placement agency representative described the type of person who might attend an institute:

> [For someone whose] dad's been a VP [vice president] of a big time company you've had sufficient exposure to culture, you've got that polish. You don't need to have that MBA but you're the one who can afford the MBA . . . but you look at a typically middle class person, he's the one who needs the MBA course. He needs to get himself polished—you know, organize his knowledge or whatever. So what happens is for these people these certificate courses and these diploma courses are really good. . . . They are not that costly and it's not so tough to get in.[17]

Many individuals I interviewed argued that they had enrolled in institutes as a strategy of upward mobility—not just to get a new job but also to enhance their chances of getting a promotion.

These institutes are part of a broader trend in the privatization of education unfolding in India. Such institutes have multiplied throughout India's metropolitan cities and small towns. The growth of such private institutes are not merely an external response to changes in the middle class labor market, they are an integral part of the everyday microprocesses of privatization. In other words, the spread of such institutes is an integral part of the restructuring of the Indian economy. At the upper tiers, such privatization can be seen in the rise of top-tier private schools and new multinational collaborations as Western universities have sought to offer their degrees on Indian campuses or through distance learning.[18] However, the core of the new middle class labor market is marked by individuals from lower to middle layers of the middle class who are attempting to gain a foothold within new economy jobs in the corporate and service sector. In some cases this involves attempting to gain credentials in fields such as business administration. However, such credentials are not markers of objective skills. They are one dimension in a broader set of requirements—such as fluency in English and the acquisition of taste, style, and manners—that make up the social capital necessary for access to the new middle class.

In practice, while such training may "add value" by providing an individual with an entry point to certain kinds of new-economy jobs, it often does not produce upward mobility within the labor market. In many instances, new business schools do not have the standing for their credentials to provide any significant job market mobility and in some cases unrecognized schools have mushroomed purely to meet lower middle and middle class demand for credentials. In such cases, credentialing strategies have not necessarily resulted in individual upward mobility in the new middle class labor market. Consider the experience that one sales officer at a multinational company recounted when I interviewed him. The sales officer was receiving a monthly income of Rs 4,000 a month (substantially lower than the inflated salaries commonly presumed to characterize multinational corporation [MNC] employment) and did not receive any sales incentives such as commissions. The officer, who was supporting a wife and child, decided to obtain a marketing diploma from one of the top private educational institutions in Mumbai with the hopes of gaining a promotion. However, as he indicated, when he gave his diploma to his manager, his manager just set it aside and never mentioned it again.[19]

As one report noted, five-figure salaries go to MBAs from leading educational institutes while individuals simply trying to gain credentials as a strategy of acquiring social capital could be employed for as little as Rs 3,000–5,000.[20] Strategies of credentialing may, in some cases, lead to limited income mobility but such mobility often occurs within a fixed structural location in the labor market. For instance, acquisition of additional skills through diplomas and certificates may enable an individual to move to higher paying employment through a move from a small firm to a larger Indian or multinational company. However, such skills do not usually change the job classification of the individual. One recruitment agent even argued, for instance:

Now take an MNC. They would like even their secretaries and even their support staff to have an MBA because they're an MNC. The support staff are doing these small time MBA courses. So they'll take these people over. . . . See a company has an image. People in customer service, if you go by and meet those customer service people you'll see a lot of them, they're all drawing salaries of about 7 and a half to 8 [thousand rupees].[21]

In this case, while an investment in credentialing allows for a higher starting salary at an MNC, additional skills do not transform the structural location of the occupational category within the organizational hierarchy of the company. In the interviews I conducted, recruitment agents as well as new middle class employees noted that such strategies of credentialing did not provide structural mobility in the labor market. For example, executive assistants were unlikely to move up into the higher managerial positions that would require traditional educational qualifications from India's reputable business schools.

Gender, Caste, and the New Middle Class Labor Market

The relationship between the new middle class labor market and the distribution of social capital intersects with and reconstitutes existing social inequalities such as gender and caste. In the current job market, reclassification of employment and skills has resulted in an expanded category of "secretarial" work that includes occupations ranging from administrative/clerical assistants to marketing executives who in effect perform the duties of higher level managerial positions.[22] For example, the skill requirements and income range for executive assistants now vary greatly, and required skills may include secretarial duties such as handling phone calls, typing, and organizing conferences all the way up to managerial tasks such as handling personnel matters and making substantive decisions on company projects. While such employees are classified as "secretarial" workers, restructuring has increasingly led companies to delegate managerial responsibilities to them. In many instances, an executive assistant will perform duties normally handled by an MBA such as meeting with clients, coordinating and organizing conferences, and performing public relations work. This transition has led to increasingly rigorous recruitment procedures. As one placement agent put it, while earlier personal referrals were sufficient for employment, now

> [Companies] want to see an in-depth analysis, to meet the candidate, to give them a test, to give them an aptitude test. Most companies have this. Even if they're taking on a secretary they are not only giving her a shorthand and a typing test, they're giving her a computer test. They're giving her a basic general knowledge test. For comprehension. . . . Today even if you're hiring a secretary . . . the guy is going to see whether you can think. Whether you're looking good. Whether you want to move into a larger role. Whether your computer knowledge is good. What other jobs can I hand over to her? Can she make a decision if I'm not there. Or do I still need to keep calling ten times and ask are you fine? Are you fine? Can you handle something more? . . . There are secretaries who are upgrading themselves—taking managerial courses.[23]

In some instances, multinational companies demonstrate a preference for even their secretarial and support staff to have MBAs or some form of managerial training. This is in line with the gendered nature of economic restructuring in comparative contexts (Bakker 1994; Deshpande and Deshpande 1992; Ghosh 1994; Jenson, Hagen, and Reddy 1988). Female workers, in such cases, must meet increased demands on productivity and skill requirements without corresponding forms of income and occupational mobility.

There is currently little systematic published quantitative data on salary scales for women working in white-collar or service-sector employment; published statistics on female workers are limited to organized sector industries such as factories and plantations. My analysis draws on interviews with recruitment agents, women employed at a range of companies who I contacted through networks at one managerial diploma granting institute, as well as numerous interviews and informal conversations with women employed at two working women's hostels where I resided during my fieldwork.

My research suggests that in the late 1990s, a monthly income of Rs 4,000 (approximately $100) was an average estimate for executive assistants who performed secretarial and some managerial duties, a salary that would place them in the lower middle class category of NCAER survey categories that measure class and income. Women who were employed in managerial positions earned substantially higher incomes, particularly if they were employed in multinational corporations. However, the work experiences of lower-tier clerical workers represent a larger segment of middle class female workers.

In this context, liberalization has produced a contradictory set of gendered effects. On the one hand, the expansion of service-sector and private-sector employment has produced opportunities for middle class women in metropolitan centers.[24] However, such opportunities often represent coping strategies as households attempt to negotiate increasing household costs and new lifestyle standards that correspond to public representations of the new middle class.

Moreover, shifting employment patterns do not necessarily transform household gendered divisions of labor. For instance, middle class women adopt a wide range of flexible labor market strategies including the use of part-time and informal work in order to negotiate household labor and marital and childrearing responsibilities. This has produced familiar gendered pressures as middle class women must perform a dual shift of paid and unpaid household work. The form of such pressures varies considerably depending on the income level of the individuals in question.

Consider the self-reflections of one woman employed as a journalist writing for a new print publication specifically targeted at the new middle class. Radha describes herself as a "slightly upper middle class person living in a metro. Dual income and still trying to make ends meet." As she indicates:

> I simply cannot give up my job. My mother gave up her job. I cannot do that because it is unthinkable. I don't like this rush but I cannot quit this race. I'm running. I don't want to run but

I cannot stop running... Out of a total monthly income of Rs 30,000 for us we are supposed to be on the premium segment of society. But a third of it goes in just running the family monthly expenses. And then you set apart another quarter for savings for tax purposes or compulsory savings or whatever and what are you left with? What all will you do with it? You would invest in infrastructure for your house or you will flash it. I mean go on a vacation or something. You'll buy dresses you'll buy jewelry. See today's avenues for spending is [sic] more but the avenues for earning has not increased to that level and so I'm more frustrated.[25]

This snapshot points to the anxieties of the segment of the middle class closest to the idealized representations of the new rich in India.

These anxieties of the new upwardly mobile dual-income upper middle class family only serve to underline the contrast to women who are employed at substantially lower salaries in the lower tier of white-collar work.[26] For example, a well-known foreign bank routinely hires temporary staff in various departments. While individuals are hired in the securities department and paid a competitive salary, the bank requires a break in a temporary worker's employment after three or four months. After a break of six to nine months the individual can accept another temporary job at the bank. This example is typical of the employment situation of the lower tier of white-collar work—and the majority of middle class women.[27] It points to a general pattern in which companies are increasingly creating a two-tiered white-collar workforce—one compromised of permanent staff with substantial benefits and perks and one comprised of temporary contract workers. The perks that permanent staff receive, include benefits such as provident fund and insurance coverage, as well as additional perks that are status symbols for the middle classes in liberalizing India—pagers, mobile phones, credit cards, air travel, and accommodation at upscale hotels. Such perks often serve as the enticement for the aspirations of middle class individuals who are attempting to negotiate a means to attain the status or at minimum the status symbols of the new middle class. As I will demonstrate later in the chapter, the gendered nature of such processes has been intensified by global processes of outsourcing and the expansion of the call center industry in India.

While the politics of gender has been reworked in the new middle class labor market through processes of restructuring, caste distinctions shape the new middle class labor market in distinctive ways. D. L. Sheth (1999a, 1999b) has demonstrated that while there has been a significant shift in the caste composition of the middle classes, caste continues to play a significant role in creating layers of stratification within socioeconomic groups such as the middle class:

> For example, upper caste individuals entering the middle class have at their disposal the resources that were attached to the status of their caste in the traditional hierarchy. Similarly, for lower caste members, lacking in traditional status resources, their entry into the middle class is facilitated by the modern-legal provisions like affirmative action to which they are entitled by virtue of their low traditional status. (Sheth 1999a, 2509)

The reliance of lower caste groups on state policies and state employment in gaining access to middle class membership has intensified the upper caste characteristics of new middle class employment in private-sector, white-collar employment. For example, survey research conducted in 1996 showed that 53.3 percent of upper castes were employed in white-collar employment, in contrast to 26.6 percent of backward castes and only 9.2 percent of *dalits* (see Table 7). As D. L. Sheth (1999b) has argued, such data demonstrates the ways in which caste has been reworked within class-based patterns of stratification. Furthermore, as Yadav and Sheth argue:

> The data of the 55th round of the National Sample Survey shows that in urban India, out of 1,000 upper caste Hindus, 253 were graduates. Among Hindu OBCs, this figure was only 86 per 1,000. We do not have reliable information on the caste-wise distribution of well-paid jobs in the organized sector. But it is quite obvious that upper caste Hindus, who constitute anything between a quarter to one-third of our population, have

cornered around twice as many jobs as their share in population might justify. (*Times of India* 2006)

Thus, despite the paucity of data, there is evidence for a pattern in
which upper-caste groups are concentrated in white-collar employment, while lower-caste groups and Muslims are comparatively underrepresented in these sectors.

TABLE 7. Caste and middle class white-collar employment (in percentages).

Social group	Proportion of social group in sample	Education above high school	Occupation in white-collar employment
Upper castes	24.8%	44.1%	53.3%
Backward castes	39.3	34.6	26.6
Dalits	19.7	11.7	9.2
Tribals	9.7	4.0	3.4
Muslims	6.5	5.6	7.5

Source: Sheth 1999b, 355, based on a survey conducted by the Centre for the Study
of Developing Societies, New Delhi, June–July 1996.

My research suggests further that this intersection of caste and
class is being intensified in the construction of the new liberalizing
middle class. While changing patterns of white-collar employment
and the entry of lower caste groups into the middle classes has been
aided by state affirmative action policies and state employment, the
private sector has been outside the purview of such policies. The social differentiation that has taken root within middle class government jobs has occurred as the status of middle class employment has
been shifting from state to private-sector jobs. A classic example of
this shift can be seen in the changing composition of the Indian civil
service. While Indian civil service jobs were historically the preserve
of upper-caste, middle class Indians, the composition of Indian Administrative Service cadres has been shifting to include rural elites
and members of new entrants to the middle class who represent a
greater degree of caste and regional diversity.[28] However, this shift has

occurred as private-sector employment in fields such as business and information technology has replaced civil service employment as the social marker of upper-tier middle class employment in the context of liberalization. Caste-based resources are thus implicated in nuanced ways in the processes through which segments of the middle class gain access to or are impeded from membership in the emerging liberalizing middle class.

The patterns of credentialing strategies that have emerged in new-economy, private-sector jobs are located in a broader set of processes in which such social and cultural resources both shape and are intensified by changes within the labor market. At one level, representational practices that have framed new middle class lifestyles are constitutive of employment strategies and of new forms of stratification within the labor market. At another level, new forms of stratification are created through the reconstitution of long-standing inequalities such as gender and caste.[29] Individual strategies of upward mobility are not isolated or particular examples of personal experience. Rather they are emblematic of systemic structural shifts within the Indian middle class that have intensified competition over jobs and accentuated the uncertainties of employment. The implications of such patterns in new economy sectors of middle class employment are part of a more general restructuring of the Indian middle class.

Restructuring the Indian Middle Class

Economic liberalization in the 1990s restructured the Indian middle class in two central ways: The labor market was marked by a decrease in job security manifested by an increasing movement from permanent to temporary or contract-based work on the one hand and retrenchment in both the public and private sectors on the other. The shift from a state-managed to a liberalized economy has begun (albeit gradually and in hidden, informal ways) to downsize the traditional middle class basis of state enterprises. For example, in the context of middle class, white-collar, public-sector employment, the banking and insurance industries have represented sites of political contestation. The banking sector in particular has been identified as a critical arena for the retrenchment of staff in order to cut costs and make public banks competitive in the context of new financial standards of liberalization. While a strong unionized staff has prevented wide-scale retrenchment, such pressures have been felt through a freeze on recruitment and through attempts to develop voluntary retirement schemes. According to trade union representatives, there has been no fresh recruitment in public-sector banks since 1986. The All India Bank Employees Association (AIBEA—the general federation of employees in the majority of banks), which has a membership of approximately 550,000–600,000 (of a total all-India banking workforce of approximately 2,200,000)[30] represents a section of the organized middle class that has opposed processes of liberalization.

The AIBEA has participated in general trade union campaigns against liberalization and more specifically against programs geared at retrenchment and voluntary retirement programs. Union officials, in particular, argue that insufficient attention has been paid to the question of unemployment for both the middle and working classes and that current images of the new middle class has little relevance for the reality of the majority of middle class individuals. This view is captured succinctly by one official, who argued:

> The middle classes are neither here nor there. As Lenin said, the middle classes have no social basis. They have some fancies. They imagine they would become rich. Have a bungalow, have a car. But ultimately they live in a lottery; few are winners, most are losers. If employment is blocked what will our children do? Computer software engineers and doctors can be 5% or 7% of the population. What about the rest?[31]

Public sector banks have in fact been able to successfully implement a voluntary retirement scheme that has cut the workforce by 15 percent (Majumdar 2001).

While there has been significant public and scholarly discussion of the politics of restructuring public-sector enterprises as such industries have emerged as a site of contestation for the supporters and opponents of restructuring, less attention has been paid to similar patterns within private-sector and new-economy jobs. Such patterns have included processes of restructuring that have ranged from lower level white-collar employees to the upper echelons of the managerial staff. For instance, initial periods of retrenchment resulted from excessive expectations in the initial boom period of liberalization in the 1990s. Multinational companies in various sectors recruited managerial employees with high salaries and perks, a process that fed into the representational practices that identified the liberalizing middle class with "the new rich." However, the combined effects of a global economic recession with the Asian crisis and stagnation in middle class consumer demand led multinationals to reign in costs. As we saw in chapter 2, this stagnation began to produce significant cracks in the discursive image of the new middle class as public discourses began to debate and explain the lack of consumer demand.

While public discourses debated the size and character of the Indian middle class, the long-term effects of such processes were concentrated in an increase in labor market restructuring in the private sector, rather than in the realm of consumption practices. Even the English-language news magazine, *India Today,* a publication whose stories of new forms of consumption and lifestyle have epitomized the construction of the "new rich/new middle class Indian" published a lead story on the downsizing of white-collar jobs with a melodramatic opening, "Jobs relocated, work outsourced. People given golden handshakes, pushed down with a golden parachute, or plain axed. Body-slammed. Eliminated like in a Stalinist Gulag" (Aiyar 1997, 41).[32]

Increased competition in the context of liberalization and related changes in technology and management style have led to significant downsizing in the private sector. In some cases, as one human resources placement agent put it:

[T]he person who works with a secretary, he's not given a secretary. He types his own letters. He's given a PC [personal computer] to type his own letters. He makes his own calls. He doesn't have a secretary to get him somebody on the line. He makes his own calls. If a secretary is needed it's shared between four executives. That way you cut numbers. The issue of support staff so to speak to line staff is decreasing.[33]

One placement representative who focuses on managerial positions indicated that some foreign banks that initially hired people at five times their existing salary began to institute severe cutbacks after two years of operation.[34] As she indicated, "they have literally in a day's notice asked something equivalent to five to six hundred people at the management level to leave."[35] This phenomenon of downsizing foreign banks represented a general pattern across the sector in what one newspaper report termed the "pink slip syndrome" (Mukherjee 1998).

This transition from an economic boom to restructuring in an economic slowdown also characterized the consumer nondurables industry. In the initial period of liberalization in the 1990s, public debates focused on India's vast untapped middle class, with some estimates reaching as high as 300 million. This discursive production of the Indian middle class market helped fuel multinational expectations particularly in white goods as newly available commodities such as color televisions, VCRs, and washing machines were depicted as the symbols of a new liberalizing India. The inability of the Indian middle class to measure up to such inflated standards of consumption (a fact that was intensified by the economic recession in the late 1990s) resulted in cutbacks in the consumer nondurables industry. As one agent who handles managerial recruitment in the industry put it, while people were not officially fired, they

> ... had no choice but to leave. Work pressure was too much. Things were not happening and somebody had to take responsibility and responsibility always lands up at the middle level management. ... What most of them have done is they've jumped from one company in white goods to another in the last three years and realized the industry is bad and now they're looking at alternatives outside the industry.[36]

Such trends were particularly acute in multinational corporations as Indian companies did not engage in comparable drastic shifts such as doubling the wages of managerial staff. The result has been a significant increase in job insecurity and instability, which is relatively new to Indian corporate culture. This instability has taken a number of forms. First, it has resulted in an increase in job movement as younger junior managerial employees have repeatedly shifted between companies. As one agent indicated:

> See in the long run if it shows that they've moved four times in two years or even three times in three years it doesn't look good for a management student at that level. He doesn't come across well and it will reflect badly on their credibility later on . . . even though every time they move they had no choice but to move because either the division was being closed down or two branches merged and things like that. Basically people were trying to survive somehow and these people had no choice but to leave. But ultimately when he puts down in this resume that he's left three companies in the last two years the fourth company will think thrice before they see him. So there are lots of people whose careers are in a mess right now. Basically it's very miserable. I mean I can quote management students who have passed out in 1992–93 been taken on by one of these companies. Since 1993 they have changed five jobs.[37]

In contrast, upper-level managers who have not faced retrenchment have been unable to shift jobs or find alternative offers in order to negotiate improved positions. As one agent put it:

> Now no matter how good you are at your job you know that you don't have options. See security comes from knowing that I can put in my papers today if I don't like the way things are going. It's not just that people are going to throw you out . . . but you also know that they may decide not to give you an increment this year or not to give you a bonus or continue with last year's policy of something that you didn't like which they had promised to change or whatever. But you can't threaten them with leaving any more in this scenario. No matter how good, how senior you are. You can threaten them with leaving. So we get a lot of calls from most of the senior level managements. And they call us saying . . . how's the market looking? Is anything interesting happening? And we have to get back to them saying

there's nothing interesting right now. We'll get in touch with you. And we don't contact them for the next three months, which is something that would not have happened [in the past]. They know that if I had given a call to a recruitment consultant at the most three days and I would have got five calls. For maybe five different positions and maybe I would turn down all five but they would have called me back. And now they don't get a call for three months. And when they get a call after three months it's something that even we know they wouldn't be too keen on moving into. But we just check with them because they said they're open to a change. Job insecurity is a way of life right now in professional companies.[38]

Nevertheless, the upper echelons of managerial cadres have been protected by well-endowed voluntary retirement schemes. Given the finite network of upper-level managerial employees, larger companies have also attempted to use generous financial terms to counteract the negative publicity associated with the retrenchment of white-collar workers. Strong social networks of elite business school graduates have induced larger corporations to temper the potential negative impact on the upper-level managers of major corporations. As one agent put it, "If . . . somebody who is my MBA batch mate is thrown out by another company I will somewhere remember it and hold it against them. Maybe I will choose not to deal with them business-wise. It is still a close knit circle that people hold it against you and it does have a negative impact."[39] Such networks provide an informal class-based safety net for upper-tier managerial employees.

Safety nets of voluntary retirement schemes (VRSs) are not present for new MBA entrants in the job market or for smaller companies that cannot afford the financial costs of generous retirement packages. The possession of social capital through credentialing processes and social networks thus once again shapes structural shifts in the labor market.

In addition to retrenchment, a second major characteristic of the restructuring of the private-sector labor market has been an increased trend toward linking job security with productivity. Workplace cultures of both multinational and Indian companies adopt methods used to measure employees' productivity and time spent on the job, and engage in surveillance of employees. Companies use methods that, for example, require white-collar employees to use time cards to punch in and out. Companies also closely monitor phone calls to determine whether employees are making personal calls during office hours, or adopt a variety of strategies that measure productivity on a weekly or daily basis. One placement agent attempted to demonstrate the impact of the new postliberalization workplace by contrasting images of workplace in public- and private-sector banks:

> You walk into any public sector . . . bank and there are people all over just doing nothing. They're being paid but they're actually not contributing anything. . . . You go to a private bank, let's say a Hong Kong bank or a Citibank each and everybody is occupied each and everybody is busy. . . . I have a friend who is working at Bank of America—he constantly has people checking into telebanking. There are people listening into your conversation. The number of calls taken is monitored. The number of calls made is monitored. How many of these are your personal calls? Everything is monitored for each and everybody is working their optimum. So now there's this trend that you cut out any extra people and you pay the ones who are there, look after them. Pay them higher salaries, give them better benefits, give them a better environment to work in and yet cut out the costs.[40]

Reorganization of the workplace has also led to a pattern of subcontracting of tasks that were previously carried out by full-time employees. In some cases, subcontracting takes the form of franchising where, for instance, a company downsizes its sales personnel and subcontracts sales work to another organization for a percentage of the profits or revenue. Or, to take another example, payroll calculations often are no longer handled by individual employees within a company but are subcontracted to companies that specialize in such tasks. Even recruitment is increasingly subcontracted to private placement agencies.

While some aspects of this structural shift toward subcontracting within the service and white-collar sector industry are related to in-

creased efficiency through the specialization of skills, in other instances, subcontracting represents a process of the casualization of
white-collar work, which is closer to the shift from permanent to
temporary workers in the industrial sector.

The particular salience of such patterns of restructuring in the
context of contemporary economic liberalization rests on their relationship to the production of the category of the new middle class.
Labor market restructuring begins to disrupt the discursive images of
the new middle class. Such processes are not of course "new" or limited to the Indian middle class; rather, they have characterized the
experiences of working and middle class employment in a range of national contexts (Steijn et al. 1998). At one level, retrenchment appears
to simply represent a well-known pattern in liberalizing economies
and is contingent on cycles of recession and boom. However, at a
deeper level, such processes also represent a shift in the structure of
middle class employment away from earlier cultures of job stability
associated with government employment to the creation of a flexible
middle class workforce. Temporary contract work has in effect become a structural part of the new middle class labor market.[41] For
example, corporations increasingly have begun to hire white-collar
employees through intermediary recruitment firms. While the employees work for the corporation in question, they are paid by and are
officially employed by the recruitment firm.[42]

At another level, the patterns of labor market restructuring in
many ways conform to comparative models that have characterized
both advanced industrialized and late industrializing countries
(Crompton and Jones 1986; Godement 1999; Jenson et al. 1988; Mills
2002; Savage, Dickens, and Fielding 1992). However, the rise of the
new Indian middle class and its relationship to new economy jobs is
shaped by processes of globalization in ways that distinguish the
significance of such microprocesses from Western contexts. In particular, the relationship between new economy jobs, labor market restructuring, and the distribution of social capital has provided the
basis for more recent trends in global outsourcing. Such trends have
begun to change the structural relationship between the new middle
class in India and its counterparts in the United States and Western
Europe, and caution us against returning to older assumptions of

modernization theory that have sought to view trends in countries such as India as echoes of existing patterns in advanced industrialized countries.

The Politics of Outsourcing: The New Middle Class and the International Division of Labor

The structural politics of the new middle class have been both intensified and globalized through the effects of the international division labor on white-collar employment. The outsourcing of white-collar service-sector jobs from advanced industrialized countries such as the United States and the United Kingdom to India has expanded many of the micropatterns of the restructuring of middle class work. At one level, outsourcing has boosted new economy sector jobs and consolidated the structural basis of India's rising new middle class. The most significant sector in this process has been information technology and India's visible successes in its export-oriented software industry. In the period 1994–99, the information technology sector's compound annual growth rate exceed 40 percent; in 1999, the software industry alone accounted for 65 percent of India's total information technology revenues and employed more than 200,000 workers.[43]

The much-publicized success of India's information technology sector has accentuated an association between entrepreneurship and new middle class employment, particularly in cities such as Bangalore, India's "Silicon Valley."[44] However, while the economic success of the industry is notable, much of the information-technology-related growth in employment has been produced by outsourcing and concentrated in the growth of call centers.[45] While outsourcing includes a wide range of occupations including accounting, transcription, and more highly skilled work in the software industry, call center work has been estimated to account for 70 percent of outsourced jobs in India (Doshi and Ravindran 2004, 38).

New middle class employment that has been boosted through outsourcing mirrors patterns of the restructured middle class labor market. The organization of work (in terms of the structuring of time and space) and the temporary, casualized nature of employment are a central characteristic of such work. In addition, particular forms of social capital such as language and style are critical elements in gaining access to such employment. For example, in the much publicized call center industry, employment is structured along strict lines of discipline in ways that parallel the organization of industrial work in important ways. Employees generally work in night shifts (in order to accommodate the time difference for U.S. and British customers) that run from 6:00 PM—4:00 AM or 10:00 PM—8:00 AM, and generally work six nights a week (Puliyenthuruthal 2002). Employees have rigorous quotas and must make around 160–180 calls per shift and are strictly supervised through the surveillance of calls and control of breaks (Islam 2002). Such rigid working conditions have produced a high turnover rate that has been estimated to range from 35–40 percent to as high as 50–60 percent attrition in the first year of employment (Bhatia 2001; Doshi and Ravindran 2004, 39).

However, despite high turnover rates and difficult working conditions, such jobs have provided an important employment opportunity, particularly for college-educated youth in cities and small towns. While such employment provides restricted long-term employment potential for individuals within the middle class (as there is limited upward mobility within the industry), the short-term salaries provide a relatively high income for middle class individuals who may be unemployed or just entering the job market. Salaries start at Rs 7,000 per month and can rise up to Rs 10,000–13,000 per month, representing relatively high incomes particularly for students or recent college graduates. In the case of students and younger individuals employed in such jobs, the salaries have fueled disposable income and intensified the significance of young urban Indians as an important segment that has the potential to measure up to idealized visions of India's "consuming class."[46]

The outsourcing boom has helped address unemployment pressures on English-educated urban middle class individuals—the core of the new Indian middle class. The public attention given to outsourcing has intensified the significance of English education and the corresponding cultural resources that are needed for middle class individuals to negotiate the labor market in the context of liberalization (McMillin 2006). For instance, call center employment requires specific kinds of cultural training in American linguistic patterns and styles of speech and interaction. Such cultural training ranges from the use of Americanized names for employees, to more nuanced training in using American accents and linguistic colloquialisms. Such techniques of accent training including hiring teams that consist of a person who is solely responsible for examining the speed, clarity, and pronunciation of speech of job applicants and an "accent neutralization" training of new recruits (Shaloff n.d., 15). As Rebecca Shaloff (n.d.) notes, such strategies "can often include 'punishments' for using one's local verbiage" (16). On a visit to a training facility, an instructor who spoke in a forced American style described how she made her students dance in front of the class every time they used an "Indianism" (Shaloff n.d., 16).

Such workplace strategies are clearly extreme versions of the ways in which social and cultural capital are being redeployed and transformed by global processes of outsourcing. However, as we have seen through the various examples of local institutes that provide training on cultural style and personal speaking, this training predated the current focus on outsourcing and is linked to broader changes in corporate and private sector cultures. While outsourcing has intensified such changes, they in fact form part of a broader pattern in which new forms of social capital have become associated with a liberalized middle class labor market.[47]

The advent of outsourcing has consolidated and transnationalized existing patterns characteristic of the restructuring of the middle class labor market in India. The significance of the existing public debate on outsourcing rests more on the national and international political dynamics it sets into motion than on a sharp empirical contrast between shifts in employment that have been taking place since the 1990s, or the nature of outsourced jobs. To assume that such shifts in the middle class labor market have been causally produced by recent trends in outsourcing is to mistake national and global political rhetoric with the socioeconomic transformations associated with liberalization that have been occurring in the Indian nation-state. In other words, outsourcing is an extension of earlier processes of liberalization, rather than a cause of the restructuring of the Indian middle class.

Consider some of the nationalist narratives that have surrounded the question of outsourcing. In the United States, the outsourcing of jobs to India has been transformed into a potent symbol of the uncertainties of the American middle class. Images of young urban Indians sitting at computers has become an iconic symbol that routinely appears in media reports and has entered the everyday lexicon of public discourses in the United States (Rohde 2003). For example, in the 2004 U.S. presidential elections, as John Kerry (the Democratic presidential candidate) sought to deploy the problem of outsourcing as a nationalist issue that could tap into middle class anxieties, and George Bush followed suit (Padmanabhan 2004b). The symbolic nature of such rhetoric is underlined by the fact that in this context, India accounts for only 2 percent of the global outsourcing industry (Doshi and Ravindran 2004, 38). Nevertheless, some U.S. state governments have attempted to adopt legislation that could curb outsourcing, and the federal U.S. government passed a law preventing private companies doing subcontracting work for the departments of treasury and transportation from outsourcing to companies outside the United States.[48]

While the overall impact of such measures is unlikely to affect the outsourcing industry, such images have become an important part of the symbolic terrain of American politics. Meanwhile, Indian nationalist responses have converged with existing pro- and antiglobalization rhetorical positions, with proponents asserting that outsourcing is part of the norms of a free trade regime[49] and opponents depicting outsourcing as a new form of the global exploitation of labor which involves, as critic Praful Bidwai has put it, the transformation of young Indian undergraduates into "cyber-coolies."[50]

The potency of the politics of outsourcing is embodied in the public debates the issue has set into motion both in the United States and in India. Such nationalist narratives effectively juxtapose a rising Indian middle class in the same temporal moment with an American middle class that appears to be in decline as it faces growing anxieties in relation to its national economy and security. In ways that have disrupted the normal teleological views of developing countries always placed in a temporal space lagging behind the West, the new Indian middle class is cast, in such narratives, as a competitor and threat to the American middle class.

An analysis of the rise of the Indian middle class, however, cautions against such an easy attempt to reverse this teleology. As I have argued, while outsourcing is an important factor in shaping the socioeconomic boundaries of the new Indian middle class, it is part of a broader pattern that has shaped the restructuring of the labor market. Analyses that simply start with the rhetoric of globalization and its symbolic politics miss the internal, local, and national dynamics that shape and intersect with the visible, public issues such as the politics of call centers. The point at hand is not to dismiss the significance of such transnational processes, it is to underline the ways in which such processes are part of complex, long histories that shape labor markets and the politics of national development.

National and transnational shifts in the structuring of the new middle class have underlined the complex linkages between conventional forms of labor market restructuring that conform to local and national comparative trends on the one hand and distinctive patterns shaping the distribution of social capital on the other. Such linkages demonstrate the ways in which the framing of the liberalizing middle class in India cuts across traditional analytical boundaries between the cultural and economic realms. Representational practices of middle class lifestyles and the acquisition of social capital such as English skills are constitutive of systemic structural shifts in the labor market. The structural dimensions of such shifts also highlight the disjunctions that exist between idealized discursive representations of the new middle class and the socioeconomic uncertainties of employment patterns.

Such disjunctions do not, however, translate into opposition to restructuring. Rather, individuals aspiring to new middle class membership develop individualized strategies of upward mobility as they attempt to negotiate cross-cutting fields of cultural, social, and economic power. In fact, it is the middle class aspirations to conform to shifting representational practices of consumption, lifestyle, and status that shape individual responses to their socioeconomic circumstances. Let us further consider these processes by turning from a discussion of such general patterns of restructuring to specific case histories of middle class employees.

Work Histories and the Strategies of New Economy Workers

The "new" middle class, as I have argued, represents a central social group that has been targeted by processes of workplace restructuring that have unfolded in the context of liberalizing India. However, such processes have not led to political opposition to economic reform.[51] On the contrary, middle class employees often turn to individualized strategies in the context of an increasingly competitive labor market. These strategies are shaped, as we will see, by the normative model of the autonomous rational actor implicit in the structure and distribution of social capital.

Consider the work history of A. L. Rao, a white-collar worker at a leading multinational company.[52] Rao is a first-generation entrepreneur, attempting to start his own machine tool business in Karnataka. He started the project in the preliberalization period in 1990 and had developed the blueprint and obtained all of the government licenses required for a medium-scale manufacturing company with a workforce of 100 workers. The project was finalized just prior to the dawn of India's first phase of economic reforms in the 1990s. In a trend typical of start-up companies during that time the rising costs of imports due to the devaluation of the rupee and increased competition transformed the company into an economically unviable project. The company began to fail within a year. New financial norms in the period of liberalization prevented state lending institutions from bailing the company out and it was eventually shut down in 1992. Rao interprets this in terms of new obstacles that liberalization placed on first generation entrepreneurs:

> We tried to go through a lot of institutions . . . [but] even those institutions became very tight because of liberalization. Some day I came to a feeling that there's a sudden shift like before if they were very helpful to see that OK your company continues now they were more keen to see that we close down. . . . I can understand . . . maybe you don't want the economy to bleed but the question of welfare was gone. That was government point of

view but for an individual for the trauma which you go through of losing a business it's terrible. . . . [W]e lost all our money because we were first generation entrepreneurs. See there are two classes I find in India—one is the people who already have industries who have big industries and who go in for projects in terms of diversification. There's another class which I feel is kind of entrepreneur class which has product which says OK let's build a plant small plant and let's manufacture and start selling. I belong to the second [class].

Rao's story points to an important move away from earlier state strategies toward the middle class; state supports for small-scale enterprises produced a significant segment of the "new rich" from a diverse regional and caste groups. As Salim Lakha (1999) argues, "the small scale sector was regarded as a means of broadening the 'entrepreneurial base' and counteracting the concentration of wealth and resources" (254).

Rao's attempt to enter the ranks of the "new rich" through this strategy faltered due to India's shift to a liberalizing economy. The bankruptcy of his business led Rao to migrate to Mumbai as he was unable to find a job in Bangalore.

First what happened was . . . getting a job was difficult again and people [knew you had a] . . . failed project and so that was one of the reasons why I've come [to Mumbai]. This project was in Bangalore so I had to leave that state and come here to Mumbai. . . . [T]here are cases now running against me . . . for recovery of loans more than 3 crores and I don't even [own] property worth even 30,000 Rs. I told you first generation entrepreneurs we put all our savings into this the whole thing and we couldn't recover the whole thing so I had written a letter to the court saying that I have nothing so if if you feel that you can recover anything from me let me know anytime I'll show you all my assets. So in effect let's say in American terms it would be bankrupt. And a job in the machine tool was impossible because I [could] go into marketing, let's say, but again the trauma of having a failed product was very big . . . everybody knows about your project in the industry . . . [and] you can be in machine tools but someone will know where you are from. These are some of the things which made me leave machine tools and come into an IT [information technology] field so I started again back from scratch. And for one year I couldn't do anything. I was just trying to recover from what had happened and where I went wrong. Now I'm in a different city so I'm totally in a different field which I've never done before.

Rao was eventually able to obtain a job with a leading American multinational company in the field of information technology. He works as part of the managerial-professional staff in the marketing department of the company and is a dealer in charge of handling accounts in the western region of India. However, Rao's position within this multinational is not one of a regular managerial position in the company's marketing department. Instead Rao's situation represents a significant pattern within multinational companies in which white-collar workers are hired through a process of subcontracting that mirrors the structural pattern of subcontracting used for the industrial working classes. Rao is hired and paid by an intermediary company, which then subcontracts his services to the multinational company in question. He has been working for over a year and a half on the basis of an oral contract, which provides him with a fixed salary but none of the additional perks and benefits provided for permanent employees.

The process of subcontracting among white-collar service workers occurs in two main forms. First, in keeping with conventional patterns of outsourcing, a company may provide certain specialized services that are routinely subcontracted to other companies. For example, such companies may provide services such as bookkeeping and payroll accounting, or advertising services such as exhibitions or road shows. A second form of subcontracting occurs when multinational companies hire individuals and place them in the formal employment of a second independent company, as in Rao's case. A distinctive characteristic of this form of recruitment is that the individual does not approach the subcontractor to obtain a job with the multinational. Instead, the multinational directs its recruits to the subcontractor rather than placing them on their own payroll. As Rao put it:

> The agency which pays me . . . if you think that if I approach this agency I'll get a job in _____ [an MNC], no, it doesn't work that way. . . . [It's] the managers [in the MNC that] decide whether [they want you]. . . . [My job] came through a friend to me. My friend is one of the managers. It usually comes like this. It comes as a temporary job for six months. [It is not openly publicized and] is through word of mouth. You're looking for a six-month job. That time I was thinking, OK, I'm going to the U.S. I want some IT experience so when I joined in March I had time for six months so I came in, OK the company also grows and you are also getting used to the company they want you to [be retained] because [the] training process . . . is quite a headache so you continue. . . .

Despite Rao's unstable position within the company, he perceives his job as a potential opportunity for upward mobility rather than as a situation of structural exploitation. He subscribes to the notion that he is merely selling his services with, as he puts it, "total freedom." He believes that either experience in a leading multinational will provide him with future job opportunities or that his performance will eventually lead to a permanent position in the multinational company; if they have an open position, "maybe they will take me," he says.

Rao's case history points to the paradox of such contradictory positions that segments of the urban middle class occupy in the context of liberalization in India. While the restructuring of the white-collar labor market provides a structural parallel to the casualization of labor in the industrial working classes, white-collar workers continue to subscribe to the potential for upward mobility that liberalization holds for the urban middle class.

Consider the following symbolic representation of Rao's position. In the middle of our interview, Rao paused and indicated that he wanted to show me something. Pulling out his wallet, he removed his business card and a company identification card. The business card is a blank company card on which he has handwritten his name. He is not allowed to print his own business cards, as he is not an official employee of the company, but he is able to borrow the symbolic status of the multinational company. This status as a temporary sojourner in the company is contrasted to an official plastic identification card the company mistakenly issued him through a bureaucratic error. Pointing to the plastic card Rao says:

> Legally in India if I'm going to take this and fight and say I'm an _____ employee they will have to agree . . . somebody didn't know what was happening. It's a mistake . . . It's a proof that I'm an employee. You need not have given me any contract. . . . In disguise there are more nonemployees than permanent employees. . . .

Rao views the plastic badge as a symbol that will, ironically, give him access to the state protection of the very labor laws that have been eschewed in the context of the new liberalizing market; a market in which he must sell his services in "total freedom." The material fragility of this presumed symbolic protection presents an ironic reflection of the situation of segments of the urban middle class that confront the contradictions between the uncertainty of labor market restructuring on the one hand and the aspirations of the discursive images of prosperity and consumption that characterize the new middle class dream in liberalizing India on the other hand.

Despite such paradoxes, Rao adheres to the notion that economic liberalization has been beneficial for India. While he places the blame on the state for not cushioning the effects on entrepreneurs like himself, he insists that he is "totally for liberalization."

Rao's case history points to a wider pattern that has begun to characterize the restructuring of the white-collar labor market. While Rao's job is among the managerial ranks, restructuring has also characterized a larger segment within the lower sectors of this market— employees who serve as the secretarial, administrative, and executive assistants in the private sector. As we will see below, individuals in these segments fall into a pattern that mirrors Rao's work situation. These individuals form part of the contract workforce in the private sector, employed in restructured work situations. Yet like Rao they echo a strong support for liberalization as they point to the new potential for commodity consumption that liberalization has brought to the urban middle class.

Let us consider more case histories of employees to examine the ways in which members of the new middle class negotiate the dislocations of the restructuring of the middle class labor market. As we have seen, a primary strategy of the middle layers of the urban middle class consists of acquiring skills and credentials at various private institutes.

One such program, affiliated with one of the oldest and most prestigious liberal arts colleges in Mumbai, offers postgraduate diplomas in business management primarily designed for students without the time, educational credentials, or financial means to enroll in an MBA program. The year-long course costs approximately Rs 8,500–10,000, in contrast to a three-year MBA program, which can cost an average of Rs 30,000 a year. The course is officially designed for individuals who are already employed (although on occasion new college graduates are able to use personal connections to circumvent this policy); professionals and management representatives from various industries deliver the lectures. During the course of my fieldwork I interviewed a cross-section of graduates from this program.

Alumnae of the program occupy a variety of jobs ranging from lower-level positions as executive assistants to managerial positions in some of the top multinational and Indian companies in fields such as information technology, media corporate groups, recruitment agencies, advertising, leisure and entertainment, consumer nondurables, and other manufacturing industries. These employees, who are generally young college graduates, make up a significant segment of the middle class flexible workforce in the private sector.

Sujata is an executive employed in an Indian company in the entertainment and leisure industry. She obtained a managerial diploma immediately after graduating from college and since then has been employed in the marketing department of a well-known amusement park, and is responsible for booking corporate or private group events in the park. While she is considered a permanent employee and receives benefits such as provident fund (retirement) benefits, after four months of employment she has still not yet received a formal letter of employment. According to Sujata this represents a general strategy the company uses to maintain a temporary workforce (the company retrenches staff during the slack season because park attendance drops significantly during the monsoon season).

Significantly, this retrenchment does not merely occur at the lower rungs of employment but represents a restructuring of the workforce through the replacement of senior permanent managerial representatives with young temporary executives like Sujata. For instance, in Sujata's case, she began in the marketing department under two senior marketing managers. However, both managers have since been displaced and Sujata—as the only remaining member of the marketing department—has taken on their duties. Like the three other senior managers in the office (maintenance, security, and personnel) she reports directly to the managing director.

The contradictory nature of Sujata's position is underlined by the conditions of her employment. While her duties are characteristic of white-collar managerial work, her working conditions in many ways reflect the workplace organization of working class employment. The company tightly controls her workplace time and movements. Sujata must punch in and out on a time card and if she leaves early or arrives late she is given a late mark. After three late marks her salary is cut by a half day's wage. However, she is not paid overtime if she works late. She works six days a week and is not provided any sick leave. Meanwhile, while on the job her telephone calls are strictly monitored in terms of number and length. Although her job primarily involves contacting clients she must provide explanations for local phone calls that last more than five minutes. As she states:

> They record on the computer the time and the number. . . . They think business is a short-term process. But business is an ongoing process and it's a long-term thing. If you don't keep your relationship with your client you are not going to be a success. I've faced such a problem because of the telephone calls. I get a firing every time. Even if I get a call and I'm talking for fifteen minutes and your bill is not increasing I'm questioned on that.[53]

Such controls over Sujata's work extend to the lack of managerial authority she holds, although she must perform managerial duties. While Sujata must negotiate with individuals scheduling events in the park she does not hold any authority over the rates and discounts she can provide and must continually consult with her managing director. As Sujata indicates, this often undermines her credibility with her higher-level corporate clients. While Sujata complains bitterly about such conditions, she indicates that she hopes the experience she gains from her job will allow her to move to a better company in a year or two. Her job is relatively stable, in contrast to individuals who are increasingly employed on a temporary contract basis.

Consider the case of Maya, a young woman who received a diploma from the same institute as Sujata. Maya had completed her college degree from a small rural college and migrated to Mumbai in search of employment. She obtained a job as a secretary at a car dealership. After a few months, a placement agency got an interview for her in the customer support department at a well-known multinational corporation in the information technology field. After three interviews with various managers conducted over a span of three weeks, the vice president of the customer support department conducted a final interview and offered her a temporary job. As Maya puts it, "He kept saying you'll be a contract employee but you'll get credentials from _____ [a well-known U.S. company]. It'll only be for six months and if we need you for longer time maybe we'll keep you."[54]

After accepting the job, classified as a customer service executive with a salary of Rs 4,200, she enrolled in the management institute. However, after three months of employment Maya fell ill with jaundice and, in the absence of sick leave privileges associated with a permanent contract, she had to quit her position. Several months later, however, she received a call from the company asking her if she wanted to return for a one-month period. As she had not obtained employment elsewhere she agreed and was taken back at a reduced salary of Rs 4,000, despite an initial promise to pay her original salary of Rs 4,200. Once she was reinstated, the company extended her contract and finally offered her an ongoing contract position. While Maya was promised that she would be put on the payroll with a higher salary and benefits, such as a bonus and insurance coverage, she in fact never received this employment status. She was maintained as a temporary worker and paid from the company's petty cash fund.

While Maya's employment was never legally formalized, as a customer support executive she had a wide range of duties including contacting customers about the status of their orders, handling billing, ordering parts from regional offices in India and in Southeast Asia, overseeing annual maintenance contracts with both individual and corporate clients, dealing with customer complaints, and managing an assistant.

The company monitored her work closely, with daily assessments. They also frequently increased her productivity targets in terms of the number of customers contacted on a daily basis. For instance, the company informed Maya that she had to make 160 calls a day to inform customers about the status of their order.

Maya's work experience is typical of the Janus-faced nature of the effects of liberalization for the urban middle class; the other face of the idealized image of the new middle class consumer is the new middle class worker who must serve this consumer and handle the intensive workplace requirements of a restructured service economy. As Maya describes it:

[T]here was a lot of paperwork involved. It became too much because the other girl [her assistant] also couldn't pick up fast and [with] just two people you get crazy. , , , [E]very day you have to call up . . . one day it would be 160, maybe the next day it might be 180 customers. You have to do it. Sometimes we used to just say we called them, we called them. But sometimes the customers call up and tell [the supervisor] "we haven't received calls." . . . I was also handling what we call escalation cases as in it gets so heated up in Mumbai—if the customer gets so agitated—it . . . gets escalated [to Delhi] and once it goes to Delhi you're in boiling water. Because Delhi will come down on you like fire and you have to handle the situation. There was this one engineer who used to handle it and plus I had to help him with that. Like he would ask me the case history. You have to remember cases that happened a long time back also. You can't afford to forget things you know you have to look at every word the customer says.

The stress and anxiety of Maya's work responsibilities were compounded by a highly volatile work culture. One of her main complaints was the personal treatment she received from her supervisor. As she describes it:

> I don't believe you need to treat somebody that way. [M]y first boss . . . used to scream and shout so I guess this woman [the supervisor] thought that's the way you need to go about it, but that's not the way you deal with people especially because the customer support job is a very tense job. Your nerves are always like that because you're having people screaming down on your throat most of the time and you have to be calm you have to listen to what they're saying. You can't scream back at them. And if you have somebody else screaming at you I mean you know the environment you're working in can drive you up the wall.

Maya continued in this situation for six months and yet was still unable to attain a formal position on the company's payroll, despite earlier promises. Finally, she quit her job even though she had not obtained another job.

The work histories of Sujata and Maya point to the significance of the gendered nature of labor market restructuring in the private sector discussed earlier. Both Maya and Sujata occupy positions that are officially classified as secretarial work, a classic model of feminized work in India, as well as in comparative contexts (Crompton and Jones 1986). In the context of restructuring, their "secretarial" positions have increasingly expanded to include managerial responsibilities.

However, such expanded responsibilities do not provide them with occupational mobility in the labor market. They are not considered part of the company's managerial workforce, nor are their extensive duties reflected in substantially higher salaries. In the context of exorbitant real estate and housing prices and high cost of living standards in Mumbai, for instance, Maya is only able to afford to rent a shared room (typically called a paying guest) in a private residence. Such women workers who increasingly comprise a significant segment of service-sector and white-collar employment typically reside in such paying guest accommodations, or in working women's hostels if they are single and do not have family members to reside with in Mumbai.

These case histories raise a deeper question regarding the political implications of the patterns of labor market restructuring. If the restructuring of white-collar jobs in many ways parallels the organization of industrial work, the question that arises is to what extent such middle class employees will begin to identify as workers or potential members of new service-sector unions. While advanced industrialized countries have witnessed the rise of service sector unions, such patterns have been slower to develop in contemporary India. Historically, traditional organized sector unions ignored workers in the informal sector, India's traditional "service sector." While this has changed in recent years with the rise of new unions and nongovernmental organizations, independent of ties to political parties, there are no immediate indications that such organization will inevitably spread to white-collar, middle class employees. In contrast to public sector middle class workers that have historically been the core of organized labor in India, individuals negotiating the new middle class rely on individualized strategies of upward mobility.

Navigating Liberalization: From Privatization to Privatized Middle Class Strategies

My research findings suggest that individuals in new middle class jobs who are dissatisfied with their employment revert to individualized strategies of upward mobility.[55] Regardless of their levels of job dissatisfaction, the individuals I interviewed confirmed that liberalization had, on the whole, provided more opportunities and choices. These individuals do not translate their dissatisfaction with their work into an opposition to liberalization. On the contrary, as we saw in the case history of Rao, some workers point to the presence of consumer choice as a mark of the benefits of liberalization.

Consider the case of Naresh, another graduate of the business management institute I studied. Naresh has been employed in the marketing department at a well-known biomedical engineering company. The company, while a multinational, is one of the oldest companies in the field based in India and is run as an Indian private manufacturing company with operations primarily based in India. As one of the older companies based in India, liberalization has to a large extent meant a loss in protection and competitiveness for the company. With liberalization and the increasing availability of cheaper imports with more sophisticated technology, the company has had to confront the growing problem of maintaining its once-profitable manufacturing orientation. However, despite this impact on his company, Naresh's analysis of liberalization is based on an individual identification with a consumer-based identity. Although he notes some disadvantages, he emphasizes the benefits of liberalization:

> Because of reforms everyone is getting lot of benefits. We have a choice. We have various price brackets available. . . . We have international brand satisfaction. We have a quality product that is very important. If reforms could not have taken place then we would have missed all that. We would not have any options but to buy what they're manufacturing. Today the concept is different; today people know multinational people who are in India they're saying "we produce what you want." Ten years back things were different. [Companies said] "We produce—that you buy." That's the difference. But today customer is the king.[56]

Sujata and Maya echo this perception of the consumer-oriented benefits of liberalization. Their job dissatisfaction did not translate into opposition to liberalization. Rather, individuals employed within or attempting to gain access to such new economy jobs attempt to use individualized strategies of upward mobility to negotiate the restructured middle class labor market. Such examples point to the broader transformation of the identity of middle class employees, one that has moved away from a unionized public-sector worker to the new middle class consumer. As we have seen, these strategies include the attempts to acquire and use various forms of social and cultural capital to gain upward socioeconomic mobility.

For example, new informal work through direct marketing corporations has attracted a wide range of individuals.[57] The well-known direct marketing corporation Amway has specifically attempted to tap into individual strategies of gaining access to new middle class status. In one meeting that I attended during my fieldwork, more than a thousand people filled a large auditorium on a Saturday afternoon. The session began with a successful American Amway marketeer showing a video of his large house and luxury cars with the audience applauding loudly at various points. The speaker then posed the question to the audience, "Do you want to live like that, have a lifestyle like that?" The crowd chanting back, "Yes!"[58]

During the course of my fieldwork, I found that many individuals had tried direct marketing (usually without much success). In addition to such emerging informal strategies, middle class individuals also resort to older strategies of getting ahead, such as overseas migration. For example, middle class employment-based migration to Persian Gulf countries provides an attractive short-term strategy because this is a form of return migration that provides individuals a flexible way of leaving and reentering the labor market in India.[59]

The individual labor market strategies I analyzed form part of a broader pattern. The new middle class has responded to socioeconomic changes associated with liberalization by using a set of privatized strategies. This is not limited to employment but also includes arenas such as education and health care. Despite the relatively privileged status of the middle class (in contrast to low-income rural and urban workers) access and quality of both health care and education has varied widely, with significant disparities between different segments of the middle class as a whole.[60] However, despite historical dependencies on the state, the middle class has increasingly resorted to privatized strategies designed to gain individual benefits, rather than through organized political pressure on the state. Such patterns have been intensified in recent years as privatization has intensified in realms such as education, health care, and municipal facilities (Donner 2005; Kapur and Mehta 2004; Kapur and Ramamurti 2005).

Consider the case of higher education which, as I have noted, has historically represented a significant site of mutual dependency between the state and middle classes. In recent years, higher education in India has been undergoing a form of unplanned privatization, with segments of the middle classes increasingly shifting to the use of privatized strategies to obtain education. As Kapur and Mehta (2004) note:

> According to NSS [National Sample Survey] data, the government's share in overall education expenditure has been declining steeply, from 80 percent in 1983 to 67 percent in 1999. . . . Many students who formally enroll in publicly funded colleges and universities, barely attend classes there. Instead, they pay considerable sums to the burgeoning private sector vocational IT [informational technology] training firms such as NIIT and the Aptech. (5)

This is compounded by the shift in emphasis toward fields such as business administration since the majority of business schools are within the private sector.

Furthermore, privatization of education is also intensified by the attempt of segments of the middle class to use migration strategies and overseas education as a means of upward mobility.[61] The result, as Kapur and Mehta (2004) suggest, is that paradoxically, "On the one hand, the middle classes clearly have been a powerful lobby in maintaining lower fees and lower recouping of costs by the state. The middle classes have as much a stake in preventing a regime where higher fees are collected as newly aspiring entrants do. On the other hand, the middle class de facto is paying higher costs for education" (13).

While Kapur and Mehta identify institutional dimensions in the field of higher education and a breakdown of state accountability and policy as key factors that have produced this trend, my research suggests that an explanation of this paradox also requires a deeper understanding of the nature of middle class formation itself and the complex ways in which middle class agency has converged with broader ideologies and patterns of privatization. Everyday forms of privatization in arenas such as education and health care are part of the broader pattern of privatized middle class strategies designed to gain upward mobility through the acquisition and deployment of various forms of social, cultural, and economic resources.

While middle class use of informalized strategies such as private tuitions (used to supplement or replace classroom education) and coaching strategies have predated recent policies of liberalization, such processes of privatization have intensified in recent years. Ethnographic evidence from my field research demonstrates that a reliance on some form of privatized strategies in gaining access to education is an integral part of middle class strategies across segments and income distinctions within this social group.[62] In some cases, the line between "privatization" and corruption is effectively blurred. For example, it is commonly known that middle class families must also routinely rely on the deployment of "private donations" for their children to gain access to more prestigious schools.[63]

In some instances, local civic organizations have tried to use the courts to bar teachers from teaching coaching classes on the grounds that this informal privatization of education gives affluent students an unfair advantage (Seshu 1998). For instance, in 1998 a Bombay High Court order barred college teachers from providing coaching and other private classes. However, such state restrictions have not produced widespread changes in the context of the broader expansion of privatized education.

A stark illustration of the significance of the privatization of education in Mumbai can be seen in the steep decline of local vernacular municipal schools (run by the local municipal council, the Brihanmumbai Municipal Corporation, or BMC). Schools in this sector (estimated at 1,300 in 1998) have been in a significant state of decline with cases of choked drains, blocked toilets, broken windows, unusable blackboards, and high dropout rates (estimated at 35 percent in 1998; Rayani 1998). For example, lower middle class families have sought access to English-language, private schools. In light of shifting patterns in the new middle class labor market, such pressures have been significantly intensified.

Health care is another arena being shaped by privatization processes. In a similar pattern to the case of education, the growth of private health-care facilities has been expanding in the context of liberalization, and as in the case of education, middle class families deploy a range of individual strategies to gain access to quality health-care services.

Also as in the case of education, middle class individuals and families continually recount their frustrations with gaining access to quality health-care services. In conversations I had in Mumbai, individuals from a range of segments within the middle class would describe bad experiences or pass on rumors of corruption in the health-care industry, pointing, for example, to cases in which particular doctors would allegedly demand bribes prior to (and in one case during) treatments or surgery.

While it is impossible to confirm such allegations, these narratives nevertheless point to the ways in which the middle class perceives that their interests are not being served either in state or private educational and health-care institutions. Nevertheless, this social group continues to rely on personalized responses rather than systematic or organized efforts to gain state accountability in preserving minimal standards. For example, Henrike Donner's (2004) findings based on ethnographic research on health care in Calcutta note that middle class individuals would rarely choose a government hospital despite their perceptions of corruption in private facilities:

In this rather problematic environment personal relationships between doctors and patients are vital, and hold the promise of sufficient services and care. Far from being a mere consideration of financial means, doctors and nursing homes are chosen because the family of the potential patient knows the doctor working there and feels more secure in the knowledge that he or she takes a personal interest. This produces a double standard in public discourses, where private health care is concerned, and while doctors are accused of greed, individual households cultivate personal links with specific doctors, who are seen as reliable and whose advice even if it includes costly treatments and tests, goes unchallenged. (122)

Such personal networks in effect rest on the ability of middle class families to gain access to social capital. The result is a significant degree of differentiation within the middle class as lower middle class families often have less access to the social networks necessary for the cultivation of such personal relations with doctors.[64]

Internal socioeconomic differences within middle class extended families then intersect with and complicate such networks; for instance, lower middle class families often must rely on a network of gifts and favors from more well off members of extended families and kinship networks in order to gain access to such resources. Such patterns of differentiation both caution us against reifying homogenized discourses on "middle class elites" and point to the significance of the ways in which consumption-based models of new middle class behavior shape privatized strategies of the middle classes. In one tragic incident during my field research, a lower middle class family had taken a relative to an emergency room in a private hospital in Mumbai. However, they were not able to provide payment to gain access and the relative died due to the delay in moving him to a municipal hospital. As a friend of this family noted, if they had taken the individual to the government-run hospital emergency room, they would have received treatment (as access could not be denied in a state-run emergency facility). While this is clearly a stark example it nevertheless signals the costs that emerge when privatization and declining state accountability in realms such as health care and education are addressed purely through informal, privatized strategies.

Conclusion

My analysis of the restructuring of the labor market in Mumbai's private sector has pointed to a significant contradiction in the position of the new middle class in liberalizing India. On the one hand, new economy labor market experiences of the urban middle class have been characterized by a significant degree of differentiation that belie the idealized images of affluent consumers that are characteristic of public representations of the new Indian middle class. On the other the hand, individual strategies and responses of white-collar workers demonstrate the effectiveness of these representational practices that have been shaping new middle class identity, as individual dissatisfaction has not led to political opposition to India's economic reform policies.

The individuals I interviewed consistently pointed to the importance of new choices available to consumers as a sign of the benefits of reform. Such responses are part of a broader pattern in which individuals resort to privatized strategies in negotiating arenas such as employment, education, and health care. While such strategies predated liberalization, they have intensified since the 1990s postliberalization period and form a significant component of practices associated with the new middle class. Middle class individuals must acquire and deploy forms of social and cultural capital from both older sources (such as caste and kinship networks) and new arenas (skills/credentials and aesthetic knowledge) in order to navigate changes in the new economy.

The new middle class identity shapes both the valuation of different forms of social and cultural capital (that is, by shaping what counts in the new economy labor market) and the nature of middle class responses to the shifts and uncertainties associated with liberalization. It is this new middle class identity that has begun to manage the intersections and tensions between the discursive images of the new middle class consumer on the one hand, and the restructured and differentiated character of the middle class. The contradictions and shifts in behavior that arise out of these empirical patterns raise broader political questions of how the tensions within the idealized image of the Indian middle class dream shape the political behavior of the liberalizing middle class. This requires a closer analysis of the political identities and practices of the new middle class, one that I will turn to in the remainder of this book.

4

State Power, Urban Space, and Civic Life

————————❋————————

Citizens Forum for Protection of Public Space, better known as Citispace, now has over 500 paid members who are consulted by the BMC [Brihanmumbai Municipal Corporation] each time an issue of open space arises in the city. . . . Citizens are indeed stepping out. In a departure from the past, Mumbaikars aren't resigning to their fate or escaping to the suburbs. Worsening civic and environmental conditions and burgeoning corruption in Mumbai have nudged citizens across the city out of their slumber. They have come together in groups to raise issues and fight for their rights.

—*Raval (2002)*

The identity of the new middle class has become a critical arena for the negotiation of uncertainties, anxieties, and resistances that arise from changes sparked by India's program of economic liberalization and the broader cultural and social dimensions of globalization that have been associated with this set of policies.[1] The growth of civic organizations such as the Citizens Forum for Protection of Public Space represents an emerging trend in which the new middle class has begun to assert an autonomous form of agency as it has sought to defend its interests. The result is that the new middle class has begun to emerge as a distinctive political actor—one that attempts to reconstitute the meanings of civic life and provokes new forms of political contestation in return. In this process, the formation of new middle class identity has sparked political and social conflicts as segments of the middle class, the state, and subaltern social groups negotiate competing responses to broader changes in the liberalizing Indian nation.

In this chapter, I examine the dynamics of this process of identity-formation through an analysis of the spatial reconfiguration of social relations in urban India. As Doreen Massey (1994) has noted, "phenomena such as globalization" can be understood as "changing forms of the spatial organization of social relations. Social relations always have a spatial form and spatial content" (168). Drawing on this approach, I focus on the ways in which the creation of the identity of the new middle class unfolds through local forms of spatial politics and contestations. These spatial practices contribute to the production of a vision of a liberalizing India that centers on the visibility of the new Indian middle class.[2]

New middle class identity, as I have argued in previous chapters, is not simply a product of individualistic responses to advertising images of changing lifestyles. Therefore I begin by analyzing the relationship between the politics of middle class lifestyle and the restructuring of urban space in cities such as Mumbai. Recent research on urban processes has begun to point to the domain of urban space as a critical (and often understudied realm) that provides a broader understanding of contemporary India, one that "stands at the cusp of both the interpretive and the material" (Sarai 2002, vii). As Gyan Prakash (2002) has noted, the assumption that urbanization represents the highest objective for a nation's development has had a long history, one that was incorporated into Nehru's vision of national development (4–5).

A focus on the restructuring of urban space in India is not an isolated or singular example but a central arena in which negotiations over national identity, development, and middle class formation unfold. In line with my conceptualization of practices as embodiments of broader symbolic-material processes rather than as individual acts, I argue that the spatialized production of middle class identity is linked to the changing relationship between state and capital in the context of economic restructuring.

The production of the identity of the new middle class is linked to a politics of "spatial purification" (Sibley 1995), which centers on middle class claims over public spaces and a corresponding movement to cleanse such spaces of the poor and working classes. This process represents an emerging dimension in Indian politics, one in which middle class individuals and social groups now consciously claim that the Indian middle class is a distinctive social group with its own set of social, political, and economic interests that must be actively represented.

Drawing on an analysis of the politics of neighborhood beautification programs, I demonstrate that such civic organizations, which have been formed in various metropolitan cities, represent a central arena for the creation of a distinctive political identity for the new middle class. This assertive middle class identity is articulated through public discourses in a range of cultural and social formations (such as the development of new urban aesthetics and assertive claims on public urban space) and through the emergence of middle class civic and community organizations.[3]

The politics of distinction plays a central role in the shaping of this identity and politics of the new middle class. The internal uncertainties and instability of the new middle class are, in effect, managed through the reproduction of sociospatial distance from the urban poor and working classes. While new consumption practices form a significant aspect of the production of a new middle class identity, they do so more as a set of sociosymbolic status markers that individuals can display in order to preserve this segregation.

Local spatial practices are an instance of a broader range of strategies, associational activities, and everyday politics that shape middle class civic culture. Such practices exemplify a broader pattern in which civic life in contemporary India is reconstituted through the intensification of social exclusions and hierarchies. On one level, this process represents a new dimension in Indian politics, one in which middle class individuals and social groups now consciously claim that the Indian middle class is a distinct social group with its own set of social, political, and economic interests that must be actively represented. On another level, these practices draw on and reconstitute middle class anxieties, interests, and identities through the politics of gender, caste, and religion.[4]

The political significance of such practices and activities is underlined by the centrality of state strategies in shaping and managing this process of identity-formation. My analysis specifically builds on recent research that has questioned the presumption of distinct boundaries between state and civil society (Migdal 2001; Mitchell 1991a). As Joel Migdal (2001) has argued, the state can be thought of both in terms of an image of a unified, distinctive entity and in terms of "the practices of a heap of loosely connected parts or fragments, frequently with ill-defined boundaries between them and other groupings inside and outside the official state borders . . ."(22). Drawing on this approach, I demonstrate that state practices are centrally implicated in the politics of spatial restructuring, as the state oscillates between an active ally of new middle class aspirations on the one hand and manager of spatialized political conflicts between the middle class and subaltern groups on the other.[5] For instance, the state participates in the production of a new middle class identity when local state strategies actively promote new models of urban civic development that conform to and help create middle class models of civic life. Yet at another level, subaltern resistance to such models brings competing pressures on the state. The result is that political discord stemming from economic restructuring unfolds through spatial conflicts that are not necessarily explicitly discursively coded as contestation over policies of economic reforms.

Political scientists concerned with the mediation of conflict and consent to policies of economic reforms have tended to study them primarily by assessing electoral responses to such policies in democratizing polities, or by attempting to measure public attitudes to particular kinds of policies.[6] While such analyses have provided important explanations of the relationship between the consolidation of economic policies and contestation within the formal democratic political arena, they have neglected a broader range of social and cultural sites in which such contestation unfolds. For instance, the political significance of this new middle class does not lie in its numerical electoral strength; national patterns of political participation have shown that the Indian middle class in general has been characterized by relatively lower voter turnout. A narrow focus on electoral politics misses the nuanced ways in which the relationship between the state and middle class is shaped in fundamental ways by informal politics and everyday practices in civil society.

As I will demonstrate in this chapter, conflicts stemming from change associated with liberalization, or with broader processes of globalization, are managed by state negotiations of middle class social and cultural identities. These state practices are engaged in political processes that shape the boundaries of middle class identity and participate in the production of a new middle class–based vision of the Indian nation—one that is based on a reconstitution of inequalities of gender, caste, and religion.

Urban Space and the Politics of Middle Class Lifestyle

The distinctiveness of the new middle class has rested on a range of representational practices centered around particular characteristics of consumption, style, and social distinction. The lifestyle of the new middle class is in many ways the most visible symbolic representation of the benefits of India's embrace of globalization. As we have seen, this middle class is not simply a new socioeconomic group; it embodies a changing set of sociocultural norms for the Indian nation. This politics of lifestyle signifies a complex configuration of symbolic, material, and attitudinal changes that resonate with global discourses on the "new rich" in Asia (Robison and Goodman 1996). Such changes have ranged from conventional shifts in patterns of urban redevelopment with the rise of shopping malls and upper middle class housing complexes to more subtle changes in aesthetic and cultural practices such as new forms of dining practices and idiosyncratic leisure activities like white-water rafting.

The visibility of such lifestyle changes that have been reshaping metropolitan cities and spreading to small towns has sparked a wide range of public commentary and scholarly analysis—one that conjures up some of the conventional symbols of globalization such as McDonald's or shopping malls. This public ethnographic fascination with the middle class has intensified the presumed identification (and slippage) between the middle class, the new middle class, and the sphere of consumption. It is now commonplace for public discourses and scholarly writings to refer to the affluence of the middle class and to point to visible lifestyle shifts as evidence of this affluence. An analysis of this politics of lifestyle provides us with a conceptual lens that can grasp the informal terrain of the politics of liberalization. The significance of the politics of middle class lifestyle must be understood in terms of the broader socioeconomic processes that have unfolded in the context of liberalization. In other words, lifestyle practices are not simply an autonomous sociocultural sphere in which middle class individuals express their subjectivities or negotiate the contingencies of everyday life. Rather, new middle class lifestyles are shaped by structural socioeconomic shifts that have been unfolding in the context of liberalization.[7]

Let us consider this process in the context of contemporary Mumbai, which is perhaps the best example of an Indian metropolitan city that appears to fit the lifestyle image of the new middle class. Consider the sphere of leisure, a critical space for the production of such social distinctions. The leisure and entertainment industry grew significantly in the context of liberalization in the 1990s.[8] The proliferation of leisure and other service-sector-related industries has contributed to the growing public and social focus on questions of lifestyle.[9] In Mumbai, the expansion of the services sector and the leisure industry in particular has included a growing bar and restaurant culture. In contrast to smaller restaurants and Irani shops, which have catered to working class and lower middle class individuals, the city now boasts a wide range of upscale bars and restaurants.[10] Dining out, in this context, has become a status marker of the new middle class. Consider the following example of the transformation of a local restaurant, which an advertising executive described to me as an example of the ways in which the production of this lifestyle shift is encoded in wider processes of urban restructuring:

It's a little seafood restaurant. It's a Manglorian restaurant. In 1991–1992 Mahesh was this crummy little place with the downstairs where they served food with *thalis*[11] and upstairs was air-conditioned . . . but I liked the place. When you're eating and drinking you don't care what's around you. What happened was Mahesh got discovered by the yuppies. You had bankers coming in and lawyers. I haven't been to Mahesh in three years because the Mahesh that is there now is quite different. There's the guy who takes the order he wears a bloody suit . . . that's not the Mahesh I know. What happened to Mahesh? It was a reasonably good place but discovered by the yuppies . . . if you look at Mahesh as a brand with a very hip yuppie crowd they made the place an "in place."[12]

At one level, this anecdote simply seems to reflect the cultural tensions between the aesthetic tastes of the old bourgeoisie and the politics of style associated with the new middle class. Indeed, much of the moral lamentation regarding changing lifestyles is part of an internal conflict within the middle class over the nature of its public social identity. However, at a deeper level, this representation of changing tastes is also linked to the restructuring of urban space in contemporary Mumbai. The changes in the forms of distinction that shape middle class identities and lifestyles represent changes in classificatory practices that also shape the structure of social space (Bourdieu 1984, 175) and are not simply products of individual consumers responding to representational practices in the media and advertising industry.[13] In the context of liberalization, this reorganization of social space can be analyzed through the restructuring of urban space.

Consider the example of the refashioning of the restaurant Mahesh. At a surface level, this process appears to embody a conventional pattern of gentrification and urban redevelopment that social geographers have analyzed in cities such as London, Los Angeles, and New York (Davis 1992; Smith 1996; Wynne 1998). This pattern of gentrification contributes to the reproduction of new middle class lifestyles. For instance, exorbitant real estate prices in South Mumbai, the heart of the city, have increasingly pushed middle class individuals into suburban areas. The result has been the production of distinctive forms of suburban cultural and social communities. High-priced restaurants, shopping enterprises, and movie theaters have appeared in neighborhoods in Bandra and other western suburbs,[14] which are now considered upscale areas. These new upscale movie theaters in the suburbs, for instance, depart from the traditional fee structure of regular theaters. While regular theaters provide different scales from expensive balcony seats to cheaper seats at the bottom level of the theater, such theaters offer only a flat, higher price for all seating. The pricing system effectively keeps out poorer working class or even lower middle class individuals from such theaters. Meanwhile, in these wealthy suburbs a new club culture of what are called "upmarket" clubs has arisen (Chaudhry 1999). This club culture is of course not new to the city and in fact stems back to colonial times when the British introduced private clubs. In the postindependence period, these clubs became the preserve of upper class and upper middle class Indians. In addition, a number of older social clubs, such as the Islam gymkhana and the Catholic gymkhana, also represent middle and upper class community-based social and cultural spaces. What is new then is not the presence of exclusive membership-based clubs for the reproduction of class distinction but the expansion of such social spaces as well as the stark increases in membership fees. Thus, an "upmarket" club in an outer suburb such as Thane or Navi Mumbai exceeds Rs 50,000, whereas prestigious clubs in South Mumbai can run in the *lakhs*.

The expansion of such sociocultural spaces for the new lifestyles of the middle class in liberalizing India have contributed to the production of a new aesthetics of class purity. Discursive representations of new middle class lifestyles have been increasingly interwoven into the creation of an urban aesthetic based on the middle class desire for the management of urban space based on strict class-based separations. This desire for sociospatial segregation cannot, of course, be viewed as an outcome causally produced by the policies of liberalization in the 1990s. As I showed in chapter 1, the relationship between middle class civic identity and the politics of urban space stems from historical processes that first emerged in the colonial period. Furthermore, in the postcolonial period, conflicts over urban space have been present in earlier events such as the coercive demolitions of squatter settlements associated with Sanjay Gandhi in the mid-1970s (Tarlo 2003).

While this politics of spatial purity has been contingent on broader historical processes, the imposition of such spatial class-based norms has been transformed by the rise of a new middle class identity in ways that distinguish it from conventional patterns of gentrification that have unfolded in cities such as New York and Los Angeles. The distinctiveness of such spatial practices stem from the specificities associated with the conditions of economic transitions that characterize late-industrializing nations. On one level, such specificities arise from historical differences that distinguish postcolonial and late-industrializing contexts such as India. Historically, in contrast to modern urban cities in the advanced industrialized countries, metropolitan cities in India did not develop into strict class segregated spaces. While cities like Mumbai, Delhi, and Calcutta have certainly reproduced spatial distinctions between wealthier, middle class and poorer, working class neighborhoods, such distinctions have historically always been disrupted by the presence of squatters, pavement dwellers, and street entrepreneurs such as tailors, shoe repairmen, and hawkers. Such street entrepreneurs and pavement dwellers were generally located in these neighborhoods in order to provide services to their middle and upper class residents. Given high levels of poverty and the dependence of middle class families on working class labor for household work (such as *dhobis*—washerwomen and men, sweepers, and cooks) the class-based management of urban space in contemporary India developed in patterns distinctive from the advanced industrialized countries.[15] Patterns of workplace–residence separation that have historically characterized advanced industrialized countries such as the United States (Katznelson 1983) cannot for instance provide the conceptual means for analyzing the experiences of pavement dwellers who perform services for the middle class neighborhood where they reside. These distinctive spatial patterns are structural effects of unequal patterns of development in late-industrializing nations that have intensified patterns of rural–urban migration and led to the expansion of squatter settlements and the growth of large informal sector workforces in urban areas in comparative contexts.[16]

On another level, the distinctiveness of the Indian case lies in the way in which urban conflicts are a spatialized form of contestation over liberalization. Space, in this case, does not merely serve as a physical container or transparent mirror of social relations—it is both a substantive component of a liberalizing economy and a realm in which the state attempts to manage consent and resistance to liberalization. An analysis of spatial practices provides a means for understanding the significance of the new middle class in shaping broader processes of privatization and the redefinition of older models of state-led development in transitioning economies. In this process, historical patterns of spatial organization have been disrupted and replaced by an intensified set of conflicts over spatial forms of segregation. I turn next to an analysis of such spatial practices in Mumbai and then use this case to draw out the larger implications for an understanding of the relation between the state, the new middle class, and economic restructuring.

State Practices, Spatial Politics, and the Reconstitution of Middle Class Civic Culture

In metropolitan cities such as Mumbai, Delhi, Calcutta, and Bangalore, there is growing political conflict over public space. Local state governments, middle class organizations, and the urban poor have increasingly been battling over scarce urban space and models of urban development. A significant example of local spatial practices is the case of "beautification" projects undertaken by middle class civic organizations and local state officials in Mumbai.[17] In these projects, the state and new middle class engage in a shared conception of the city as a central sociospatial site that can manifest an idealized vision of an India that has been transformed by globalization; the global city in effect, represents the new city–nation. Consider for example the following vision of the former sheriff of Mumbai:

> There will be no slums. The streets will be clean with wide pavements unencumbered by hawkers. People will stroll through pedestrian plazas. The night will be brilliant with majestic buildings and fountains. (Seabrook 1996, 48)

This imagined city captures the aesthetic of the civic culture of the middle class in liberalizing India—one that attempts to manifest the image of the new Indian middle class by cleansing the city of any sign of the poor or poverty. The drive to "clean up" the city has been centrally constructed around such class-based discourses.

Such processes of spatial purification are not simply an expression of the private desires of middle class individuals. They represent a political project that centrally involves the exercise of state power within an emerging civic culture of the new middle class. For instance, beautification drives in Mumbai have been organized both by middle class civic organizations and by local state officials through Maharashtra's Cultural Affairs ministry. The drive aimed at "cleaning up" public spaces and land such as beaches, promenades, *maidans* (public grounds), and other public areas represents official policy of the state government and has explicitly sought to cater to the lifestyle model of new middle class identity. For example, in the affluent suburb of Bandra, one such project spearheaded by Cultural Affairs Minister Pramod Navalkar focused on developing a jogging strip with plants and seats on the seaside promenade.[18] This example points to a wider pattern in which local state strategies have attempted to restructure space in ways that cater to the wealthier segments of Mumbai and to the lifestyles of the new Indian middle class. Proposed plans to restructure parks and *maidans* have involved the drawing of clear social boundaries through the construction of gates that control access to what were once accessible public spaces. In one such plan, the BMC developed a Rs 6,000,000 beautification project that would transform one of Mumbai's most well known *maidans,* Shivaji Park, by constructing seven gates, "VIP" parking, tiled jogging tracks, and elaborate fountains and pavilions (Karkaria 1997).

While state government officials have sought to construct such projects in terms of a broader public drive for sanitation involving a cross-section of areas across the city,[19] the boundaries of the "public" constituted by such beautification drives have in fact been dependent on the politics of socioeconomic class. Consider the following description of the beautification and cleanup drive of Chowpatty, one of Mumbai's most well-known beaches:

> Yes, it's possible to now take a relaxing walk along the Mumbai coastline at Girgaum Chowpatty. Finally, the sand looks and feels like sand. Years of neglect and unsuccessful cleanliness

drives later, the city's most famed beach is free of muck, debris, urchins, beggars, lepers and hutments, thanks to state culture Minister Pramod Navalkar. The entire 1km stretch of the beach has been bulldozed and cleaned, illegal slums removed, fishermen relocated and dustbins installed. (*Bombay Times* 1998a)

In this discursive construction, which is an instance of a broader set of public discourses, urchins, beggars, and the residents of hutments are viewed as interchangeable with the "muck and debris" which must be "cleaned up." What is particularly significant in such class-based discourses is the role of the state in defending middle class claims to an unfettered access to public space. As part of the Chowpatty "beautification" drive, plans were also developed to ensure that the relocated poor would not reenter the beach. Such plans included the construction of a 120-foot-high watchtower and a permanent presence of two policemen (Sharma 1998). The result is a convergence between state strategies and the development of middle class civic spaces. Middle class civic culture in this context becomes the terrain for the expansion and exercise of state power (Sharma 1998). Such examples also demonstrate the ways in which state practices participate in the production of the identity of the new middle class, in this case through the preservation of a spatialized form of urban aesthetics.

Such examples demonstrate the blurring of the boundaries between state and civic life.[20] However, the state does not represent a passive instrument of the middle class; nor does it consistently operate with a unified set of interests (Migdal 2001). On the contrary, the dynamics of democratic politics often place contradictory pressures on the state. Consider the way in which the convergence between the exercise of state power and the production of a middle class civic culture through the management of public space has unfolded in relation to hawkers (street vendors) and their unions. Increasing pressures on urban space have in recent years produced significant conflicts between hawkers (Bhowmick 2002a, 2002b) and middle class civic organizations demanding greater access to public street space. The result is that the state government in Maharashtra has begun to significantly crack down on hawkers through a series of actions including confiscating their goods and demolishing their stalls.

Despite this convergence between state and new middle class models of urban development, the state agency involved, the local municipal corporation, Brihanmumbai Municipal Corporation (BMC), is in a conflicted position. Unlike the hutment dwellers and "beggars" who have been driven away from public spaces such as beaches and *maidans,* Mumbai's hawkers are unionized and thus have been able to wield more political clout in the contest over public space in streets and neighborhoods.[21] In addition, the BMC has used an official system of daily charges, as well as an unofficial system of bribes for unlicensed hawking as a financial source. In an attempt to mediate between the hawkers' unions and middle class civic organizations, the BMC has developed a plan that will manage claims to public space through the creation of legal "hawking" zones. Such plans have produced significant political conflicts as both hawkers' unions and civic organizations contested the plan during negotiations and via legal avenues.

Such conflicts have furthered the development of new networks of middle class associational life. Middle class organizations have sprouted up throughout the city with a range of objectives from cleaning up particular neighborhoods, to lobbying local state officials to keep public spaces free from street vendors, to dealing with urban environmental issues. In contrast to traditional formal organizations such as labor unions and nongovernmental organizations that work on questions of social justice and equity, such associations are marked by their specific concern with the conditions of middle class life.

Such civic organizations specifically battle against a state that they perceive as catering to or captured by unions and workers, and claim to represent the interests of the middle class. Middle class activity in the form of such citizen's groups and media representations of these contentious issues have largely constructed hawkers as a threat to the civic culture of the middle class (Bhowmick 2002) on a wide array of middle class interests, including inconvenience, sanitation, fears of social disorder, and the threat of declining real estate prices for residential areas set aside for relocating hawkers.

Such associational activity begins to provide specific organizational mechanisms for the political representation of the new middle class. In this process, the new middle class emerges as an independent political actor that assertively makes claims on the state. Several middle class and residents' and citizens' associations have put forth legal challenges to the BMC's zoning plans in order to prevent hawkers from being relocated to their neighborhoods (Devidayal 1998b). For example, in one case, a "citizen's forum for protection of public spaces," representing fifty citizen organizations, filed legal petitions to prohibit hawkers from operating in residential neighborhoods and near major public areas such as railway stations, hospitals, educational institutions, and places of worship.

These newly emerging forms of middle class activity have fallen under the radar of contemporary political science research because they have unfolded at the local level without national formal organizational frameworks similar to those of labor union federations or recognized nongovernmental organizations. Furthermore, political scientists have been more preoccupied with organized interest groups that have lobbied against economic reforms than such emerging organizations that are associated with new middle class visions of modernity and national development.

While this network of state strategies and middle class associational life unfolds at the local level, it is not unique to the particular case of Mumbai or to the specificities of Maharashtra's state government.[22] Similar patterns have unfolded in cities such as Bangalore and Calcutta. State strategies in Bangalore, for instance, have successfully transformed it into a model "Silicon Valley" city.

Drawing on an existing pool of managerial, technical, and professional segments of the middle class, state and private capital collaborations have accelerated a model of urban development that parallels Manuel Castells's (1996) conception of an "informational" model of economic development. Such processes have included the growth of technology parks, new forms of urban development catering to the middle class, and similar cross-pressures between new middle class cultural spaces such as a well-known club culture and a large pool of workers and urban poor concentrated in the informal sector of the industry.[23]

Mumbai and Bangalore are in many ways similar cases given that they have had longer historical traditions of commercial and scientific–technical growth, visible English-speaking middle class professional urban cultures, and sought private and multinational capital prior to the 1990s period of liberalization. However, these kinds of patterns of urban restructuring are not limited to such typical examples of modernized cities. For example, Calcutta has been defined by uninterrupted communist rule, an ideological orientation toward agrarian reform,[24] and formal ideological opposition to economic reforms. In patterns that parallel those of cities such as Mumbai and Bangalore, the Communist Party of India-Marxist (CPM)-led state government has sought to promote a new form of urban developmentalism in an attempt to recast the city's image and has engaged in similar strategies to promote new middle class housing development projects, clean up public spaces, and evict hawkers through its "Operation Sunshine Drive."[25] As Ananya Roy (2003) has argued, "the Left's newfound agenda of urban developmentalism can be read as an attempt to recover the "public" from the *pablik* [the colloquial idiom for a democratized, inclusive public sphere], reinscribing space as middle class and subject to civic control" (11). Such processes constitute a generalized pattern that underlies the disparate array of localized spatial politics.

Spatial practices and the convergences and tensions between state and middle class civic culture rest on a shifting urban-based model of economic development. While I have provided a sense of the texture of these practices, my underlying argument is that such processes are characteristic of new middle class identity because they are shaped in distinctive ways by more recent processes of liberalization. For instance, I argue that the politics of middle class lifestyle is not constituted by private tastes and preferences but is inextricably linked to the material restructuring of urban space. This distinction is significant because emerging forms of urban middle class environmentalism often adopt an individualistic language of responsibility. For instance, in a discussion of urban environmentalism in Delhi, Awadhendra Sharan (2002) notes the synergy between "environmental self-help and a new emphasis on 'caring for the self' (e.g., reiki/yoga, no smoking, safe water, exercise diet, etc.), which is addressed to the health of the middle class through deploying the language of a larger urban public" (34). However, despite the expansion of such languages of individual responsibility, I argue that the materiality of lifestyle is not the result of changing individual "cultural" tastes of the middle class. In other words, the restructuring of urban space is not merely a result of changing attitudes and preferences of the middle class. Rather, as I will demonstrate, such changes embody broader processes of restructuring that have been intensified by policies of economic liberalization.

Urban Space, Economic Restructuring, and the Redefinition of State-Led Development

Projects of urban spatial restructuring in metropolitan cities represent what Saskia Sassen (2002) has termed the "strategic geography of globalization [that] is partly embedded national territories, i.e., global cities and Silicon Valleys" (96). An analysis of urban restructuring moves us away from conceptualizing the politics of liberalization through facile juxtapositions between states and markets.[26] My discussion of the links between new middle class identity and state strategies has shown the ways in which liberalization has opened up new spaces for the exercise of state power, for instance in realms that are conventionally defined as "civic space." An analysis of the identity of the new middle class provides a lens for the ways in which liberalization has produced a restructuring of the state and a reworking of older models of state-led development.

Liberalization, in other words, does not lead to a decline in the significance of state intervention as is sometimes assumed by theorists of globalization and scholars of economic transitions.[27] The kinds of spatial practices discussed above are part of a reconstituted model of state-led development.

Consider the structural dynamics of the reorganization of urban space. I have argued against an understanding of such dynamics as an effect of individual middle class consumer choices. This is consistent with comparative scholarship that has sought to explain the structural basis of middle class-oriented urban redevelopment. Writing about gentrification in the United States, Neil Smith (1996) cautions against deploying a "consumer preference model" (108), which reduces explanations of urban restructuring to an effect of individual choices and middle class demand. As he argues, "To explain gentrification according to the gentrifier's preferences alone, while ignoring the role of builders, developers, landlords, mortgage lenders, government agencies, real estate agents—gentrifiers as producers—is excessively narrow" (57). However, as noted earlier, in late-industrializing countries such as India, such dynamics are distinguished by the specific conditions of economic transition. Structural changes in land usage are shaped by the dynamics of liberalization.

Local spatial practices in cities such as Mumbai reflect wider structural shifts in land usage and the real estate market. At one level, the effects of globalization on the real estate market have often been embodied in stark visual and spatial forms. For instance, in metropolitan cities such as Mumbai, construction of luxury apartment complexes targets both the top tiers of the new India middle class and the global Indian middle class usually termed "NRIs"—non-resident Indians.[28] Meanwhile, rising real estate prices have also accelerated the shift from older declining manufacturing industries such as the Mumbai textile industry—one of India's oldest manufacturing industries—to new-economy industries such as the service sector and media enterprises. The 1990s, the first decade of new economic policies in India, produced steep speculative rises in Mumbai's real estate. As Jan Nijman (2000) says:

> The partial opening up of Mumbai's market in the first half of the nineties meant that the market had to find the "right" price of Mumbai real estate. The "right" price was escalating upwards due to the much talked about scarcity of office space in the city in combination with rapidly increasing demand, an equally popular topic of conversation. The search for a stable market was complicated by the entry of global capital, because now Mumbai was now not only compared to places such as Delhi or Pune, but also to New York or Hong Kong. Thus, when Nariman point became as expensive as Manhattan and five times as expensive as Bangalore, who was to say that was not "normal"? (580)

Mill owners have found it more lucrative to sell land used for textile mills than to try and revive sick mills in the face of strong international competition (D'Monte 2002).

The transition was vividly evident to me during my fieldwork as I conducted a series of interviews with journalists working for a new consumer magazine targeting the new middle class. The offices were housed in a converted textile mill while other sections of the former mill were being used as a television studio.

Such shifts from manufacturing to service industries have also skewed the benefits of India's new economy toward the new middle class and away from the working class. As one public commentator put it:

> The transition from a manufacturing to a service sector economy is being hailed as a sign that Bombay is maturing into an international city. But it has left mill labourers and the rest of the working class bewildered. The service sector demands skills that they simply do not possess. "All these jobs have been created in this area, but hardly any of them have gone to mill workers or their children. Do you think these people want to become copy writers?" asks Meena Menon, an organizer of Girni Kamgar Sangarsh Samiti (Mill Worker's Struggle Committee). (Fernandes 1996, 21)

According to one estimate, employment in the textile industry has dropped from 250,000 in 1980 to 57,000 in 2000 (Saran 2000). A critical contradiction in this process is that unemployed mill workers are often forced to turn to alternative forms of employment, such as hawking, in order to support themselves.[29] However, as we have seen, middle class-based definitions of the service industry have constructed hawking as a threat to the social order rather than as an integral consequence of processes of restructuring unfolding in liberalizing India. The kinds of local spatial conflicts discussed earlier are an explicit product of structural contradictions in the Indian economy.

State strategies have helped to consolidate these structural processes either through a passive form of complicity or through more active forms of intervention. For instance, in Maharashtra, local officials have not enforced laws that prevent the sale of textile mills despite stringent legal restrictions on such sales. An analysis of such practices is critical for scholars interested in assessing policies of economic reform. Scholars have often evaluated the success and extent of such reforms by analyzing formal shifts in policy regimes or legislation. However, this assessment is based on an analysis of legal activities. In practice, laws and formal policies often do not correspond to informal practices, many of which may fall outside of the boundaries of legality. For instance, while analysts cite strictures on the sale of textile lands as an example of state controls that need to be removed, such sales have in fact already been carried out (Kakodkar 2003; Raval 2000).

Similar processes can be seen with regard to India's "exit policy." Despite the lack of an exit policy (the ability of companies to engage in labor retrenchment as part of restructuring processes), such retrenchment is in fact a longstanding pattern conducted either through official programs such as voluntary retirement schemes or through extralegal means.[30] While scholars of Third World nations have often analyzed the problems of state corruption, less attention has been paid to the ways in which "corruption" has served as an arena for state practices of liberalization. The state, in effect, undermines its own legal authority in support of restructuring processes.[31] The state thus remains a crucial actor in shaping liberalization, often through such unconventional and extralegal activities. This role of the state also extends to a more active promotion of new models of urban development that are associated with a liberalizing economy.

The restructuring of public space in liberalizing India is thus not merely an effect of middle class desire but is also an aspect of new strategies of state-led development in the context of liberalization.[32] In India, local state governments in states as ideologically varied as Maharashtra and West Bengal have sought to promote privatized models of urban development.

Liberalization, in this context, does not lead to a decline of state intervention but to a shift in the nature of the exercise of state power. Consider the ways in which this shift is shaped by processes of privatization. A central dimension of the model of urban development that caters to the new middle class is the emergence of new forms of collaboration between the state and private sector. For instance, the state-led beautification projects such as in Chowpatty were carried out with financial support from the corporate sector, while private security firms carry out the surveillance of such "beautified" public spaces.

The local state government has also tried to privatize other public spaces, such as municipal gardens, and made a controversial attempt to demolish Mumbai's Aquarium and replace it with an elaborate underwater aquarium to be constructed though a joint venture with a Singapore-based firm—a shift that was estimated to potentially raise entrance fees from Rs 4 for adults to Rs 140 per person (Deshmukh, 1998a). Furthermore, in the state's antihawker drive, the BMC employed private guards to evict illegal hawkers from public places, a tactic that was used for the first time in the BMC's history (*Asian Age* 2001; Bunsha 2002).

State reliance on the private sector is not limited to the BMC but is part of a broader pattern in which both central and state governments have been increasingly subcontracting work to private agencies (Kapur and Ramamurti, in press). Such processes are part of a broader pattern of the "privatization of the state" which, as Kapur and Ramamurti (in press) argue, can be seen in a variety of activities ranging from "the growth of gated communities, to the private provision of social services, to private modes of transportation replacing public modes, to privately appropriating public assets as in the power sector and the "sale" of public jobs. . . . Private townships and buildings with their own water, power and sanitation systems have exited the public sector" (26). It is this kind of everyday privatization that specifically converges with the identity and civic culture of the new Indian middle class. In other words, a substantial part of these forms of local privatization target members of the new middle class. Thus, there is a growing intersection of interests between the state, the private sector, and this rising social group.

Spatialized state practices represent one case on a broader range of state strategies that have sought to manage the effects of liberalization. The politics of urban development reflect the ways in which the state shapes middle class identity and consequently helps consolidate a base of support for economic restructuring. The exercise of state power in this context does not take the form of an external force that is protecting or catering to a predefined set of interests of the middle class; rather, it is inextricably engaged in the production of a distinctive identity for the Indian middle class. Kirin Aziz Chaudhry (1994) has noted that it is often the nature of the state's involvement in the economy that shapes outcomes of economic liberalization programs.

However, while comparativists have focused on a range of variables such as political coalitions, institutions, and state policy (Haggard and Kaufman 1995), less attention has been paid to the ways in which the politics of identity formation and the state management of identity politics shapes such processes. While I have focused thus far on identities of social class in order to foreground the structural dimensions of the politics of space, group identity is always constructed through multiple, intersecting identities.[33] The relationship between state practices and the identity of the new middle class is also constructed through identities such as gender and religion. In the final sections of this chapter I examine the reworking of such identities and the ways in which state strategies have deployed and responded to such identities in an effort to manage some of the tensions and anxieties associated with economic policies of liberalization and the broader sociocultural dimensions of globalization.

Managing the New Indian Middle Class: Gender, Culture, and the Politics of Identity

The state's spatial practices are part of a broader set of political dynamics in which the disjunctures and transitions of liberalization are negotiated through the management of this middle class identity. This process takes a form of cultural politics shaped by identities of gender and religion. For instance, some state-driven policies of spatial purification have rested on a notion of cultural purity and a reaction against "sexual deviance." As the Cultural Affairs Minister indicated in relation to new timing restrictions imposed on access to beaches, "'The beach has become a haven for *hijras,* beggars, homosexuals, commercial sex workers and homeless people at night. I want to put an end to this nuisance immediately," he said, adding that the restriction would not affect law-abiding citizens. 'No decent man or woman is interested in strolling out on the beach after midnight'" (*Times of India* 1998b). This example points to the state involvement in the production of dominant conceptions of middle class respectability and a normative gendered conception of public civic life.

Consider the following example of the state government's management of the disjunctures of liberalization through the invocation of a politics of purity.[34] On July 10, 1996, thousands of women workers, employed as waitresses and dancers, marched to the Maharashtra state government's office in Mumbai to protest state laws that would prohibit them from working in bars and restaurants after 8:30 PM.[35] The law, which represented a reactivation of a 1948 act barring the employment of women from establishments such as shops and restaurants before 6:00 AM and after 8:30 PM, was part of a "morality drive" launched by the conservative Shiv Sena government in Mumbai.[36] The Maharashtra Government's Cultural Affairs Ministry, which spearheaded this endeavor, began to revoke the licenses of establishments that held late-night dance shows.[37] The clubs and bars that cater to middle class men (ranging from "regular" middle class constituencies to "VIP" rooms that serve wealthy businessmen) and are mainly concentrated in the suburban areas around Mumbai.[38]

In the context of the creation of middle class civic culture that I have outlined, such local state strategies provide a clear attempt to redefine the boundaries of Indianness, boundaries that rest on the purification of "Indian cultural life." Government officials, for example, argued that the offending establishments had distorted accepted cultural norms as they had obtained licenses by classifying the dances as "classical dances"; according to local officials, dances set to popular film songs did not fit the category of legitimate cultural activities.

The state's move to police the boundaries of cultural life was fundamentally dependent on the deployment of a set of gendered discourses. Public rhetoric from government officials and some newspaper reports located the rationale for this middle class morality drive in terms of the protection and purification of women's sexuality. On the one hand, officials indicated that the 1948 law was being reactivated in the name of the safety of women. Indeed, this act is related to wider "protective labor legislation" which has also prohibited women from working in night shifts in factories. As in the case of factory night-shift regulations that threatened the employment of women workers, women protesting the law in Mumbai argued that such restrictions would cause significant losses in wages as a substantial portion of their earnings were comprised of tips earned in later hours of the evening (when businessmen visit the bars after work).

This "politics of protection," which has been a central ideological strategy of state policy in comparative contexts (Alexander 1994; Brown 1995), has provided the symbolic capital for the state government's efforts to displace the disjunctures of liberalization onto a gendered terrain of public cultural life. This process of displacement is highlighted by the paradoxical situation in which the government was imposing restrictions on women workers in bars and restaurants whereas the export-oriented jewelry and electronics industries (which are in line with the export-oriented growth strategies of the new economic policies) were successfully able to modify the Factories Act, weakening national labor law that had prohibited the employment of women workers in factory night-shift work.

The politics of purity in Mumbai have been shaped by the dominance of the Shiv Sena both as a party in power in the state government, and as a powerful independent organizational and ideological force in civil society. For instance, Thomas Hansen (2001) argues that the "Sena's target was neither consumption nor capitalism. As with Sena's resentment of artistic refinement, the crux of the matter was the rejection of 'urban excess'; immoderate enjoyment and overt sexuality marked the intimate enemy" (216). Indeed, the Shiv Sena's ideology and politics of purity have not been limited to questions of globalization. They have included earlier campaigns of ethnic exclusion that targeted South Indians and mobilized an aggressive Marathi identity and more recent Hindu nationalist activities that have concentrated on the threat of Muslims (Gupta 1982; Katzenstein 1979; Katzenstein, Mehta, and Thakkar 1997; Lele 1995). While the specificities of this political organization have been a crucial element in the state government's spatialized purification of "Indian culture," the general significance of such strategies cannot be fully grasped solely in terms of the uniqueness of the Shiv Sena's extremist cultural and political ideologies. What is at stake is a broader gendered national definition of middle class civic culture—one that is shaped by both the dynamics of religious nationalism and the cultural politics that have characterized more traditional secular political organizations and sites within middle class civil society.

Let us examine the ways in which the rise of Hindu nationalism and the BJP's growing political significance began to shape middle class civic culture through a set of gendered practices and discourses. Consider the events following the 1996 national elections in India when the BJP, one of the central opposition parties and proponents of a form of economic nationalism (*swadeshi*), was asked to form a government.[39] During this initial tenure in government, the party whose anticonsumerism election slogan on the new economic policies had been "computer chips not potato chips," appointed a finance minister well known for his pro-liberalization policies in a critical move signaling that the BJP would not reverse the existing direction of economic reforms initiated by the previous Congress-led party government.[40]

However, during the BJP's rule, the central force of the government's anti-reform rhetoric was concentrated on the cultural sphere, particularly in relation to television and advertising. The focus on "obscenity" and calls for increased censorship of film and media images has periodically comprised a significant and consistent component of the BJP's political rhetoric and activities.[41] During the BJP's early stint in power in 1996, for instance, the Information and Broadcasting Minister, Sushma Swaraj, launched a series of attacks on supposed sexualized representations within the media, ranging from advertisements for contraception—which she directed were not to be aired during times when young children might view television, to a television advertisement that depicted a woman with a billowing skirt (modeled on the well-known Marilyn Monroe scene), to asking Doordarshan (state television) announcers to refrain from wearing revealing clothes during newscasts.

Such events are not merely particular characteristics of religious nationalist parties but represent instances of a wider set of processes associated with the politics of globalization in India. Various forms of cultural spectacles have provided a rich terrain for the expression of resistance to globalization. Consider, for instance, the ways in which widespread protests over the "Miss World" contest held in Bangalore were framed through a set of gendered nationalist discourses.[42] Orga-

nizations from a wide ideological spectrum—from women's wings of
the Communist Party of India to the BJP—protested the pageant on
the grounds that it represented a threat to the Indian nation; while
the BJP depicted this threat as an assault on Indian national culture
and womanhood, organizations from the ideological left argued that
the contest encouraged the entry of foreign capital into the country.[43]
Such responses on the ideological left inadvertently converge with the
Shiv Sena's culturally based drive for the preservation of moral standards in Mumbai. The threat to the purity of women's sexuality becomes a central trope that places these ideologically disparate instances
of the cultural management of the liberalizing middle classes within
a shared discursive space.

Cultural management is not limited to the official realm of the state
but also extends into more conventional realms of civic life. Consider
public discourses on barmaids in the print media. Newspapers simultaneously began to transform women's labor rights into a problem of
protection by reporting on rapes of women working in bars. However, such reports focused on women's vulnerability to assaults during late-night hours rather than on violence against women as a
social problem. The incidents of rape were recast as evidence of the
dangers of women traveling from work at night rather than in terms
of patriarchal domestic ideologies that attempt to confine women to
the home. Such media representations converge with national patterns of judicial discourses on rape, which as Veena Das (1996) argues,
"mediate the everyday categories of sexuality and sexual violence,
sorting and classifying the normal and the pathological in terms of
marriage and alliance (2412).

Hence, both state and civil discourses contributed to the transformation of working women into deviant figures implicitly displacing
the responsibility of sexual violence to the sociospatial transgressions
of the women in question. This transgressive quality to women's
nighttime employment was underlined by a second trope deployed
by government officials and news commentators who speculated on
the link between women employed in bars and restaurants and the
supposed spread of prostitution.[44] The state government's attempt to
rescue Indian cultural life rested on both the protection and purification of women's sexuality and the corresponding attempt to manage

the boundaries of the middle class public sphere—a process that parallels the convergence between state and middle class civic life that we have seen unfold in the case of class-based spatial conflicts.

Such gendered ideologies that permeate the state, media, and political organizations are, in effect, attempting to police the boundaries of the middle class public sphere in the context of changing gendered roles produced by liberalization. The expansion of service-sector and private-sector employment has produced opportunities for middle class women in metropolitan centers. In the case of married women, a combination of rising costs of living, high real estate costs, and increasing pressures of lifestyle and consumption standards have also produced significant economic pressures on middle class families and have led to a shift toward dual-income families.[45]

Such shifts, along with changing norms for the new Indian middle class, appear to have produced important changes in lifestyle norms for urban women. Media representations of "Mumbai women" have focused on career women as socially and sexually liberated with lifestyles that revolve around bars, parties, and discos.[46] The following media report, for example, attempts to link changing lifestyle roles (including late marriages and increased alcohol consumption) to breast cancer among urban women:

> They were your average millenium yuppies. He was a securities banker, she worked as an accounts executive in a Mumbai advertising agency. Their day was mechanically programmed: wake up at 7 AM in a matchbox suburban apartment, crawl into town through peak hour traffic, deal with clients over endless cups of coffee and grab a Coke and sandwich for lunch. Then, when the day is done, meet with friends at a pub to unwind over greasy tandoori chicken and a couple of vodkas, and crawl back again to their cubbyhole. Life was tough but the money was good, marriage was OK and babies were definitely not on the personal projects page of this year's planner.
>
> Then one day in April this year, 32-year-old Anita Desai found a small hard nodule on her left breast, just under the armpit. A biopsy showed it was malignant. . . . Now Desai can ask only one question, "Why me?" At the Tata Memorial Hospi-

tal and Research Institute (TMHRI) in Mumbai, the largest cancer research centre in the country, Dr. Indraneel Mittra tersely provides the answer: female emancipation. It is not a sexist pronouncement or even a conservative verdict. Just a neutral assessment of neutral statistics. (Baria 2000)

Such constructions suggest that liberalization has produced significant changes in gendered norms for the new Indian middle class—particularly in relation to a break from the joint family structure, deviations from social expectations of early marriage and motherhood, and the breakdown of the predominantly masculine preserve of public spaces (such as bars). While such changes are indeed evident in metropolitan cities such as Mumbai, the actual experiences of working women are in fact structured around familiar patterns of dual shifts of labor within the workplace and household. As one woman employed as a secretary in a well-known firm described her daily routine, "We have very long days. It takes two hours to come to work. We have to leave at 8:00 in morning and we reach [home] at 8 o'clock at night. By the time we see to the cooking and the children's education and things like that, there's no time left. There's hardly any time for family life."[47]

In practice, in contrast to public national anxieties about shifting gendered social codes in the context of globalization, women's lives continue to be constrained by the reproduction of gender inequalities. Consider the gendered politics of space and residence of working women who form of a significant section of service sector workers in India's new economy. Single women employed in Mumbai who have migrated there from outside the city or from distant suburbs must deal with significant social and spatial constraints that shape their residence options. They must either rent a room from a family as a "paying guest" or they must apply for residence at one of Mumbai's working women's hostels. While these options place significant social restrictions on women, economic and social constraints prevent most single women from being able to rent an entire flat (apartment) on their own. One woman residing in a hostel described the following experience of the coercive gendered restrictions that lurk beneath the discursive stereotypes of the partying "Mumbai woman":

Actually we have a flat in Bombay and my sister and I were stay-
ing there. But we had a lot of problems. I had to work late. By
the time we finished practicals I used to come back at 10 or
10:30 PM. Then we used to work and sleep by 12 or 12:30 PM.
One night a gang of men came to the door and started banging
on the door and calling out to us. The neighbors had to come
out and drive them away. The next night again they came. So
my dad said you better just stay in a hostel.[48]

The hostels have a set of strict set of social codes. Applicants must undergo a careful application procedure that in many cases includes an
interview (often accompanied by parents or relatives acting as her
guardians). In some instances, parents themselves are interested in
ensuring that hostels adapt strict screening procedures in order to
maintain the "good character" of the hostel residents. Some hostels
preserve class boundaries through the designation of minimum
salary requirements for residency. In most hostels, residents are only
allowed to reside for a three-year period and must shift to a new residence at the end of the three years. Indeed, working women often develop extensive social networks and friendships as they move from
one hostel to another.

Working women residing in hostels must usually adhere to strict
restrictions such as curfews and limitations on visitors. At one hostel
for working women, for example, residents must return by 10:30 PM,
at which time the front gates and doors are locked. However, in practice, most women residing in that hostel are not bound purely by
such formal regulations but by a set of informal gendered social codes.
The women in charge of running the hostel expected the residents to
be back for dinner on a regular basis (dinner would be served until
8:00 PM). Residents were categorized according to a "good girl/bad
girl" dichotomy based on whether they returned to the hostel in time
for dinner. It was in fact not uncommon for individual women to be
publicly scolded in front of other residents for too many late nights or
for skipping dinner too many times. Even in the case of another hostel
known to be more liberal in its attitude, a strong system of surveillance was present. Residents were given a limited number of late

passes they could use and male *durwans* employed by the hostel were responsible for checking late passes of the hostel residents.

These social restrictions must be contextualized within a larger social milieu in which single working women must contend with strong gendered ideologies that construct them as a potential threat to the social order. Women residing in some hostels indicate that in when they apply for jobs, it is advisable to lie to employers rather than reveal that they reside in hostels. In such cases, women provide their employers with an address of a relative residing in Mumbai instead their hostel address.

Women who *have* told employers that they reside in hostels indicate that they usually receive a strong negative reaction from employers or coworkers as the notion of an unmarried woman living on her own continues to provoke a stereotype of a socially or sexually immoral woman.[49] It is not only individual employers that have strong negative reactions; as many hostel residents argue, these responses stem from broader public perceptions of hostel residents as "loose" (sexually promiscuous) women. Women I interviewed describe the discomfort of standing on the street at night waiting for a bus and being perceived as a prostitute. As one woman put it, "Girls don't like to tell employers or colleagues that they live in a hostel. No matter how much we progress if you are a woman living alone you are always hassled. People always think the worst."[50]

Jaya, who resides in a working women's hostel, describes the experience of being interviewed in a large private-sector firm.[51] During the interview she was asked about her residence in a hostel and the lack of a permanent residence in Mumbai. According to Jaya, the interviewers expressed strong reservations about this and indicated to her that they required what they classified as a "permanent residence" in order to vouch for her character. In hindsight, she expresses a great deal of regret that she did not provide them with her sister's address in Andheri, a suburb of Mumbai. Jaya is currently employed as a secretary in a small Indian firm in Mumbai and is faced with a problem of residence once again as her hostel has just raised its minimum monthly salary requirement from Rs 3,000 to Rs 4,000, an economic requirement she is unable to meet. While her family has been attempting to arrange her marriage, so far the prospective grooms had either not been interested or had made large dowry demands in the *lakhs* of rupees, which her family—from a small town in a neighboring state—cannot afford.

The anxiety of middle class working women like Jaya often has less to do with romanticized notions of marriage than with questions of economic security embodied in the need for access to housing. As Jaya put it, "I want a house. More than being married first I want a house. In Bombay that's the main thing to have. I told you even if I save my whole lifetime, I won't be able to afford a house." Women residing in such hostels would often speak of the problems associated with isolated individual cases of older professional women who were still residing in hostels. In one instance, two older women in their fifties with steady jobs were facing pressure to move out of their hostel. The women were paying double the regular fees in order to remain as hostel "guests" beyond the official three-year term. However, the nuns running the hostel, fearing the responsibility of having to care for them in their old age, were trying to get them to leave. Such instances present a stark counterpoint to the gendered construction of the threat of social disorder associated with economic and cultural globalization.

I have analyzed the gendered politics of the new middle class identity that shape both religious nationalist and secular discourses and practices. The politics of this social group unfold through a dynamic process as social identities of gender, class, and religion converge and produce instances of contestation and ambivalence. These points of contestation have already been evident, such as when hawkers' unions have sought to reclaim public space and women's organizations have contested both secular and religious nationalist strictures on gender roles.

The layering of social identities unfolds in complex ways that cannot be cast in a homogeneous mold. For instance, middle class women are not merely symbolic boundary markers (McClintock 1995) of social processes, they also actively participate in the dominant construction of middle class identity and civic life. The formation of middle class women's identities is constituted at the intersection of caste and class inequalities.[52] Middle class women who have moved into new-economy jobs continue to rely on the labor of domestic workers who are largely comprised of lower caste, low income women.

However, everyday discourses of middle class women often revolve around a perceived threat of the leveling of caste/class. During my field research, both single women residing in hostels as well as women in households whom I interacted with would comment on what they viewed as changing practices of female domestic workers. As I noted in chapter 2, in some instances, middle class women would comment—with a sense of discomfort—about domestic workers engaging in new cultural/lifestyle practices such as using "modern" beauty salons. In the working women's hostels in which I resided, conflicts would often break out between middle class residents and domestic workers responsible for cleaning their rooms. Middle class women would indicate that they could not instruct the domestic workers on how to clean their rooms because they were unionized— a complaint that echoes broader middle class rhetoric on unmanageable, unionized workers.

Women's concerns for public safety are often constructed through caste- and class-based discourses that converge with the politics of spatial purification embodied in state strategies and civic organizations. For example, during the course of my fieldwork, a series of attacks on women riding local commuter trains was gaining a great deal of public and media attention. In a highly publicized case, a young college student was pushed out of a train by an individual trying to snatch her purse. The woman lost her legs and the incident became emblematic of wider middle class women's concerns with public safety. However, although the woman was in fact the daughter of a mill worker, the case was constructed through middle class discourses on crime and the need to "clean up" the city. While the caste-based dimensions of such narratives often remain hidden, the predominantly lower-caste composition of groups such as domestic workers, street vendors, and the urban poor and the discourses of purification that permeate middle class conceptions of civic life serve as important reminders of the ways in which both gender and class in India have historically been coded by caste-based discourses and inequalities.

My analysis of the spatialized politics of liberalization has illustrated the ways in which the construction of the identity of the new middle class is produced through a set of gendered politics in both secular social spaces and religious nationalist sites. This gendered convergence points to the ways in which new middle class civic identity is shaped by practices that cut across secular and religious frames of political life. Such convergences between dynamics of religious nationalism and the secular boundaries of middle class civic life unfold in striking ways through the spatialized politics of new middle class identity. An analysis of such spatial practices thus provides a significant example that helps provide an understanding of the ways in which the formation of the new middle class identity has been shaped by two of the central national trends that have shaped contemporary India since the 1990s: the rise of Hindu nationalism and the politics of economic liberalization.

Liberalization, State Practices, and Hindu Nationalist Spatial Politics

Contemporary spatial politics consist of a complex set of intersections between the secular boundaries of new middle class civic life and an intensifying relationship between Hindu nationalism and middle class identity.[53] For example, the politics of spatial purification that have targeted the urban poor with the secular objective of producing a sanitized middle class civic culture have also been adopted by Hindu nationalist organizations and local governments. Both the BJP and Shiv Sena have used civic strategies designed to clean up cities to target Muslim immigrants from Bangladesh. In such cases, constructions of class impurity have converged with xenophobic constructions of "illegal" Muslim immigrants in the discourses of Hindu nationalist organizations. Consider for example "Operation Pushback," a government campaign in Delhi in the 1990s designed to forcibly return alleged illegal immigrants to Bangladesh. As Sujata Ramachandran (2002) has argued, such immigrants living primarily as slum dwellers in Delhi were characterized as threatening infiltrators invading the Indian nation-state. In Mumbai, the Shiv Sena has attempted, with varying degrees of success, to use the political rhetoric on Bangladeshi immigrants to further its long-term antimigrant/anti-Muslim agenda.[54] This campaign, based on the politicization of religion and ethnicity, has merged with local state strategies that have targeted working class squatters. The local state agency—the BMC—has now begun to deploy the rhetoric of the threat of Bangladeshi immigrants in conjunction with its project of evicting squatters from public lands (Ragunath 2003). In such cases, since the urban poor usually do not have formal documents for identification, many of the targeted individuals in Delhi and Mumbai have been Indian (rather than Bangladeshi) Muslims.

These local strategies have also become nationalized political issues. Consider the example of recent political discourses on the threat of illegal immigrants crossing the border from Bangladesh. At the beginning of 2003, India's Union Home Minister, L. K. Advani, a leading figure in the Hindu nationalist party (the BJP), signaled that illegal immigration would be a central political issue for the government and party. As one news report put it, the minister, "asked states to identify the estimated 15 million Bangladeshi illegal immigrants and 'throw them out'" (Chengappa 2003, 41). In this process, constructions of class impurity converge with xenophobic constructions of "illegal" Muslim immigrants.

More recently, state strategies of purification have been intensified and transformed in light of the U.S.-declared global war on terrorism. The BJP-led government in effect deployed the United States' agenda in conjunction with its own Hindu nationalist project of constructing Indian Muslims as an alien threat to the Hindu-Indian nation. Consider, for instance, the ways in which the state and some media representations have constructed the question of Bangladeshi immigrant workers through the rhetoric of terrorism. These constructions depict such workers as a threat to national security and define immigration flows produced by poverty in terms of the threat of cross-border terrorism from Islamic nations such as Bangladesh and Pakistan. This construction is succinctly captured in the analysis of one mainstream media report:

> The fear that, along with innocuous "economic refugees," the Pakistan Inter-Services Intelligence and Al-Qaida-linked terrorists

may also be crossing over is all too real. Internal security concerns are now inextricably linked with the "Bangladeshi problem." Terrorism and underworld tracker, Delhi's JCP Neeraj
Kumar says, "Pakistan is increasingly using Bangladesh as a base
for its nefarious activities in India."

The police are investigating Bangladeshi crime syndicates in
the national capital. Fourteen Bangladeshi citizens who were ar-
rested in Delhi last year have confessed to a series of robberies.
(Chakravarty 2003, 20)

This discursive construction presents a series of associations between
Bangladeshi immigrants, the Pakistani government, al-Qaeda terrorism, and urban crime. Immigrant workers in effect become the embodiment of both the threat of global terrorism and of internal social
disorder associated with crime. The news report is captioned "The
Immigrants" with a detailed title "Banglo-Indians: The Bangladeshi
immigrants are everywhere. They even have crime syndicates in Delhi."
This association between Muslim (Pakistan-sponsored) immigrants,
terrorism, and crime is particularly significant as it attempts to link the
external security of the nation-state with middle class discourses on
crime and social disorder.

The politicization of the "Bangladeshi immigrant" worker enables
a convergence between three central political processes: (1) the construction of a middle class definition of civic life that has been intensified in the context of liberalization, (2) the Hindu nationalist
agenda of producing a purified Hindu citizenship, and (3) the global
"war on terrorism." Political parties such as the BJP and Shiv Sena
have attempted to use the "threat" of Bangladeshi immigrant workers
to engage in political agendas that reinforce exclusions of religion
and ethnicity. In Delhi, for instance, local officials have attempted to
remove Muslim voters from electoral lists by alleging that they are illegal Bangladeshi workers rather than Indian Muslims from the state
of West Bengal. Since individuals from poor and working class communities often do not have official documentation proving citizenship, this has enabled local Hindu nationalist officials to engage in
strategies of disenfranchisement. In this context, racialized, xenopho-

bic discourses of threatening "Muslim invaders" produce a form of purified Hindu civic space that converges with the dynamics of spatial purification.

These dynamics demonstrate the complexity of the formation of the identity of the new middle class as it mediates its points of affiliation with Hindu nationalism, on the one hand, and more secular images of a cosmopolitan, high-tech, consuming class. This has led some scholars to emphasize a form of identification between the politics of liberalization and the politics of Hindu nationalism (Rajagopal 2001a). While such points of convergence constitute an important part of the formation of the identity of the new middle class, they are part of a more complex and varied political field that draws on both secular and religious nationalist models of the nation-state. The politics of India's new middle class cannot, as we have seen, simply be reduced to the politics of Hindutva, nor is it necessarily the case that Hindu nationalism will inevitably serve as a vehicle for the expression of new middle class interests. The politics of liberalization shape the boundaries of middle class civic life in autonomous and exclusionary ways that are defined as much by secular forms of class politics.

While new middle class politics intersected with the rise of Hindu nationalism in large sections of the middle class in the 1990s, the interests and political orientation of this social group rest on a more complex set of processes. New middle class politics are shaped both by the tensions and interactions between the discursive and socioeconomic boundaries that are specifically associated with liberalization on the one hand and the reworking of enduring social inequalities and identities on the other. It is this set of processes that has marked the rise of the new Indian middle class and that plays a central role in shaping the politics of liberalization in contemporary India.

Conclusion

The formation of the identity of the new Indian middle class is part of a broad process of cultural and economic change that was set in motion through the economic policies of liberalization in the 1990s.

Spatial practices produce a vision of a liberalizing India that centers on the visibility of the new Indian middle class. The management of liberalization, in effect, occurs through the production of the boundaries of this new middle class identity, boundaries that are constructed through a politics of distinction of gender, caste, and religion.

The exercise of state power is an important political force in this process. Local state practices play a central role in attempting to manage the transitions of liberalization through the production of a purified middle class civic space that can represent the globalizing Indian nation. The state is often fragmented and conflicted as it oscillates between responding to the organized demands of middle class communities and workers' organizations such as hawkers' unions. At another level, the state actively participates in attempting to produce a middle class–based vision of a beautified, globalizing city in which signs of poverty can be forgotten in both spatial and political terms.

There are two central conclusions regarding the politics of liberalization. One is that state and middle class practices begin to create the underpinnings of exclusionary models of community and civic life— models that cut cross the arenas of secular civil society and politicized religious nationalism. Second, such processes are disrupted by social groups that do not accept dominant constructions of the new middle class vision of the Indian nation. This contestation continually disrupts and highlights the more coercive aspects of exclusion and purification of this process. Such political dynamics point to the ways in which processes of economic liberalization, and the rise of the new Indian middle class in particular, are reshaping meanings of citizenship and democracy in contemporary India. It is this question regarding the relationship between economic transitions and political democratization that I turn to in the next chapter.

5

Liberalization, Democracy, and Middle Class Politics

—✳—

Every party is looking for ways to seduce India's most capricious set of people: the urban middle class. No one party can claim to have this section in its pocket. That's because the middle class has no defining characteristic: there is no identifiable vote-bank on the basis of caste, religion, or reservations. But the middle class counts. It counts because it dominates the media; because its opinions are the ones that politicians have to hear; and because every election in Indian history has been determined by issues that were first raised by the middle class.

—*Sahgal (1998)*

The growing visibility and assertiveness of the new middle class in India's emerging political culture of liberalization has intensified public interest in the political behavior and leanings of the middle class. The quotation that opens this chapter captures some of the contradictions and confusions in identifying discernible patterns in the formal electoral and political behavior of the middle class. Levels of electoral participation for the middle classes have been relatively low when compared to subaltern social groups. For example, survey research has demonstrated that voter turnout is below average for upper castes, urban dwellers, and graduates and postgraduates—all segments that are traditionally identified with middle class status (Jaffrelot 2000, 378).

However, recent political trends have demonstrated that the political responses of the middle class have played an important role in shaping the direction of contemporary Indian politics. For instance, studies have shown that a form of political alienation of the urban middle classes played an important role in the rise of Hindu nationalism as the middle class switched allegiance from the Congress to the BJP (Hansen 1999; Jaffrelot 2000; Yadav 1999).

In the late twentieth century in India, middle class protests increased. These protests were defined by the politicization of identities of caste and religion and were aimed at curtailing a perceived expansion in the political participation of backward caste and Muslim communities. Meanwhile, as we have seen, public discourses have sought to construct the middle class as a political proponent of liberalization. Such trends have led to the emergence of two complementary narratives that cast middle class politics as a story of alienation and resurgence. In this depiction, on the one hand, the middle class, alienated by the political assertion of lower-caste and class groups retreated both from the Congress party and from the conventional terrain of formal electoral politics. On the other hand, this alienation has led to a resurgence of middle class politics or what Corbridge and Harriss (2000) have termed "elite revolts" as the middle classes sought to reassert themselves through their support for both Hindu nationalism and economic liberalization in the 1990s.[1]

The rise of an assertive new middle class identity has indeed been shaped by this surge in middle class protest politics that unfolded in late twentieth century India. Emerging in the context of such trends, the expansion of a new middle class political identity in the public sphere and the growth of middle class associational activity has also translated into a process aimed at narrowing the boundaries of participation. As we saw in chapter 4, new middle class discourses, identities, and practices have sought to reclaim the "public" in ways that have intensified social inequalities and exclusions.

The political significance of such processes does not lie in a deterministic trajectory in which middle class interests are translated into electoral results. As I have noted, the middle class has expressed a more contradictory relationship with the nature of formal political democracies. Although formal democratic processes have enabled marginalized groups to gain access to political power, the political power of the middle class has rested on its growing condemnation of such democratic processes and its successful attempts at claiming access to citizenship and the state through nonelectoral means. In other words, as the expansion of democracy has enabled subordinated groups to gain access to political power, groups such as the new middle class have been able to find ways to circumvent such formal processes and reconstitute the political mechanisms that provide access to the state. The new middle class can indirectly shape policy agendas in ways that do not rest on the results of electoral politics—a process that may partly explain relatively low elite voter participation rates.

In any endeavor to understand middle class politics, the task at hand is not simply to assess whether the new middle class (or the middle class in general) is an essentially democratic or authoritarian social group. As I have argued earlier, such classifications usually rest on overdetermined constructions in both public and academic discourses of ideal-typical and deviant models of the middle class. Rather the question I explore in this chapter is: How has the rise of the new middle class begun to shape the content of categories such as democracy, citizenship, and participation through specific practices and strategies?

The objective of this chapter is to analyze the political significance that the creation of this new middle class holds for a more general understanding of middle class politics and of contemporary democratic politics. I begin with an overview of the narratives of alienation and resurgence that have shaped middle class politics since the late twentieth century. I then analyze the implications that new middle class practices have had for these patterns of political activity.

My analysis of the political implications of this emerging social group is based on three central arguments. First, I argue that the late twentieth century narratives of middle class alienation and resurgence both shape and are reworked through identities based on class and consumption. I demonstrate the ways in which existing forms of middle class protest politics have been recast in distinctive ways through an emerging new middle class model of consumer-citizenship.

Drawing on an analysis of the 2004 India Shining campaign, I examine both the significance and the limits of newly formed linkages between the state and new middle class in attempting to reframe the terms of contemporary democratic politics.

Second, I argue that an understanding of the political significance of this group requires a move beyond these narratives of alienation and protest and a deeper conceptual understanding of the relationship between the state and the middle class. Such an understanding, I argue, requires a move away from static generalizations that suggest either a form of middle class retreat from the state or an uncontested form of middle class capture of the state.

Finally, I conclude with a discussion of alternatives to these dominant models of middle class politics. Drawing on an analysis of a cross-class women's consumer protest, I point to moments of contestation of dominant new middle class models of citizenship. Such moments, while often transitory, nevertheless serve as a caution against rigid formulations that cast the middle class as a homogeneous elite. Such formulations often miss the heterogeneous nature of middle class interests and conflate the hegemonic construction of a new middle class identity with the highly differentiated groups that constitute the middle class. As I have demonstrated throughout this book, the singularity of identity that is implied in a phrase such as "the rise of the new middle class" is politically significant precisely because of the variation it seeks to manage.

Narratives of Alienation and Resurgence: Late Twentieth Century Patterns of Middle Class Politics

The rise of the new Indian middle class has unfolded in the context of a broader political field that shaped middle class politics in the late twentieth century. During that period, dominant middle class constructions of their interests and political activity were cast in terms of languages of alienation and resurgence. According to these middle class political narratives, the growing political assertiveness of subaltern social groups led to an increasing sense of middle class alienation both from formal democratic politics and from the Congress party.

This sense of middle class frustration and alienation helped catalyze a resurgence of a public Indian middle class identity in the 1980s. The dynamic of alienation and resurgence of the urban middle class rests at the heart of many of the central trends of contemporary Indian politics in the last decades of the twentieth century. These trends were centered on the growth of a form of middle class protest politics that was based on and intensified distinctions of caste and religion. The most visible and well-analyzed of such trends was the growing middle class support for Hindu nationalism and the middle class backlash against the political assertion of lower caste groups centered around the Mandal Commission report and the question of expanding caste-based reservations.[2] Scholars and political analysts have exhaustively studied these defining events.[3] However, while such events will be familiar to specialists on India, an analysis of the distinctiveness of new middle class politics cannot adequately proceed without an understanding of the continuities and defining influences of these late twentieth century trends on middle class politics. I use my analysis of these narratives of alienation and resurgence to point to the ways in which such political trends also represented important internal debates and conflicts within the middle class and were not purely a middle class backlash against subaltern groups.

One of the central political trends in the 1980s and 1990s was the rise of a self-perception of the urban, upper-caste, Hindu middle class that Indian democracy had been corrupted by a political field that catered excessively to subordinate social groups such as Muslims and lower-caste groups such as *dalits* and other backward castes (OBCs). Middle class political responses unfolded in two central ways. First, this sense of political frustration took the form of a growing alienation from the Congress party, which was increasingly perceived by the urban middle class as a party that depended on the politics of votebanks and that pandered excessively to Muslims and to the lower classes and castes. Second, these urban middle classes were also threatened by an increasingly diversified political field with both

smaller regional parties and autonomous political and social movements providing mechanisms for *dalits* and OBCs to gain both political voice and electoral representation.[4]

The growth of middle class support for the Hindu nationalist
party, the BJP, in the 1980s and 1990s has been widely documented by
a large literature on Hindu nationalism.[5] The urban middle classes
increasingly began to turn to the BJP as a party that could represent a
strong middle class–oriented nationalist party—one that could provide an alternative to a Congress party that the middle classes viewed
as corrupt and captured by subordinated social groups. For instance,
in the 1980s the urban middle class grew alienated from Rajiv Gandhi's
regime as he became mired in corruption scandals and as he turned
away from earlier promises of economic reforms in favor of more
populist electoral strategies. Rajiv Gandhi failed to live up to his
promise as a new urban middle class–oriented prime minister and
failed to meet the rising expectations of an increasingly vocal middle
class that had begun to identify itself as a distinctive group with specific interests that needed political representation. This middle class
frustration was constructed through a political perception of a
democracy that was decaying because it had abandoned middle class
interests and been muddied by the demands of subordinated social
groups (Hansen 1999, 58).

The well-publicized Shah Bano case gained much scholarly and
public attention as a defining event that helped the BJP gain public
support and helped delegitimize Congress rule.[6] The Congress' role
in using parliamentary means to overturn a Supreme Court ruling in
this case enabled the BJP to effectively portray the Congress as a party
that pandered to conservative Muslim leaders. Analysts have widely
discussed the complex political implications such events had for
debates on secularism as the BJP was effectively able to portray the
Congress as a "pseudosecular" party (in the language of BJP leader
L. K. Advani) because of its protection of Muslim personal law and its
rejection of a uniform civil code.[7]

At another level, the Shah Bano case in many ways represented a
deeper middle class debate on the terms of democratic politics. The
controversy about the meaning of secularism, in effect, became the
symbolic terrain for an underlying debate on the terms of democ-

racy. In other words, BJP rhetoric that the Congress had contaminated secularism by pandering to Muslims dovetailed with broader middle class perceptions of a democratic political field that had been captured by special interests and subordinated social groups. The public outcry over the Shah Bano case brought to the surface the underlying political frustrations of the upper-caste Hindu middle class. The rhetoric of rescuing secularism from pseudosecularism effectively tapped into a broader middle class desire to rescue Indian democracy from the corruption, patronage, and "special interests" of rising politically assertive subaltern groups that diverged from middle class models of citizenship and civic and political life. The result was a consolidation of the interests of upper-caste Hindu middle class conceptions of democracy and citizenship with the language of Hindu nationalism.

Such processes dovetailed with and were intensified by the other major national political controversy of this period—the Mandal Commission recommendations for caste-based reservations in government jobs and educational institutions (Jaffrelot 2000). The recommendations, and National Front Prime Minister V. P. Singh's decision to implement them, produced a range of upper-caste middle class protests particularly in urban areas. While the most sensational of such protests involved the self-immolation of upper caste middle class students, at a deeper level, the public outcry once again dovetailed with upper-caste middle class perceptions of a democratic polity that was failing to protect its interests. As with the Shah Bano case, the BJP was able to effectively respond to such perceptions in its opposition to Mandal, culminating in its departure from the coalition government that brought down the National Front government (Corbridge and Harris 2000, 126).

These events in the 1980s and 1990s were transformed into a broader middle class discourse that both merged with and transcended the specific interests and strategies of the BJP. Consider the satirical representations of regional leaders such as Bihar's Laloo Prasad Yadav and U.P.'s Mulayam Singh Yadav. These political figures became public symbols of the new leaders who were corrupting urban middle class standards of democratic representation. Laloo Prasad Yadav's cultural and linguistic rural style, for instance, became an unending source of political humor for English-educated upper-caste urban middle class individuals, particularly with the expansion of television. For the middle class, such figures in effect became the antitheses for iconized figures such as Rajiv Gandhi (in his early years) and Chandrababu Naidu.

The politics of "Mandal and Mandir"[8] outlined above have become iconic events in contemporary narratives on the resurgence of an angry, alienated middle class that has sought to reclaim its national primacy. However, at another level, such definitive events in the late twentieth century were as much an internal struggle over identities and interests within the middle classes as they were a backlash against various subordinated social groups. As Zoya Hasan (1998) argued in her study of contemporary politics in Northern India, the growing significance of regional political parties and caste-based politics have also been linked to the upward mobility of newly emerging groups that have contested the social and political dominance of the traditional upper-caste English-educated middle classes (136). Political conflicts over government jobs and reservations have fundamentally been about access to middle class status and corresponding conflicts over the socioeconomic and cultural definition of the middle class identity in the face of new upwardly mobile social groups. An analysis of the politics of such internal differentiations—of caste, language and urban/rural cultural styles—provides an important cautionary note against tendencies to assume that the middle class is associated with a homogenous form of identity and politics.

Internal differentiation has also characterized middle class electoral behavior. As Suhas Palshikar (2001) notes, middle class voting patterns since the 1990s show a trend toward middle class support of the BJP. The BJP has consistently received a greater share of upper-caste middle class support, a pattern repeated in the 2004 elections (Yadav 2004, 5392). The success of the BJP in gaining middle class support has been achieved through the conscious construction of a particular form of an upper-caste Hindu middle class identity or what Yogendra Yadav (1999) termed the BJP's new social bloc.

However, significant sections of the middle class have also voted for the Congress. For example, according to survey data of the Center for the Study of Developing Societies, between 1996 and 1999, while middle class electoral support for the Congress did decline from 32.1 to 28.2 percent, it was nevertheless higher than support for the BJP (which changed from 23.9 percent in 1996 to 28.2 percent in 1999) (Palshikar 2001, 173). This general pattern has also characterized the results of the 2004 elections as the BJP lost support among the upper and lower middle classes (see Table 8). Thus, upper middle class support for the BJP in the 2004 elections declined by 7.5 percent (compared to 1999) and lower middle class support declined by 4.2 percent.

TABLE 8. Middle class voting patterns in 2004 elections.

	Votes for Congress (%)		Votes for BJP (%)	
	2004	Change from 1999	2004	Change from 1999
Upper middle class	26	0.3	31	−7.5
Lower middle class	28	−0.5	25	−4.2

Source: Yadav 2004 (5391), based on National Election Study data.

Such contestations over middle class identity and political representation provide the political context in which the creation of a new middle class identity is being shaped in liberalizing India. It is this trend of middle class frustration, protest, and self-assertion that has simultaneously intersected with the emergence of the pro-reforms identification of India's assertive new middle class. The simultaneity of these trends in the formation of middle class identity have led some scholars to argue that there is a convergence between the politics of middle class support for Hindu nationalism and for economic reforms (Corbridge and Harriss 2000; Rajagopal 2001a). Corbridge and Harriss argue that it is possible to "describe both economic liberalization, and Hindu nationalism, with their sometimes contradictory but often surprisingly complementary agendas for the reinvention of India, as 'elite revolts.' Both reflect and are vehicles for the interests and aspirations especially of the middle class and higher caste Indians" (xix).

However, the heterogeneity of the middle class and the contestations over middle class identity suggest that assumptions of a natural or essential correspondence between Hindu nationalism and economic liberalization are premature. For instance, conflicts over caste-based reservations represent conflicts within the middle class as new entrants into the middle class attempt to gain access to benefits that the upper-caste Hindu middle class has historically enjoyed. The electoral movement of the middle class toward the BJP was the outcome of the BJP's success in linking politicized Hinduism, support for reforms, and political rhetoric that has effectively tapped into the anxieties of the upper-caste Hindu middle class. However, successful strategies such as these cannot lead to a self-evident inference that a pro-liberalizing middle class will inevitably support the BJP or a politicized Hindu identity. While new middle class identity has intersected and been shaped by identities of caste and religion, the political behavior of this group is not reducible to the politics of religious nationalism. Rather, as I will argue, the politics of the liberalizing middle class is shaped both by continuities with late twentieth century narratives defined by caste and religion, and by new patterns of class politics.

Consumer-Citizenship and the Politics of the New Middle Class

The contours of new middle class politics have reshaped narratives of middle class alienation and protest through the production of a new model of citizenship, one that rests on a continual struggle to reclaim the terms of democratic politics from subordinated social groups. This hegemonic role of the liberalizing middle class coexists with and is challenged by numerous forms of political mobilization of marginalized caste and class groups in contemporary India. New middle class politics therefore rest on more active processes of exclusion that are in turn contested by these marginalized groups. This has unfolded through the emergence of a distinctive middle class model of consumer-citizenship. In effect, the identity of a consuming-liberalizing middle class is transformed into a generalized form of consumer citizenship, one that is marked by a shift from workers' rights to the rights of the consumer.

Consider the following instance of public political discourse on workers' activity that occurred during my fieldwork in Mumbai. On October 6, 1998, the Brihanmumbai Electric Supply and Transportation (BEST) workers, led by well-known labor leader Sharad Rao, went on a three-day strike to press for various demands, including a higher bonus and better medical facilities for workers. In the context of economic liberalization, which has been accompanied by a growing defensiveness of labor unions particularly in public-sector industries such as banking and insurance, the strike represented a visible counterexample of the political strength of labor. The strike, which mobilized workers of the BEST buses, a central mode of transportation for both middle class and working class individuals, crippled bus services across Mumbai. According to one estimate, out of a total of 3,201 buses, only three were on the road on the first day of the strike (*Bombay Times* 1998b). In a measure of the political power of labor leader Sharad Rao, one report noted that "Only one other person has been able to bring the city to a halt in the last two decades—Sena chief Bal Thackeray" (Barucha and Singh 1998), referring to the notorious leader of the Shiv Sena party. While the BEST Corporation attempted to use legal means to subvert the strike by getting the industrial court to stay it and declare it illegal, the success of the strike was evident when the Shiv Sena mayor agreed to an increased bonus after only two days.

In this series of events, public discourses in the mainstream media are significant for an understanding of middle class politics. Such public discourses were predominantly centered on the consumer-oriented implications of the strike. With headlines such as "Mumbai-ites are Held to Ransom," and "Strikes—We've Had Enough!" the English-language print media catering to the new middle class presented a vivid construction of the strike as an anti-middle class, anti-consumer event. Consider the following narrative:

The "strike" appears to be a recurring phenomenon in Mumbai. As strikers justify their grievances and authorities refuse to bow down to pressure, the common man bears the brunt of the impasse.

He finds himself torn between two warring sides, one that displays lack of public conscience and the other, which gives incompetence and indecisive administration a new name. The list of public woes is predictable: if the motormen strike the common man will stand in serpentine queues to reach office, if BEST goes off the road, he will travel in crowded trains or shell out extra cab and auto fare. If auto rickshaws agitate he prefers to walk, if banks are closed, he'll borrow. . . . His amazing capacity to be patient is commendable even in the face of unscrupulous people who want to make a fast buck out of this desperation.

The public apathy has made the trade union, which has no conscience, even stronger. "The threat has grown," says leading consumer activist, M. R. Pai. (Deshmukh 1998c)

The narrative above presents an example of the transformation of the middle classes into the figure of the Indian consumer-citizen, the new "common man." This figure represents an innocent victim of an ineffective government on the one hand and greedy, lawless unions on the other. Both unions and the government in this representation embody the corruption and incompetence of the political system.

The representation points to older patterns of middle class alienation and what Thomas Hansen (1999) has described as middle class perceptions of a "plebianization of the political field" (8) in which, as he notes, "From the 1960s onward, the public construction of politics has increasingly been transformed toward that of an 'immoral vocation,' a site of unprincipled pragmatism, corruption, nepotism and greed—in brief, as the profane antithesis to the sublime qualities of the cultural realm"(56). These late twentieth-century patterns of middle class frustration and alienation have been reconstituted by the production of this consumer-citizen as an iconic figure of liberalizing India. Discourses of social disorder and political corruption echoed through all of my interviews and informal interactions during my fieldwork and were targeted at both the poor and lower-caste communities as well as perceived cultural and political elites.

Such constructions were pervasive in the contexts of the working women's hostels. Many of the individual women would complain about the difficulty of dealing with domestic workers who cleaned the hostel and worked in the cafeteria, attributing this difficulty to the unionization of the workers. As one woman complained, "Some girls chat with them so they think everybody should. But they need to know their place." This question of "knowing their place" and the notion that the working poor were transcending the socioeconomic boundaries that distinguished them from the middle class point to the underlying class-based anxieties of the middle class in the context of liberalizing India.

In addition to this fear of socioeconomic leveling, the construction of the new consumer citizen also rests on a perceived corruption of Indian elites. Discourses on the corruption of political elites and the criminalization of politics in particular form a significant thread in the construction of such class-based anxieties. These attitudes are not isolated examples but are also manifested in middle class community-based activism. On the one hand, middle class individuals would argue that the decline of public and civic standards was linked to the social disorder produced by the poor and working classes. As one middle class public-sector employee put it, "These people [pavement dwellers] will never change. Even if you give them a free house they will sell it and go back to the footpath."[9]

Such constructions of the poor center around two main elements. The first dimension rests on a notion that the poor choose their poverty and are essentially unwilling to work in order to gain social mobility. A second dimension arises from middle class frustration based on perceptions of excessive state support for the poor and working classes. The mention of free housing in the quote above refers to attempted local government schemes to build low-income housing for pavement dwellers being displaced by the processes of spatial restructuring. Middle class individuals I interviewed, ranging from white-collar professionals to small business owners, would consistently insist that taxi drivers and domestic workers earned more than they did and simply chose to live in slums. As P. K. Das (2003) notes:

Outfits of "citizen" groups (representing small and exclusive groups of middle and upper classes) are now intervening in the housing sector. Their strategy is to oppose those policies of the government relating to the campaign to the right to housing, upgradation of slums and protection against eviction. These

groups and the leadership influence the media too; they campaign in the press against the interests of the slumdwellers. In
the recent past, many such groups have organized campaigns in
the press to oppose government policy to recognize the residential rights of slum-dwellers and the right to rehabilitation of
those who are evicted by the development programmes of the
state. (208)

The examples of political activity listed in the excerpt above point to
the ways in which segments of the urban middle class have opposed
what they perceive as a state that caters excessively to the poor and
working classes—a process that echoes the normative political culture of liberalization that advocates the downsizing of the role of the
state through privatization and cutbacks in subsidies.

Middle class frustration and anger is not simply a reflection of cultural anxiety but is also linked to middle class perceptions that their
interests are not being served by politicians and by the state. Consider
the following response of a journalist from a consumer-oriented
magazine as I discussed my interest in interviewing members of his
staff for a book on the Indian middle class: "Anger. The major feeling
is anger. You can call one chapter "anger." The middle classes are two
percent of the population and they are not being represented. There
is no representation. The interests of the middle classes are not being
represented by politicians." As another staff member added in clarifi-
cation, the "politicians may be from middle class backgrounds but
middle class interests don't shape their policies and agendas."

These anecdotes are not isolated examples. They underlie the attitude of emerging middle class organizations. Consider for instance
the comments of the general secretary of one middle class citizen's
group, the Chembur Citizen's Forum, "In fact, it is a matter of shame
that the administration is more concerned about illegal hawkers than
about tax-paying citizens. People, specially those belonging to the
middle-class have put up with this kind of high-handedness far too
long. But not anymore" (Balakrishnan 2001).

Such examples also reflect broader national trends that shape
middle class attitudes toward democratic politics. As Christophe Jaffrelot (2000) notes, survey research has demonstrated that the middle

class has expressed a growing dissatisfaction with parliamentary democracy, with a majority of those surveyed agreeing with the proposition, "if the country is to progress, it needs a dictator" (369). It is this middle class anger and the corresponding question of the representation of middle class interests that lies at the foundation of the emerging consumer-citizen in liberalizing India.

New middle class identities and practices have begun to reconstitute the meaning and boundaries of citizenship by reproducing and intensifying exclusions based on hierarchies such as caste, religion, and gender. An understanding of the political implications of the everyday new middle class practices, attitudes, and discourses requires a conceptualization of democratic citizenship in terms of substantive political practices rather than in terms of purely formal or legal parameters of parliamentary democracy. As Evelyn Glenn (2002) argues, it is such "localized, often face-to-face practices that determine whether people have or don't have substantive as opposed to purely formal rights of citizens" (2). By cementing the boundaries of exclusionary forms of citizenship and creating new terms of public political discourse, the new middle class is in effect engaged in an attempt to reclaim Indian democracy from demands of groups such as unions, subordinated castes, and Muslims. This reclamation is based on long-standing middle class perceptions that the politics of "vote-banks"[10] leads state elites to excessively cater to these subaltern social groups. From this middle class political perspective, democracy must be dissociated both from the corrupting influences of mass-based participation and mobilization and from the constraints of democratic electoral considerations.

The middle class consumer-citizen is in effect the new "common man," victimized both by a corrupt and ineffective political system on the one hand and the supposedly privileged and protected poor and working classes on the other. The production of the consumer citizen as the common man in the national public discourses of the new middle class points to the ways in which the production of consumer-based identities in the context of liberalization have rested on a politics of distinction between the middle class on one hand and the poor and working classes on the other. This politics of distinction between the middle and working classes is of course a historical phenomenon that is not causally produced by liberalization. However, the creation of the new middle class identity has intensified these processes.

Consider the shift in middle class identity that has taken place in postcolonial India. In the early decades of the postindependence period, strong levels of unionization among middle class employees often produced a normative political culture focused on workers' rights. Critics of the Indian trade union movement have argued that the focus of a great deal of unionism on the more privileged white-collar and middle class public-sector unions weakened the legitimacy of Indian trade unions and diverted energy away from less privileged, particularly informal sector unions (Chatterji 1980; Rudolph and Rudolph 1987). Writing in the late 1980s, Lloyd and Susanne Rudolph (1987) described the "islands of privilege"(266) among organized sector workers and argued that the "disproportionate organization and mobilization of white-collar professional and skilled labor reveals that organized labor has elected to follow the path of least resistance" (266). Such criticisms have been important because they have pointed to the historical blindness of unions to the structural inequalities and hierarchies between workers (Fernandes 1997).

However, what critics of unionized middle class and white-collar workers have often left unanalyzed is the wider sociopolitical meaning of the production of the identity of the middle class as workers rather than consumers. The creation of this identity, I suggest, represents an important factor in the production of a national political culture, which maintained a public normative interest in questions of poverty and workers' rights.

The shift in middle class aspirations from public-sector to private-sector jobs I discussed in chapter 3 thus holds broader political significance. To point to this significance is not to engage in an antiquated defense of overstaffed, inefficient public-sector units, which are vivid figures in the current Indian public imagination. The political significance of the restructuring of public-sector middle class workforces is easily caricatured in terms of irresponsible unions struggling to uphold the privileges they have gained from outdated economic policies. What I am suggesting instead is that the significance of this transition must also be understood in terms of the resulting reconstitution of democratic civic life; that is, through the production of a normative civic culture based on notions of the rights of consumer citizens rather than the rights of workers. It is this shift from the identity of the middle class as workers to that of consumers that captures the politics of the new middle class in liberalizing India.

The emergence of a new middle class model of consumer-citizenship points us to an understanding of the ways in which economic liberalization has resulted in an expansion of political space for the urban middle class to redefine the terms of democratic politics. In other words, the political assertion of this middle class unfolds through everyday discursive, cultural, spatial, and organizational practices that seek to define the terms of citizenship and, implicitly, of Indian democracy within the sphere of civil society. This can begin to help us understand the seemingly paradoxical situation in India in which subordinated social groups have tended to take voting more seriously than elite groups.[11] The new Indian middle class is, in effect, able to redefine the boundaries of citizenship in the public sphere and gain access to the state through practices and discourses that do not need to rely directly on electoral politics. We have already seen such processes foreshadowed in chapter 4 through examples of ways in which the new middle class has created exclusionary models of civic life that have defined its new relationship with a liberalizing nation. These processes are fundamentally linked to questions of citizenship and democracy as they are explicit instances of middle class claims on the state. Middle class claims redefine the terms of political discourse in ways that strengthen specific kinds of social exclusion.

Reframing Democratic Politics: Consumer-Citizenship and the 2004 "India Shining" Campaign

The emergence of a dominant new middle class conception of consumer-citizenship in many ways appears to confirm the identification of middle class political activity with associational life and social practices within the sphere of civil society.[12] However, associational life and social practices within civil society enable the new middle class to attempt to change the symbolic registers of democratic politics through informal points of access to state power.

Consider the case of the much publicized "Indian Shining" media campaign launched in the prelude to the 2004 national elections—a campaign that encapsulated new middle class visions of a prosperous liberalizing India becoming, as Prime Minister Vajpayee put it, "an economic powerhouse . . . and a land of opportunity and achievement" (Perry 2004, 2). When the BJP-led coalition unexpectedly lost the 2004 election, with the Congress Party emerging as the winner and the India's Left Front parties performing strongly, national and international media representations and some analysts focused in particular on the impact of the BJP's miscalculated India Shining campaign. They focused on the ways in which the campaign's glorification of India's strong economic growth associated with liberalization was out of touch with the vast socioeconomic inequalities and intensified structures of poverty, particularly in rural areas. Satirical newspaper headlines such as "NDA Shrinking" and "Sonia Shining"[13] reflected the ways in which the India Shining campaign had come to symbolize a deep discrepancy between new middle class perceptions of a prosperous, booming economy and socioeconomic measures of unemployment and poverty in both rural and urban India.

While the factors leading to the electoral results are more complex, the case of the India Shining campaign demonstrates both the political significance of new middle class visions of the Indian nation and the ways in which such visions can shape contemporary political processes albeit in unpredictable ways. The campaign, as I will argue, demonstrates both the power and the limits of political constructions associated with the new middle class, particularly when such constructions coexist in tension with the complex layers of socioeconomic differentiation that shape the political economy of India.

The India Shining campaign, initiated by the government of India (originating from the finance ministry), was geared toward marketing India's successful economic performance, an endeavor linked to BJP's campaign for reelection. The government of India, led by the BJP coalition, hired the well-known multinational advertising firm, Grey Worldwide, to launch the campaign in order to "project what the Government of India had done in terms of economic reforms and thereby the opportunities that exist for the people at large."[14] The advertising campaign was one of the biggest in Indian television history. According to one report, the India Shining advertisement was the most frequently broadcast brand on television between December 2003 and January 2004.[15] The ad also appeared in the print media; in the first fifteen days of January the campaign ranked fourth amongst top brands in newspapers.[16]

The advertisements depicted idealized images of both rural and urban prosperity. In line with the representational practices I analyzed in chapter 2, the ads attempted to weave together nationalist narratives with both local and global cultural symbols. While rural representations depicted farmers, urban-oriented advertisements showed domestic scenes of urban middle class families as well as images of India's newfound success in the global economy. For instance, in one advertisement there was a compass with the caption, "opportunity has a new geography." Echoing the broader pattern of images of a middle class-oriented conception of a globalizing nation, such ads sought to link together images of nationhood, globalization, and prosperity.

The India Shining campaign in effect attempted to produce a nationalist vision that could encourage a political mobilization based on the emergence of the middle class model of consumer-citizenship that, as I have argued, has emerged in the context of liberalizing. The campaign literally sought to turn the BJP-led government's vision of liberalizing India into a brand that could be marketed to Indian citizens. Echoing middle class constructions of the new "common man," Nirvik Singh, CEO of Grey Worldwide, noted, "It seemed that all the [economic] indices had come together after really long, and it seemed like people were on a roll. And we felt that nothing captured the feeling better than a phrase called 'India Shining.' The feel good factor came from the politicians when they used the term to describe how the average man was feeling."[17]

The government's campaign was linked to the BJP's drive for reelection in 2004. While this linkage was denied both by the BJP and Grey Worldwide, the campaign dovetailed with the BJP's political rhetoric for reelection and was specifically adopted in a *yatra* (cross-country journey) that L. K. Advani embarked on, Bharat Uday Yatra

(India Shining on Wheels). The electoral strategy of the campaign in effect rested on a conception of the Indian voter as a consumer of a new "Government of India" brand.

However, in a striking parallel to the ways in which middle class versions of consumer-citizenship have been contested by various local workers' organizations, the electoral plan based on the consumption of a nationalist model of Shining India produced various forms of political contestation. Sonia Gandhi and the Congress were effectively able to deploy populist language condemning the campaign for ignoring groups such as farmers, the poor, and unemployed that had not benefited from strong economic growth rates. Sonia Gandhi was in effect able to evoke a politics of forgetting implicit in the India Shining campaign by arguing that the campaign ignored the majority of Indians that did not benefit from call centers, shopping malls, and technology parks (Perry 2004).

The power of this rhetoric was intensified by the financial controversy surrounding the campaign given its high costs (Rs 100 crores budgeted; $20 million) and the fact that a Rs 17 crores shortfall for the campaign that had to be garnered by reappropriating funds for publicity in various ministries and departments.[18]

The India Shining campaign brought the politics of visibility associated with the new middle class consumer-citizen within the realm of formal electoral politics. It represents an importance instance of the ways in which the everyday practices, representations, and discourses of the new middle class can shape the more traditional realms of democratic and electoral politics, although with unpredictable consequences.

What then are the implications of this case for our understanding of the relationship between economic reforms and democratic politics? At first glance, the case of the 2004 elections seems to confirm traditional assumptions that economic reforms are contested by political opposition within democratic contexts. However, a closer analysis of this case belies such an easy assumption. On one level, reasons for the electoral shifts in 2004 varied widely based on regional differences and cannot be reduced to the miscalculations of the India Shining campaign.

More significantly, at another level, my analysis suggests that the power of the new middle class and its vision of a shining, prosperous, liberalizing India reaches beyond the realm of electoral politics. While the 2004 elections demonstrated the contestation of this middle class dream, it has not displaced this vision. Consider the question of reforms. The shift to the Congress-led government in alliance with Left Front parties is unlikely to stop the government from pursuing reforms, a fact underlined by the appointment of the architect of the 1990s generation of reforms, Manmohan Singh, as prime minister. At a broader level, the politics of the India Shining campaign demonstrates that an understanding of the relationship between reforms and democracy must rest on the ways in which both formal and informal spheres of politics shape arenas such as economic policy.

The power of the new middle class vision of India implicit in this campaign rests on its ability to shape both India's national identity (as a liberalizing nation) and its policy agendas through various informal practices. While the crystallization of such practices in the India Shining campaign produced a political backlash, the electoral shifts have not displaced this vision or the economic policies associated with them. On the contrary, the failure of the India Shining campaign may underscore the ways in which the politics of the new middle class may be more effective in shaping policy agendas and gaining access to state power through the cultural, sociospatial, discursive, and organizational practices within civil society rather than through electoral politics.

Election analysts have noted the low turnouts of the middle class voters in democratic elections in India. As my analysis of the power of everyday informal practices suggests, segments of the middle class may have different avenues and mechanisms for exercising power that do not necessarily have to be contained within the conventional act of voting.

Exit, Voice, or Capture? Middle Class Strategies, Interests, and the State

The direction of new middle class politics, we have seen, is shaped by a set of processes in which this social group is able to gain access to the state through particular mechanisms, discourses, and strategies within the sphere of civil society. Such processes have been accompanied by electoral patterns of low middle class participation rates. This pattern suggests that large segments of the middle classes have engaged in an exit from participation the formal political system and has led to the emergence of theoretical conceptions that have identified civil society as the sole preserve of the middle classes.

Partha Chatterjee (2004) suggests that contemporary democratic politics in India rests on a distinction between "civil society" and "political society." He argues for a distinction between these two categories in which "One is the line connecting civil society to the nation-state founded on popular sovereignty and granting equal rights to citizens. The other is the line connecting populations to governmental agencies pursuing multiple policies of security and welfare" (37). This formulation rests on an assumption that the associational life of civil society is the preserve of the middle class, whereas political society shapes a relationship of political management (rather than citizenship rights) that exists between the state and subaltern groups.

Chatterjee rightly points to the power differentials between elite and subaltern groups, differentials that intrinsically shape conceptions of civil society and citizenship. However, the limitation to this formulation is that it assumes that the elites (what he terms "bourgeois society") form a homogeneous group whose interests are represented in self-evident ways in civil society. For example, he argues that "civil society as bourgeois society" can be understood "in the Indian context as an actually existing arena of institutions and practices inhabited by a relatively small section of the people whose social location can be identified with a fair degree of clarity" (Chatterjee 2004, 38). Chatterjee's conception rests on an assumption of a naturalized identification between civil society, elite middle class expression (voice), and the representation of a homogeneous set of middle class interests. In effect, such a notion conflates dominant conceptions of elite or middle class identity (such as the hegemonic identity of the new middle class) with the broader and highly differentiated group that constitutes the middle class. Moreover, as we have already seen, in practice, subaltern groups such as workers and unions in fact actively contest middle class models of citizenship within the sphere of civil society.

My research suggests that the relationship between the middle class and the state is shaped by a more complex set of processes that cannot be captured by simplified narratives of exit from democracy, voice in civil society, or capture of the state. Let us review the range of strategies that segments of the middle class use in order to both pursue their perceived interests as well as to gain political access to state power. The most visible set of middle class strategies are the wide range of associational activities within civil society including conventional organizational practices through civic organizations, public narratives, and discursive practices within the media and public sphere.[19] As we have seen, such practices form part of a broader set of discourses and mechanisms that have constructed a middle class model of consumer-citizenship. The delineation of a form of citizenship that does not rest on electoral politics or on the formal-legal dimensions of political democracies, in effect provides a distinctive mechanism that links the middle classes with state power. It is dominant middle class practices and discourses that determine access to this form of citizenship—a process that contests the formal model of citizenship that the middle class has perceived as being captured by the politics of votebanks.[20]

A second set of practices consists of privatized strategies that various segments of the middle class use to pursue their interests in areas such as the labor market, education, and health care. Such practices converge with state discourses of liberalization as the middle class engages in individualized attempts to acquire various forms of capital to gain specific advantages in the context of liberalization. However, the fact that a rising new middle class identity has been shaping the nature and direction of strategies and practices does not automatically imply that the interests of the middle class are being represented in a self-evident way either by the state or by dominant representations of this new middle class. The differentiation of interests within the middle class is such that vast segments of this social group in practice do not benefit from state policies. For instance, in realms such as health and education, while the intensification of privatized strategies may benefit upper tiers of the middle class, state cutbacks or the absence of state accountability does not inevitability serve a generalized set of middle class interests.[21] Furthermore, as we saw in chapter 3, in the realm of employment, large segments of the middle class continue to depend on state employment and do not necessarily benefit from privatization or from the increased status of fields such as information technology.

This differentiation of the middle class is perhaps best seen in the ways in which large segments of the middle class must continue to rely on networks of political patronage, party connections, and mobilizations, as well as—on occasion—ethnically based social movements such as "sons of soil" movements.[22] In the case of middle class segments from the *dalit* and backward caste communities, state policies of reservations as well as networks of patronage (for instance through civil service appointments) continue to represent important strategies that middle class segments of these communities rely on even as they try and gain access to forms of capital such as English education (Weiner 2001, 213). The political significance of such processes cannot be grasped by an assumption of homogeneous middle class interests. Rather, there is a more dynamic and ongoing set of political contestations unfolding between segments of the middle class as competing members of this group attempt to gain access to resources and delineate their relationship with the state. Consider one prediction of potential conflict:

> Should the Indian economy continue to expand significantly in the next decade, with a contraction of employment in the public sector and an expansion of employment in the private sector, we can anticipate that scheduled caste and OBC leaders will demand reservations in the private sector. . . . The result could well be an acute political struggle, this time involving not only the excluded [from reservations] higher castes, but the business community whose involvement in the earlier debates over Mandalization was minimal precisely because they were unaffected. (Weiner 2001, 222)

Regardless of whether such conflict is borne out in the future, it points to the broader political significance of contestation among segments of the middle class. In this context, the state is not merely a passive actor responding to active middle class citizens making political claims. Rather, state practices also engage in the political management of middle class practices and identities. For instance, state practices (such as the spatial practices and state strategies analyzed in chapter 4) that contribute to the production of the new middle class are instances of this form of management. The broader political significance of the rise of the new middle class lies precisely in the way in which it represents a key arena for the ongoing negotiation and management of interests of the state and of the highly differentiated social locations that are glossed as "middle class" or "elites."

This kind of political negotiation has produced important points of convergence between middle class support for Hindu nationalism and for India's policies of reforms. In other words, the political opening for the assertion of a new middle class identity that has been sparked by liberalization unfolded within the same temporal space in the politics of upper caste, middle class backlash that has been transformed into support for the BJP. Recognizing this temporal simultaneity is important as it moves us away from erroneous assumptions of causality between the rise of Hindu nationalism and economic liberalization. The link between these two phenomena, I would argue, is not a naturalized affinity between Hindu nationalism and economic reforms, but the ways in which both sites provide the political space for particular segments of the middle class to attempt to reclaim and redefine the terms of democratic politics.

My analysis of the formation of the new middle class illustrates that the direction and implications of middle class politics cannot be assumed to take a predetermined direction. The heart of middle class politics rests on the ways in which dominant constructions of middle class identity interact with and mediate such forms of differentiation. Let us consider this process of contestation through the case of an anti-price-rise campaign in Mumbai. The case illustrates the ways in which even the dominant new middle class model of consumer-citizenship is contested by competing middle class conceptions. While the case of the anti-price-rise campaign was a temporary interruption of the dominant construction of middle class consumer-citizenship, it nevertheless highlights the politicization of socioeconomic inequalities and uncertainties within the middle class that have accompanied images of prosperity associated with the new middle class.

The Politics of Onions: Consumer-Citizenship and Cross-Class Alliances

The political significance of the identity of the new middle class does not simply stem from its pro-reforms cultural ethos of prosperity but from the tensions that arise when this ethos is destabilized by the persistence of inequality and economic hardship within the middle class. The identity of the new middle class, as I have argued, has reinforced middle class anxieties and strategies geared at reinforcing sociocultural distinctions that separate the middle class from the poor and working classes.

This process of identity formation should not, however, be viewed as a predetermined outcome of the politics of liberalization. Let us consider a counterpoint to the dominant model of middle class identification through an analysis of an example of responses to a significant public consumer crisis in food security. During the course of my fieldwork in 1998, one of the most public political crises faced both by the ruling national BJP-led government as well as by local governments in urban areas ranging from metropolitan cities such as Delhi and Mumbai to towns in Rajasthan and Gujarat, was catalyzed by a steep rise in the price of vegetables. This set of inflationary pressures was symbolized by the rise in the price of onions from normal prices of around Rs 7 to highs of Rs 40–50 per kg in the space of a few months from August to November 1998.[23] The price of onions, a staple food for both working and middle class families, soon became a cross-class public symbol of economic pressures. While in this case the actual causes of the price rise were not a direct result of liberalization, the public outcry became a visible symbol that captured the economic pressures on working class and middle class families. Social groups from lower economic strata were particularly affected as onions and *roti* (bread) is usually the only staple meal that is affordable to working class families. However, the widespread use of onions in Indian food also meant that middle class household budgets were significantly affected.

During this period, public discourses ranging from everyday conversations to mainstream media reports to public satirical events such as an "onion fashion show" were singularly focused on the price of onions in a sharp contrast to idealized images of middle class consumption of commodities such as cars and cell phones. The onion debacle soon became an embodiment for traditional middle class frustrations with government inefficiency and public corruption.

While the original cause of the rise in prices could be traced back to crop failures due to bad weather conditions, a lack of administrative response transformed the problem into a public crisis of food security. The attempts of both the central and local governments to bring down prices were mired in administrative mismanagement. While the government banned exports of onions and placed onions in its "Open General License" category in order to permit imports, such decisions were taken only after the price rise had become a major national issue. In Mumbai, a shipment of imported onions was allowed to rot because of delays in customs clearance (Balakrishnan 1998). Some reports pointed to the role of traders in hoarding and manipulating prices and suggested that the government's failure to act more aggressively to stop hoarding was linked to the fact that the trader community served as an important source of financial and electoral support for the BJP.[24] Meanwhile, belated attempts by state governments to sell subsidized onions through the public distribution system were inadequate, leading to long lines and instances of violence when supplies ran out (Chakravarty 1998). As one report put it, "The lines have not grown shorter. Middle-class people line up from as much as *four hours* before the onion-bearing truck is supposed to arrive. When the truck arrives, the queue often breaks, the officials are rude and unsympathetic: all in all, it's a despicable dehumanising process that would have earned Mikhail Gorbachev's awe" (Deb 1998b, 59).

This debate, which was typical of many mainstream public discourses, did not construct any links between inflationary pressures and the government's policies of economic liberalization. The problem is depicted using the imagery of Soviet-style food shortages, producing a subtle link between the onion crisis and older elements of a planned economy. Significantly, discord in such representations was not channeled into dissatisfaction with liberalization but against the incompetence of the state management of the economy. The onion crisis struck at the heart of traditional middle class frustrations with corruption and bureaucratic inefficiencies.

However, during this crisis, another case of public political activity produced a significantly different interpretation and response. On November 12, 1998, a Women's Anti-Price-Rise Committee organized a march through a central area in Mumbai, from Churchgate station to the Azad Maidan to protest against the rising prices. The march was supported by an array of women's groups ranging from women's wings of traditional political parties such as the Janata Dal and the Communist Party of India-Marxist (CPM) to autonomous organizations such as the Young Christian Women's Association. The anti-price-rise campaign attempted to build a cross-class alliance based on the gendered nature of consumption in which women from both working and middle class households generally must manage household budgets and negotiate the inflationary pressures on daily expenses. The campaign also drew on a longer historical memory of women's activism. Mrinal Gore, one of the central leaders of the campaign, drew on her own history in a militant form of women's activism in the early 1970s in response to price rises spurned by famine in Maharashtra.[25] As with the campaign in the 1990s, in the 1970s women's organizations formed an anti-price-rise committee and engaged in a number of militant protests from within the offices of the state government to *gheraoing* (a form of militant protest where the opponent is encircled and held hostage) a minister at his residence. Gore recalls a specific protest against kerosene prices at which women were demanding that kerosene be distributed as a subsidized product on the state ration card:

> We asked ladies to carry empty tins and then that rolling pin in the bag ... [then] at the central place [in Mantralaya] where the lifts are. . . . So there we all gathered, about forty to fifty of us, and took out that empty tin and started banging. So it makes such a horrible noise the whole secretariat came running down to see what is happening. . . . We started to go up. All the ministers sit on the sixth floor ... and all of us banging went up to

the sixth floor. The staff, which had come and were on the stair-case, they allowed us to pass through. They were just enjoying. They were happy also that somebody is working for them. . . . [W]hen the police followed us they stopped them. So we could go straight away to the sixth floor, to the supplies minister's chamber and then we started banging. He got so frightened he locked from inside the door. Then we started saying "give kerosene on ration card. From today we want kerosene on ra-tion card." And naturally he rang the police. They came in big numbers because after all they had to arrest forty ladies. We were not prepared to move. Forcibly they took us but that very night the civil supplies minister announced that henceforth kerosene will be distributed on ration card. You know that sense of winning was there.[26]

The historical memory of the 1970s women's protests, which Gore brought to the 1998 campaign, is marked by a clear sense of nostalgia. While the 1998 campaign did gain some media attention and drew a group of about thirty or forty women who participated in the march, and a slightly larger crowd that gathered to hear speeches at the rally, the campaign did not have a comparable sense of militancy or wider public impact as did the protests in the 1970s.

However, while the 1998 march and rally did not measure up to the militancy of the 1970s protests, the campaign nevertheless points to an alternative to the construction of India's new consumer citizen. In particular, the campaign was effective in temporarily producing a consumer-based form of activism that subverted the traditional class and gender politics of the consumer identities and activism of the lib-eralizing middle class.[27] The campaign drew on cross-class common-alities between women in urban contexts and produced a notion of consumer identity that did not rest on the discourses of class distinc-tion and of law and order that have constructed representations of consumer activism purely in terms of middle class interests. The gendered nature of the protests pointed to the wider political possi-bilities of mobilizing women through cross-class consumer-based identities. While the militancy of the protests was limited, anger and frustration over rising prices had broader political implications that extended to an impact on the local electoral politics of ruling governments of the BJP and the Shiv Sena parties (Raj 1998). For instance, in Delhi's assembly elections one report suggested that the price-rise crisis had led close to two-thirds of housewives to vote for the Congress in lieu of the BJP.[28]

The Women's Anti-Price Rise Committee campaign points to the possibility of an alternative conception of the consumer-citizen, one that does not necessarily rely on a politics of distinction between the middle class and the poor and working classes. I have pointed to this alternative as a counterpoint to the naturalization of consumer-based images of the middle class that permeate public discourses and academic analyses.

However, the transformative nature of such a campaign should not be overestimated. The women's campaign, for instance, did not have the sustained militancy of its historical predecessor in the 1970s. In addition, it is important to note that the politics of rural and urban distinctions and inequalities continued to persist in important ways even in the context of such a campaign. Well-known farmers' leader Sharad Joshi, for instance, pointed out that a similar level of public attention was not mobilized in response to farmers' suicides that hit rural India during the crop failures and which initially led to the price rises. Even a contestation of the boundaries of India's consumer citizen is marked by the significant hierarchies that continue to characterize urban–rural divisions in postcolonial India.

In addition, attempts to draw on a notion of shared interests between the middle and working classes in the context of liberalization have not met with sustained success.[29] On the contrary, the political responses of the urban middle class have continued to center on a politics of distinction. The national direction of new middle class political behavior has still been dominated by the pro-Hindutva, anti-Mandalization attitudes of the Hindu middle class. As I have noted earlier, the rise of Hindu nationalism in the 1990s rested in large part on a shift of the urban middle class base from the Congress to the BJP (Jaffrelot 2000; Yadav 1999). Convergences between middle class interests, the rise of Hindu nationalism, and the policies of economic liberalization point to the ways in which the most effective cross-class political alliances and movements in response to the disjunctures of liberalization have been manifested in the rise of the Hindutva movement.

The direction of Indian politics has in fact been increasingly shaped by this articulation of a hegemonic notion of shared cultural-political interests between the Hindu middle and working classes, rather than the notion of shared interests between blue- and white-collar workers that shaped the politics of organized labor in earlier decades. Consider the response of one middle class white-collar union leader in the insurance industry to the question of middle class politics in the context of liberalization:

> That's why you see the growth in crime. . . . There is a lot of so-cial discontent. But what shape it will take we don't know. Social discontent may not be in the form of class struggle. There are other things like caste which are there. We don't know what shape it will take.[30]

This commentary represents a caution against a presumed assumption that the left-oriented unions and parties will necessarily be able to transform social discontent sparked by liberalization into a cross-class-based movement. On the contrary, the power of the new middle class lies in its ability to manage the disjunctures of liberalization in ways that move us away from an easy assumption that the economic costs or uncertainties will necessarily lead to political opposition to reforms.

Conclusion

In this chapter, I have examined some of the political implications of the rise of the new Indian middle class. The political practices of this social group have begun to redefine the boundaries and meanings of democratic citizenship in ways that have intersected with and intensified social inequalities. Such practices have drawn on a rise of middle class protest politics that has shaped political dynamics in late-twentieth-century India. The politicization of the middle class has concentrated on attempts to limit the participatory potential of subordinated social groups. Furthermore, I have argued that the significance of my analysis of the new middle class lies in the ways in which it seeks to move us away from easy conflations of the middle class as a homogenized elite with self-evident interests. Rather, the political significance of the new middle class lies in its interaction with and management of a highly differentiated set of interests—a process of management that also directly involves state practices.

I have argued that this emerging form of new middle class politics has not been designed in opposition to democracy but through an attempt to reclaim and redefine the terms of democracy in exclusionary ways. While scholars of comparative politics have traditionally sought to examine whether democratization has posed political obstacles for the consolidation of reforms, my analysis points to the political obstacles that liberalization poses for democratization. In this endeavor, I have sought to demonstrate the significance that an analysis of everyday politics and identity formation holds for an understanding of democratic processes.

The rise of the new Indian middle class, as we have seen, captures a deeper paradox inherent in the workings of political democracy. On the one hand, my analysis has shown that the rise of this group has produced significant contestations from subordinated groups both within civil society as well as within the realm of electoral politics. Democracies thus provide vital mechanisms for political contestation. On the other hand, my analysis shows that the new middle class has effectively been able to reconstitute the boundaries of citizenship and national identity in ways that make certain forms of exclusion intrinsic to the workings of democracy. In other words, middle class conceptions of citizenship and democracy are defined and enacted through the politics of distinction and exclusion. Any understanding of the relationship between reforms and democracy requires an analysis of the substantive operation of democracy and the ways in which such substantive dimensions shape and constrain the political implications of electoral politics. While formal voting mechanisms in democracies may enable marginalized social groups to signal their protest against the effects of particular policies, informal practices may be more significant in framing national political cultures and the policy agendas affiliated with these agendas.

While I have concentrated on providing a textured sense of political life in contemporary India, the politics of the identity formation of a group such as the new middle class holds broader insights for an understanding of economic and political change in comparative contexts. Processes related to the rise of the new Indian middle class can be discerned in comparative contexts in Asia and Latin America. Policy analysts and scholars have continued to stress the centrality of the middle class in creating a social contract that can accelerate development and promote socioeconomic security.

The middle classes continue to shape democratic trajectories as well as broader processes of globalization in ways that are often disproportionate with their numerical strength in late-industrializing countries. I thus turn in the concluding chapter to a discussion of some of the general theoretical and comparative implications that this study holds for our understanding of culture, democracy, and the politics of economic reforms.

Conclusion

----------*----------

The rise of the new middle class rests on a complex and often contradictory set of processes that began unfolding with India's push toward economic liberalization. Throughout this book I have sought to capture both the dominant and often rigid boundaries of this emerging social group and the fissures and contestations that arise when the identity of this new middle class has pushed up against both internal differentiations within the middle class and external distinctions that differentiate the middle class from subaltern socioeconomic groups. I have deliberately sought to capture the hegemonic nature of this social group through the sense of singularity implied by the phrase "the rise of the new middle class." The creation of this new middle class represents a hegemonic process in which the identity of this group serves as an idealized elite standard for a range of social strata that make up the rural and urban middle classes. The new middle class, in effect, is the social group that embodies the realizable potential of a liberalizing Indian nation.

In order to fully grasp the significance of the rise of this new middle class, I have argued for an approach that simultaneously analyzes this hegemonic process of construction and moves beyond an understanding of the new middle class purely as a cultural sign or symbol of broader economic or political processes. National and international public rhetoric about the new middle class has often mistakenly conflated this process of signification (one that associates the new middle class with the benefits of liberalization) both with the actual practices and experiences of this social group and with the middle class in general. Indeed, such commentary, ranging from media discourses to some of the quantitative projects of income measurement, has itself become part of the symbolic framing of the new middle class.

I have aimed not only to juxtapose an erroneous image of the new middle class with a more accurate one. I have sought to analyze the cross-cutting symbolic and material practices that have shaped the remaking of this middle class, as well as the actual practices and symbolic/material effects of individuals and social strata that claim or aspire to membership in the new middle class.

Such an approach both recognizes the power of symbolic-discursive construction and provides theoretical space for a conceptual understanding of nondiscursive realms of socioeconomic structure. Through this approach, I have sought to move beyond a static conception of the new middle class as a consumer group (whether defined in terms of economic measures of income or culturalist interpretations of media images). Rather, my focus on the practices and politics of the new middle class point to a conception of a much denser field of relationships and activities in which individuals and subgroups in the middle class attempt to negotiate, respond to, and shape the political dynamics of liberalization, often in ways and in spaces that may not at first glance appear to be overtly related to changes associated with policies of economic reforms. As I have argued, it is through such processes that the new middle class begins to exert various forms of agency and often acts as a unified social group with a discernible set of interests defined both in relation to liberalization and in relation to the state.

My underlying theoretical premise in this argument has been that a constructivist approach requires an analysis of the ways in which the middle class exerts various forms of social, political, and economic agency. In this case, the significance of the rise of the new middle class lies in the ways in which this emerging social group has begun to shape the politics of liberalization in India. A recognition of such agency points to the ways in which the construction of the new middle class becomes *materialized*. I have explicitly sought to move away from versions of social constructivism that have sometimes fallen short in discussions of both agency and materiality due to assumptions that any discussion of agency anthropomorphizes the construction (in this case the new middle class) or that any discussion

of materiality implies a static opposition between structure and discourse.[1] While the agency and interests of the new middle class are of
course hegemonic in nature and will not necessarily represent the
complex and varied layers of the group, such tensions and contradictions in fact form the heart of political life.

In this concluding chapter I draw out some of the wider theoretical implications that emerge from my analysis of the rise of the new
Indian middle class. I begin with an overview of some of my central
research findings on the new middle class and the significance of
these findings for an understanding of contemporary Indian politics.
I then outline some of the comparative implications that this study
holds for a more general understanding of the relationship between
class, the state, and the political economy of development. Finally, I
end with a discussion of some of the theoretical implications for a
conceptual understanding of the middle class as well as for the
broader theoretical salience of the category of class.

The Rise of the New Middle Class and Contemporary Politics in India

The rhetoric of globalization is often centered on a premise of newness, that is, on the assumption that contemporary globalization
marks a sharp historical break from past legacies that shaped the
ways in which societies organized cultural, economic, and social
practices.[2] In many ways, the new middle class is the quintessential
embodiment of this rhetoric of newness; dominant representations
of this social group depict it as the central agent that can effectively
realize the potential of a newly liberalizing Indian nation. In contrast
to this rhetoric of newness, one of my central objectives in this study
has been to engage in a more nuanced specification of both the historical continuities and the changes that have made the new middle
class a distinctive group in postliberalization India. As we have seen,
there are striking parallels between nineteenth- and early twentieth-
century debates on the new colonial middle class and late twentieth-
and early twenty-first-century discourses on the new liberalizing
middle class. In both cases, the new middle class was the site of, and
an important agent in, public debates on questions of culture, nation,

and civic life. Moreover, in both historical periods we have seen that debates on such public identities and arenas have been mediated and constructed through social and cultural hierarchies and meanings.

Inequalities in caste, language, gender, and religion that shaped the formation of the new middle class in the colonial period continue to influence the resources, practices, and identities of postliberalization India in significant and enduring ways. These continuities do not imply that such inequalities are unchanging or static components of Indian society. Instead, such historically produced social distinctions have provided particular social segments with varying forms of resources that they have attempted to use to preserve or raise their social standing.

My analysis of historical continuities underlines the significance of both temporality and agency in the reproduction of what seem like immutable social structures. Consider the question of language, education, and middle class formation. As we have seen, British educational policy shaped the formation of the colonial middle class in important ways. The acquisition of an English education represented a primary means for entry to the colonial middle class, a new elite social group that was emerging distinct from, and in an uneasy relationship with, traditional elites as well as with other less privileged segments of the middle class, particularly the vernacular, lower middle class. Access to English education has continued to shape the middle class in postcolonial India. As I have argued, the dominant construction of the new liberalizing middle class identity has rested primarily on idealized representations of the urban English-speaking middle class. The acquisition of English-language skills represents a critical means by which various segments of the "old" middle class preserve or gain access to membership in the new middle class.

The link between language and middle class formation has been intensified by globalization as an expanding private sector and outsourcing have consolidated the importance of English-language skills. Consider the dynamics of continuity and change in this relationship between language and class. Segments of the middle class that have historically had access to English education have been poised to convert this capital into new forms of mobility in a liberalizing labor market. I have demonstrated that the new liberalizing middle class is not made up of new entrants to middle class status; rather, this "newness" refers to the national ideological-cultural shifts associated with liberalization. By grasping such historical continuities we are able to analyze the ways in which enduring structures based on inequalities such as language and class are reconstituted despite the ideology of newness associated with globalization.

This analysis of historical patterns of social reproduction does not mean that the new middle class has remained a static category. On the contrary, as I have demonstrated, the power of the new middle class lies in the promise of access to the benefits of liberalization— particularly for different layers of the rural and urban middle classes. In postcolonial India, the demand for English education has spread within the middle class, as well as among upwardly mobile segments of lower-income families.

In recent years, language itself has changed in the context of shifting cultures of liberalization. With the expansion of middle class English education, language has been transformed by various forms of cultural and social capital. Shifting discourses and practices of lifestyle, manners, and taste (aesthetic knowledge) have reconfigured distinctions between the upper tiers of the English-speaking middle class (the new liberalizing middle class) and broader sections of the middle class attempting to realize the promise of access. The result, as I have demonstrated throughout this book, is a complex set of practices and strategies that individuals and segments of the middle class have deployed as they have attempted to shape, negotiate, and respond to both this new class identity and the corresponding changes sparked by liberalization. Examples of these strategies range from the accent-training programs of call centers, to the cultural and public speaking training designed to help workers adapt to changing mores in private-sector and multinational firms, to changing consumption practices that echo new social distinctions defined by the use and display of particular products. As I have demonstrated, the new middle class has been continually shaped by the reworking of social hierarchies of caste, religion, and gender.

Given the salience of historical processes in shaping the middle class, the question that arises is: What is the distinctive significance of the new middle class for our understanding of contemporary politics in India? My analysis in preceding chapters has demonstrated three central areas of significance: (1) the influence that the new middle class has in shaping public responses to liberalization, (2) the emergence of the new middle class as an autonomous actor with its own set of interests and political agency, and (3) the ways in which the new middle class sheds light on state practices under liberalization. First, I have argued that the rise of the new middle class has begun to shape social and political responses to economic liberalization. The dominant identity of this social group has rested on an image of a consuming middle class that is both the beneficiary and central agent of a liberalizing Indian nation. I have focused on a range of practices (such as representations in the media and public sphere, state policies and spatial practices in urban development, and middle class civic activities and discourses) that have contributed to the creation of this dominant identity. Through this analysis, I have demonstrated that such practices constitute a set of political processes that result in associations between the middle classes, consumption, and a pro-liberalization orientation. This dominant identity of the new middle class signifies the benefits to which upwardly mobile segments of the population can aspire.

I have also demonstrated the ways in which responses to broader questions of economic policy are coded through informal and everyday cultural and social meanings and practices. For example, research findings on postliberalization India suggested that knowledge about economic reforms in India is relatively low and that economic reforms have not been a major electoral issue. However, my findings suggest that conflict and consent over policies of economic reform do not play out only in the formal domain of electoral politics. Moreover, perceptions of reforms are often shaped by local cultural and social meanings and practices that may fall outside survey codings of formal forms of knowledge. My aim has not been to assess the responses of the new middle class or of segments of the middle class to specific economic policies (such as free trade, labor laws, or privatization). Rather, I have argued that the rise of the new middle class has shaped responses to liberalization by producing a new kind of public common sense or political culture of liberalization. An analysis of the rise of the new Indian middle class thus deepens our understanding of the political dynamics of economic reform in contemporary India.

The politics of internal differentiation within the middle class (and the tensions between this differentiation and the dominant identity of the new middle class) have been a central force in shaping the politics of liberalization. This interplay dispels the assumption often present in both scholarly and public discourses on economic reforms and globalization that the middle class benefits uniformly from policies of economic liberalization. I have specifically argued for a shift away from the assumption that the middle class is necessarily a beneficiary of economic liberalization—an assumption that conflates the dominant new middle class identity with the broader social group comprised of the rural and urban middle classes. For example, even in the realm of consumption, which is most often associated with new middle class identity, the empirical data has demonstrated that while there have been measurable increases in income and consumption, broad patterns of consumption practices have often proved to be more contradictory. In contrast to a country like China, a substantial portion of household income in India is devoted to housing, medical care, and education, and large segments of the middle class do not have the kind of disposable income associated with the upper middle class and upper classes.

The significance of my analysis of the rise of the new middle class in this context is twofold. One, it provides the conceptual space needed to avoid a conflation between this hegemonic identity and the middle class in general. Two, it demonstrates that this new middle class shapes the dynamics of consent and conflict over the uncertainties and dislocations that may be sparked by liberalization. For example, as we have seen, middle class individuals resort to privatized strategies as they attempt to convert various forms of capital into a means of gaining access both to new middle class membership and to the benefits of a liberalizing economy. As we have seen, there is a great degree of internal differentiation within the middle class, and various segments of this social group attempt to draw on both longstanding sources of capital such as language, caste, and kinship resources, as well as on new forms of cultural, aesthetic, and socioeconomic capital.

Thus an array of institutes have sprouted up in rural and urban areas with promises of new skills, credentials, and cultural expertise that can help individuals negotiate new-economy jobs that are located primarily in the service sector.

If such privatized responses of middle class individuals illustrate the symbolic power of new middle class identity in consolidating consent to liberalization, other examples have shown heightened social and political conflict through a range of sociocultural contestations over issues such as the restructuring of urban space, competing definitions of national culture, and identity-based conflicts. Thus, my research has demonstrated that the rise of this new middle class represents an important force in shaping the consent and conflict over liberalization, in ways that have traditionally been overlooked by conventional political science research on electoral responses to shifts in economic policy.

The second area of significance that the new middle class holds for an understanding of Indian politics lies in the way in which the new middle class has begun to assert agency through a range of practices and activities. I have argued that this process represents an emerging dimension in Indian politics, one in which middle class individuals and social groups now consciously claim that the Indian middle class is a distinctive social group with its own set of social, political, and economic interests that must be actively represented.[3] I have shown that this assertive middle class identity is articulated both in public discourses as well as in a range of cultural and social forms such as the development of new urban aesthetics and assertive claims on public urban space, along with the emergence of middle class civic and community organizations. My research has demonstrated that such emerging middle class activities have, in distinctive ways, reshaped the nature of democratic politics. For example, drawing on an analysis of the politics of neighborhood beautification programs, I have shown that the internal uncertainties and instability of the new middle class are, in effect, managed through the reproduction of sociospatial distinctions from the urban poor and working classes. These middle class practices attempt to reconstitute civic life in contemporary India through the intensification of social exclusions and hierarchies such as gender, class, and religion.

In many ways, these new middle class practices in the postliberalization period have drawn on and recast late twentieth-century trends in which upper-caste, urban middle class members began to engage in a form of backlash protest politics against a democratic political field that they perceived as having been captured by previously marginalized social groups. For example, I have examined the emergence of a new middle class model of consumer-citizenship that has sought to rework historical social exclusions into a new form of civic life that draws on discourses of consumption and privatization. The result is a process in which the new middle class is engaged in a series of practices and contestations aimed at redefining the boundaries of democratic politics and reclaiming the primacy of the middle class in the political field of contemporary India.

Finally, the third area of significance of the new middle class lies in the insights we gain on the nature of state practices in liberalizing India. A central finding of my research has been that the creation of this social group necessitates a move beyond a presumed opposition between the state and market (and the corresponding assumption that the orientation of the middle class has shifted from a state- to a market-oriented outlook) that sometimes appears in subtle ways in discussions of policies of economic liberalization and processes of globalization. My analysis has shown that the politics of the new middle class is shaped in significant ways by its relationship with a range of state strategies and practices; the state itself is involved in the making and management of the new middle class. For instance, the state participates in the production of a new middle class identity when their strategies actively promote new models of urban civic development that conform to and help create middle class models of civic life. Local state practices often manage the uncertainties of globalization through gendered cultural practices and discourses that seek to manage women's social roles, for example. Such state practices shape the boundaries of middle class identity and contribute to the production of a new middle class–based vision of the Indian nation—one that is based on a reconstitution of historical inequalities of gender, caste, class, and religion.

This analysis cautions us against an easy assumption of a sharp break between the state dependence of the Nehruvian middle class on the one hand and the market orientation of the postliberalization new middle class on the other. On the contrary, my research has demonstrated the importance of moving away from static generalizations that suggest either a form of middle class retreat from the state or an uncontested form of middle class dependence on or capture of the state.

Policies of liberalization and the related cultural and social processes of globalization have produced a restructuring of the relationship between the middle class and the state. The politics of the new middle class have been shaped by an assertion of claims on, rather than a retreat from, the state. The new middle class has sought to make material its national vision through demands made in the public sphere. For example, in my analysis of the India Shining campaign, I argued that the significance of this campaign is not in the public and electoral backlash it produced. Rather, its significance lies in the way it illustrates the success of the new middle class in using practices within civil society to shape the symbolic registers of democratic politics through informal points of access to state power. The India Shining campaign in effect represented an electoral manifestation of the new middle class model of consumer-citizenship. The vision of the India Shining campaign also reflected the convergence of interests between the new middle class and the postliberalization state. Both the state and new middle class have been invested in idealized visions of a liberalizing nation being transformed into a global economic giant. The new middle class is thus not simply a consumer-oriented group defined by the market, it is a social group partly being produced by and partly supporting state-led strategies of liberalization.

While such convergences between the state and the new middle class are significant, this does not imply that the state has been captured by the middle class (that is, the state does not cater exclusively to middle class interests). A central dimension of my argument has been that the dominant identity of the new middle class interacts with complex and differentiated social forces that constitute the middle class. Vast segments of the middle class struggle with the costs of the privatized strategies required to negotiate fields such as the restructured labor market, education, and health care. However, the symbolic and material power of the new middle class is precisely that it helps negotiate such disjunctures between the promise of economic liberalization and the realities of middle class life. The majority of middle class individuals I interviewed continued to express support for liberalization despite their awareness of these costs. This does not, of course, imply that the political responses of the middle class are predetermined by this dominant identity. On the contrary, the crux of my argument is that it is precisely the fluidity of the potential convergences, interplay, and conflicts between this rising new middle class and the broader matrices of social differentiation that will be a significant factor that shapes contemporary politics in India.

State, Class, and the Political Economy of Reforms in Comparative Perspective

The rise of the new Indian middle class, as I have demonstrated, encapsulates central dynamics of contemporary politics that involve the changing nature and relationship between state, democracy, and the politics of economic reforms. The Indian case holds broader implications for a comparative understanding of the politics of economic reforms. Most significantly, my study points to the need to address the centrality of the relationship between the middle class and the state in understanding the political economy of reforms. While recent scholarship has demonstrated the relationship between class and state in shaping trajectories of economic development (Chibber 2003; Evans 1995; Kohli 2004), most comparative research has tended to neglect the role of the middle class in an analysis of this relationship.[4]

A recent exception in the field of development studies is Diane Davis's (2004) important comparative study of patterns of development in East Asia and Latin America. Drawing on comparative historical research on Korea, Taiwan, Argentina, and Mexico, Davis argues that a key variable shaping trajectory and national developmental prospects is the political influence of the rural middle class. For example, she illustrates that in the case of South Korea, a strong rural middle class political base enabled the state to discipline both capitalists and urban workers and pursue its developmental goals relatively unencumbered. In contrast, as she argues, "urban-based classes had both a size and political visibility that made it difficult for

Latin American states to respond to rural middle classes, given the stark differences in their lives and livelihoods" (61). While Davis' research focuses on the significance of "rural middle-class-embedded" states in shaping developmental trajectories in the twentieth century, it nevertheless points to the broader comparative implications of the politics of the middle class in shaping the relationship between the state, class, and the political economy of development.

Davis's findings corroborate Pranab Bardhan's (1998) earlier argument that the professional, white-collar workers (that is, the upper tiers of the middle class) represented one of the central dominant proprietary classes that shaped and benefited from the trajectories of development in India.[5] As with Davis' research, Bardhan's argument points to the ways in which the political and economic influence of a particular segment of the middle class is able to shape the direction of state-led development in significant ways. While Davis points to the political role of the rural middle class in enabling South Korea's model of disciplined development, Bardhan depicts the upper tiers of the middle class as a rentier class that harnessed national development in the service of their own economic interests (1998, 52).

In line with such research that points to the significance of the middle class in shaping development strategies, my study of the Indian case opens up the significance of the politics of the new middle class in shaping the political economy of reforms and more broadly the politics of globalization. The convergences between the state and new middle class politics in India are significant precisely because they reveal the potential for the new middle class to influence broader patterns of national development, in this case by shaping responses to liberalization in the public sphere. As I have demonstrated, the dominant identity and politics of the new middle class is associated with a specific vision of national development that is supportive of India's move to liberalization. However, my theoretical framework and empirical analysis has deliberately sought to capture the complexity of the middle class in order to highlight the distinction between this new middle class project of national development and the highly differentiated set of interests within the middle class.

From a comparative perspective, two central implications stem from my analysis. First, as I have noted, state–middle class relations

form an important and understudied set of social and political interactions that shape public responses to reforms. Second, the nature of
this relationship between state and class requires a theoretical approach that can grasp both the dynamic and complex nature of
middle class politics. I have argued, for example, that the political and
conceptual significance of such processes are missed by existing studies of economic transitions that have primarily attempted to assess
public responses to economic reform either through an analysis of
formal voting behavior (that is, how attitudes to reform shape electoral politics) or have sought to measure public opinion through survey research data on attitudes to specific policies of reform. Such
methodological orientations cannot fully grasp the ways in which
middle class politics and the subtle linkages between class and state
are often forged and played out through social and cultural practices
that are not explicitly coded in the formal terms of electoral and policy arenas.[6]

This is not, of course, to advocate a rejection of the use of quantitative or survey-based research. For instance, income-based surveys
and data on consumption patterns provide an important set of parameters that can be used to gauge shifts in the middle class. Indeed, I
have used such data to provide a corrective to some interdisciplinary
approaches in fields such as postcolonial studies that have too easily
extrapolated theories about middle class behavior from data that
exclusively relies on discursive representations or localized ethnographic observations of middle class consumption. Nevertheless, studies of economic transitions in political science have tended to miss
the ways in which the social construction of groups like the new
middle class plays a significant role in shaping the political dynamics
of such transitions in comparative contexts. The emergence of this
kind of new middle class politics is not unique to the Indian context
but can also be seen in regions such as East Asia, Southeast Asia, and
Latin America.[7] Existing research on this class has been conducted
primarily in disciplines such as anthropology and sociology and has
not specifically engaged with political science debates on economic
transitions. My analysis and arguments in this book thus point to the
need for a comparative research agenda that specifically addresses the

impact that the rise (and decline) of the new middle class has on the trajectory of economic transitions in such regions. Such a research agenda specifically requires the inclusion of a constructivist approach within the existing terrain of comparative political economy.

The comparative implications of my study also extend to political science debates on the links between economic and political transitions. Such debates have tended to focus primarily on the transitions from authoritarianism to democracy, with an emphasis on the establishment of formal democracy.[8] The stability of formal democracy in India for well over fifty years makes India a useful case for a closer analysis of the relationship between economic transitions and substantive democracy. The rise of the new Indian middle class captures a deeper paradox inherent in the workings of political democracy. The rise of this group has produced significant contestations from subordinated groups both within civil society and within the realm of electoral politics. Democracies provide vital mechanisms for political contestation. However, my analysis has also shown that the new middle class has effectively been able to reconstitute the boundaries of citizenship and national identity in ways that make certain forms of exclusion intrinsic to the workings of democracy. In other words, middle class conceptions of citizenship and democracy are defined and enacted through the politics of distinction and exclusion.

Any understanding of the relationship between economic reforms and democracy requires an analysis of the substantive operation of democracy and the ways in which such dimensions shape and constrain the political implications of electoral politics. While formal voting mechanisms in democracies may enable marginalized social groups to signal their protest against the effects of particular policies, informal practices may be more significant in framing national political cultures and affiliated policy agendas. It is this reconstitution of democracy that deepens our insights regarding the consolidation of policies such as those related to economic reforms. I have argued that this emerging form of new middle class politics has not been defined by an opposition to democracy but by an attempt to reclaim and redefine the substantive terms of democracy in exclusionary ways. While scholars of comparative politics have traditionally sought to examine whether democratization has posed political obstacles for the consolidation of reforms, I have focused on the political challenges that liberalization poses for democratization.

The politics of the new middle class hold wider comparative implications for the study of economic and democratic transitions. While I have noted the methodological implications and the need for constructivist and interpretive approaches to adequately grasp the political dynamics of such social groups, the general significance of my analysis is not simply about the need for methodological diversity within a discipline such as political science. At a more general level, the theoretical project at hand is one that can successfully conceptualize the dynamics of class formation in postcolonial societies. This theoretical project is not simply one of bringing class back into our analyses but of systematically addressing how class can be theorized in ways that capture the complexities of globalization in postcolonial societies without resorting to exceptionalist arguments of cultural difference that miss both systematic patterns and the theoretical generalizability of class politics in non-Western societies such as India.

Practices, Capital, and the Theoretical Question of Class

The theoretical approach I have developed has sought to capture both the sense of liminality that characterizes middle class identity and the precise mechanisms and practices through which the boundaries around and within the middle class are maintained, often with an enduring rigidity. The liminality refers to the symbolic politics of class formation in which the promise of access to membership in a group such as the new middle class begins to shape the group's practices in material ways. The representational practices that shape class formation are clearly not epiphenomenal (mere reflections of underlying structures) in this context. However, at the same time, the ability of individuals and social segments to accumulate capital and maintain or gain access to new middle class membership are both shaped and constrained by their interaction with layered structures of inequality that have long historical legacies. Such strategies of conversion are shaped by the reworking of long-standing social inequalities such as the symbolic and material structures of caste, religion, language, and gender. One of the cornerstones of my theoretical argument is that it is this kind of symbiotic relationship between structure and discourse that underpins the dynamics of class formation. More specifically, I have argued for a practice-oriented approach that can grasp the dynamic nature of this interaction between the structural and discursive dimensions of class formation.

The mechanisms that shape class formation rest on the ways in which a range of practices produces the boundaries of social groups. Such practices are the outcome of a dynamic set of processes that are both symbolic and material and that are shaped both by longer historical processes as well as by the temporality of the everyday. However, they are not merely individualized or subjective forms of behavior that rest purely on the contingency of daily life.

Drawing on Bourdieu's (1984) explication of the classificatory practices that shape group formation, I have argued for a framework that addresses the ways in which individuals who either identify with or aspire to middle class status attempt to deploy various forms of capital in order to gain access to membership in the new middle class. This occurs through a dynamic and interactive process in which individuals and groups accumulate resources, seek to convert these resources into strategies designed to further their social standing, and respond to and draw on historically produced inequalities. The outcome is a set of classificatory practices (civic, discursive, and consumption) that structure the middle class. Previous studies of the middle class have tended to fall into two divergent streams theoretically oriented either by a structuralist or economistic conception of social groups that rests on income or occupation, or by a culturalist definition that is based on discourse or consumption.[9] However, the heart of the formation of social groups such as the new middle class rests precisely on the slippages, fractures, and tensions that arise from the interactive and mutually constitutive relationship between "structure" and "culture."

Let us consider further what is at stake in the way in which class as a theoretical category is brought back in, particularly in the study of postcolonial societies and nations. One of my central theoretical arguments focuses on the need to systematically address the category of class and the significance of the structural dimensions of class in interdisciplinary fields such as postcolonial studies. Ironically, while I have emphasized the cultural dimensions of class politics, my theoretical approach also to a large extent has represented a project of "writing against culture" (Abu-Lughod 1991). I have argued instead for a theoretical understanding of class that provides the conceptual space for an understanding of the linkages and interactions between realms such as structure on the one hand, and culture and discourse on the other.

A theoretical understanding of the structuralist dimension of class formation captures the enduring reproduction of social inequalities and the ways in which such inequalities are systematically structured by shifts in economic policy. For example, studies of the middle class that have focused exclusively on consumption and representation have missed the importance of systematic processes of restructuring in sites such as the labor market and urban neighborhoods. The approach I have developed specifically moves away from conceptions of structure that treat social and cultural identities as epiphenomenal reflections of structure. Consider the dynamics of class structuration in the creation of the new middle class in India. As I have demonstrated, class formation is substantively shaped by the reworking of inequalities of caste, language, religion, and gender. In other words, class as a category is constituted by these structures.[10]

In this book I have specifically sought to move away from culturalist approaches that conflate the specificities of postcoloniality with exceptionalist arguments that rest on notions of cultural difference. For instance, the postcolonial critique of Eurocentric assumptions that are embedded in Western theoretical conceptions of class and capitalism have led some scholars to simply shift away from a theoretical focus on class to an exclusive focus on cultural identities such as gender and ethnicity.[11] The result has been a missed opportunity in the field of postcolonial studies to develop and rethink existing conceptions of class in ways that can address the specificities of postcoloniality and cultural difference without sidelining the structural patterns of class formation that are discernible in comparative contexts.[12]

Consider my reworking of Bourdieu's theory of class formation in my analysis of the new middle class. Bourdieu's theoretical approach rests on an analysis of internal processes within the national context of France. However, the postcolonial specificities of a country like India shape class formation in distinctive ways, stemming both from the historical legacies of colonial rule that shaped the emergence of the middle class and the ways in which such colonial legacies have been reworked in contemporary national anxieties about Westernization and globalization. For example, the rise of the new Indian middle class is distinguished by national narratives (often cast in terms of debates on culture and gender) that seek to manage India's relationship with external forces such as "Westernization" and "globalization." Such specificities do not have to be cast as a narrative of Indian exceptionalism; that is, a narrative that claims that any discussion of the structural reproduction of inequalities such as class automatically implies a return to a deterministic or teleological approach to the study of postcolonial societies. On the contrary, a more nuanced understanding of the cultural, discursive, and structural dimensions of class holds important implications for fields such as South Asian studies, which have been strongly influenced by postcolonial critiques and which are grappling with the ways in which contemporary processes of globalization are reconstituting and intensifying socioeconomic inequalities.

In conclusion, I have argued that the rising new middle class represents an important social force in contemporary India, one that has been shaping conflict and consent over economic policies of liberalization and processes of globalization. My objective in this book has been both to trace the processes that have sought to remake the middle class in this singular, hegemonic image, as well as to provide a textured analysis of the practices, mechanisms, and differences that shape the formation and politics of this social group. This analysis points to broader implications both for an understanding of contemporary Indian politics as well as for a comparative and theoretical perspective. It also raises further questions and directions for future research that are beyond the scope of a single book. For instance, my argument suggests the need for further research on the responses of the middle class to specific policy arenas both in India and in comparative contexts that can be gleaned both through survey methods and qualitative research. Further research is also needed on the political implications that changing linkages between the state and middle class hold for the dynamics of economic transitions.

In the Indian context, my analysis specifically suggests that the tension between this emerging new middle class and the internal differentiation within the middle class will be an important force shaping politics in contemporary India. While this differentiation has led to conflicts over governmental caste-based reservations or has been folded into middle class support for Hindu nationalism, competition for private-sector employment represents a potentially ripe arena for political claims for access from marginalized sections of the middle class attempting to gain new benefits associated with liberalization.

As I have described throughout this book, there is a sense of fragility inherent in the middle class that marks its political role and socioeconomic position with a sense of uncertainty and unpredictability. The rise of the new middle class is always accompanied by the threat of failure for large segments of the middle class struggling to preserve their social status or simply trying to gain access to the benefits associated with this new middle class identity. It is this uncertainty that is in a sense captured by the disjointed series of images that alternatively depict the new Indian middle class as national icon of a liberalizing India, victimized workforce of global outsourcing, symbol of the consumerist contamination of Indian culture, and socioeconomic threat to the American middle classes. While the future of the new Indian middle class remains unpredictable, its imprint on contemporary India and its significance for an understanding of the dynamics of contemporary globalization have already been forged in enduring ways.

Notes

——✳——

Introduction

1. India gained independence from Britain in 1947.

2. See also Gupta 2000.

3. Such views are also present in the popular print media and in television programs such as new talk shows, which focus on youth problems, consumerism, and the Westernization of Indian culture. There are, of course, exceptions to this view of middle class consumerism. Dipankar Gupta (1998), for example, has cautioned against confusing consumption and consumerism, and has argued that the Indian middle class is too economically fragile to engage in consumerism.

4. Satish Deshpande (2003) has recently commented on this: "In the Indian context in particular, the mismatch between the contemporary importance of the middle class and the volume of reliable research on it is one of the more remarkable anomalies in our social science literature" (128). While Deshpande suggests that this may be due to a form of Indian exceptionalism, this mismatch also characterizes other non-Western countries. For work that addresses the postindependence Indian middle class see Ahmad and Reifeld 2001; Bhatia 1994; Chibber 1968; Deshpande 2003; Dubey 1992, Favero 2005; Frankel 1991; Mankekar 1999; Misra 1961; Rajagopal 2001b; Ram 1988; Rao 1981; Rutten and Upadhya 2005; Sheth 1999a, 1999b; Sridharan 1999. For non-Western countries see Embong 2002; Hsiao 1999; O'Dougherty 2002; Pinches 1999; Robison and Goodman 1996.

5. For an overview of such research see Dubey 1992. For a discussion of the problems of defining and measuring the middle class using existing quantitative data see Deshpande 2003.

6. See for example Rajagopal 2001b; Mankekar 1999. The cultural studies/ postcolonial studies literature has tended to focus on the middle classes in terms of the categories of globalization and modernity rather than in relation to specific phases of economic reform. See for example Appadurai and Breckenridge 1995.

7. See also Beteille 2001 on the importance of internal differentiation.

8. The definition of course depends on how the middle class is being measured. Income-based definitions would include both the rural and urban middle classes and include groups such as farmers, shopkeepers, and small traders. See for example National Council of Applied Economic Research 2002.

9. There are also long-term political costs to segments of the unionized middle class public-sector workers. I address some of the responses of insurance and bank employees' unions in chapter 5.

10. The new middle class thus begins to operate as an informal interest group. Atul Kohli (1989) suggests this potential for the middle classes to serve as a base of support for liberalization in his analysis of Rajiv Gandhi's policies. The point at hand is not, of course, that middle class individuals (intellectuals, activists, journalists, NGO workers) do not or cannot oppose liberalization; rather there is a political shift with the emergence of a new middle class identity that seeks to displace such opposition. Middle class critiques of globalization are thus as much a battle over the identity of the middle class as they are over the effects of globalization.

11. For work that analyzes such upward mobility see Sheth 1999a, 1999b, and Ram 1988, particularly in relation to caste and class intersections.

12. The term *middle class* itself does not have a precise indigenous linguistic equivalence; there is thus an in-built linguistic connotation to middle class identity that privileges English-educated segments of the middle class as the elite tier that defines middle class identity. See for example the emergence of the *bhadralok* as a kind of cultural upper class identity that competed with English upper class status in Calcutta. *Bhadralok,* however, connotes an upper class/caste status of the gentleman, rather than the "middle" sense of middle class identity. I return to this question of language and class identity in chapter 2.

13. Figures have ranged from tens of millions to 250 million.

14. I therefore refer to the rise of "the new middle class" precisely to underline the dominant nature of the construction even as this group—like all hegemonic formations—is continually shaped by internal and external differentiation.

15. It is this fluidity that leads to the confusion between the political identity of the "new Indian middle class"—a newly emerging interest group—and socioeconomic generalizations and measurements made in relation to various segments of the rural and urban middle classes. In other words, the emergence of this group cannot be viewed as a socioeconomic class simply acting on behalf of it interests; I analyze the ways in which the "interests" are created through specific sets of political/cultural/discursive processes. Other research has noted the significance of this group but has tended to assume the interests of the middle class are defined by their social

location rather than created through political processes (see Bardhan 1993). Corbridge and Harriss (2000) also refer to both economic liberalization and Hindu nationalism as "elite revolts" and as "vehicles for the aspirations and interests of the middle class."

16. For an overview of debates see Haggard and Kaufman 1995.

17. See for example Przeworski 1992 and 1996 and Stokes 1996a. For research on India see Jenkins 1999.

18. See also Jenkins 1999, which focuses more on the role of elites in engaging in strategies of "stealth" and manipulating democratic political processes.

19. Ibid. This includes both formal and informal political/governing elites such as politicians, bureaucrats, and party members. See also work on the role of state-level governments by Rudolph and Rudolph 2001 and Sinha 2004. For a comparative discussion of ideational factors and decision making see Weyland 2003.

20. A straightforward shift to focusing on socioeconomic elites would simply move to analyses of existing sociological groups such as the middle classes or business elites. Rather, the focus I suggest is on the political creation of a new pro-reform interest group that is not identical with the generalized sociological description of the middle class. On local elites in India see Mitra 1991 and 2001.

21. Thus, the new middle class operates in the form of an informalized interest group. It is not organized as one formal, organized interest group; rather, it is defined through informal, diverse practices that nevertheless represent a dominant set of interests associated with a pro-liberation orientation. For an overview of the conceptual literature on interest groups see Baumgartner and Leech 1998.

22. Chhibber and Eldersveld's survey (2000) indicates that 15 percent of masses and 63 percent of elites in India are knowledgeable about reforms in India, in contrast to 77 percent and 100 percent respectively in China. Sanjay Kumar (2004) has used National Election Study (NES) data to show that by 1998, 26 percent of all social groups in India had heard about economic reforms. However Kumar notes that despite negative perceptions of reform, this did not serve as an important electoral issue. Similar patterns shaped the 2004 elections (Yadav 2004).

23. For an analysis of the survey research methodology and the "don't know" responses as a reflection of socioeconomic inequality and the corresponding conditions of knowledge see Bourdieu 1984, 398–99.

24. Roderic Camp (2002) has recently noted that by "focusing on measurable consequences of elite decisions rather than ideas and values" (4) we miss key areas necessary for an adequate understanding of elite behavior. (I would add "social and cultural practices" to Camp's "ideas and values.")

25. In this analysis, my objective is not to examine responses to specific sets of policies. Policies of economic reform encompass a wide range of

issues, such as trade and financial liberalization, labor laws, the restructuring of state welfare and subsidy programs, and tax reform. Changes in India's economic policies have been uneven; for example, India has achieved greater success in financial liberalization than in restructuring labor legislation. My concern is with analyzing broader political, public consent, and resistance to the project of reforming the Indian economy and to the embrace of globalization, rather than on an examination of specific attitudes to particular policy arenas.

26. See Varshney 2003 for a conceptualization of civil society that includes both everyday and associational forms, and that moves beyond traditional dichotomies between modern secular associational activity and ethnically based forms of organization and activity.

27. I use the term *globalization* here because much of this research on the new middle class is not located in the discipline of political science and it tends to use the concept of globalization rather than economic reforms.

28. There is less literature on contemporary Latin America and Africa as most of it is historical in nature. For contemporary studies see Burke 1996; Davis 2004; O'Dougherty 2002.

29. Gerke argues that the ability of the Indonesian middle class to consume was weak even before the Asian economic crisis (2000, 137).

30. The Asian economic crisis occurred in 1997–98 as nations in Southeast Asia experienced a large outflow of foreign capital and steep declines in their stock markets and national currency exchange rates, as well as banking crises, debt repayment problems, and recessions.

31. Hagen Koo (n.d.) notes that the result has been the creation of strong internal differences "even within the new middle class, between those who rely basically on occupational incomes and those who draw on a substantial amount of income from other (like real estate and stock market) investments" (1–2).

32. The Indian middle class was not, of course, affected in the same way by the Asian economic crisis. The specificities of the effects of economic policies on the middle class varies. For instance, India has not dealt with the kinds of inflationary problems that have affected Brazil and significantly shaped the emergence of middle class consumer identity in that context (see O'Dougherty 2002).

33. The Robison and Goodman (1996) book is particularly significant as it marked new conceptual terrain in the study of elites in Asian studies and it is the first in a series of volumes on the new rich in Asia published by Routledge.

34. See also Appadurai 1996 on the postnational middle class diasporas and Ong and Nonini 1997 on transnational Chinese elites.

35. For instance, in Malaysia, Embong (2002) has argued that the new middle class is in fact a first-generation middle class. There are numerous

studies that focus on the lack of the stability of middle classes in the advanced industrialized countries. However, levels of economic development still place these groups in a more privileged location (see for example Steijn, Berting, and de Jong 1998).

36. On the growth of middle class support for the Hindu nationalist party—the Biharatiya Janata Party (BJP)—see Hansen 1999; Jaffrelot 2000; Yadav 1999.

37. As Owensby (1999) also notes, the difference from similar comparative framings within U.S. and European contexts is that the emerging Brazilian middle class is compared to a Western conception of the middle class that is already in existence. In other words, the comparison measures the Brazilian middle class against a normative idea of the middle class that operates in the form of fixed, dominant models in the West; see also Chakrabarty 2000.

38. For a critical discussion see David Martin Jones 1998; he notes that such assumptions also characterize later works that assume the middle class will serve as a key actor in the transition from authoritarianism to democracy (see Przeworski 1992).

39. For instance, such arguments have been made with regard to the Asian middle class. David Martin Jones has argued that Pacific Asia has been characterized by an "illiberal political culture" that is not suitable for the emergence of autonomous civil society. In the Latin American context, Owensby (1999) argues that "when military regimes, often with broad middle class support or acquiescence, suspended democratic governments, starting with Brazil in 1964, many scholars lost faith in the prospects of Latin America's modernization and concluded that the middle classes could not advance the region's development." As he goes on to note, scholars thus either turned away from the study of the middle class or concluded that Latin America's cultural distinctiveness precluded a middle class (6).

40. Such rhetoric intensified during the 2004 elections, but it is not limited to politician's speeches. For example, see "Exporting America," the ongoing series on CNN's *Lou Dobbs Tonight*, which has routinely attacked the outsourcing of jobs with particular references to India. For a different view that nevertheless romanticizes the Indian middle class see Friedman 2005. For a perspective on the anxieties of the decline of the American middle class see Krugman 2002.

41. See for example Burawoy and Verdery 1999; Gills and Piper 2002; and Ong, 1988. For work that does deal with gender and internal differentiation see Wilson 2004.

42. See the critical development studies literature; e.g., Escobar 1994.

43. Such analyses have tended to be driven by a lens that sometimes misses the layered and internally differentiated social structures within national contexts that shape political responses to economic reforms. See Bhagwati 2004a for a similar criticism.

44. For an insightful analysis of the relationship between the state and the rural middle class in comparative perspective see Davis 2004; for earlier debates on the relationship between class and the state in India see Bardhan 1998; Rudolph and Rudolph 1987; and Rudra 1989.

45. See for example Glenn's discussion (2002) of the ways in which everyday social practices have historically determined whether people have or don't have substantive, as opposed to formal, citizenship rights (2).

46. Recent anthropological work drawing on Bourdieu has tended to underplay the centrality of structure in his conception of practices and distinction. A central theoretical argument in this book is that an analysis of the interaction between structure and discourse is central for any understanding of class formation. See also Katznelson 1986 for a parallel view of such a layered conceptualization of class. Bourdieu's analysis of social capital differs from Robert Putnam's study of social capital (1993, 2000). For a useful critical discussion of Putnam that draws on Bourdieu's work see Callahan 2005.

47. Bourdieu (1984) terms these "structuring structures."

48. For structural theories of the middle classes see Urry 1971 and Wright 1978, 1997.

49. Bourdieu's work has thus often been adapted in a culturalist frame, drawing on his notion of distinction. See Liechty 2003 and Mazzarella 2003.

50. The postcolonial and subaltern studies' theoretical turn in studies of South Asia has tended to foreclose an understanding of the significance of structure. I discuss this in greater length in chapter 5.

51. See Chatterjee 1993 on historical salience of difference in the formulation of postcolonial nationalisms.

52. The new middle class is a theoretical concept that is not reducible to an economistic category of class; rather it is produced through the material and symbolic intersections between class, gender, caste, and religion. For a discussion of the concept of intersectionality see Barad 2001 and Crenshaw 1994. On the making of class see Thompson (1966); for a lengthier discussion of class and intersectionality see Fernandes 1997.

53. This tension is often missed by the conflation of the middle classes with a homogeneized notion of "elites"; thus contemporary discussions of the Indian middle class often refer to the upper tier of the middle class that has laid claim to the dominant identity of the new middle class (see Chatterjee 2004).

54. Such approaches tend to break down in line with trends in social theory, drawing on: (1) Weberian conceptions of income and occupation, (2) neo-Marxist and historical–sociological structural mappings of the middle class, (3) culturalist and anthropological theories, and (4) interdisciplinary postcolonial and cultural theories of the middle classes. There is, of course, overlap between these approaches in the existing scholarship.

55. There is a vast cross-disciplinary literature on the making of class. For the classic formulation see Thompson 1966.

56. This moves away from an assumption that only strict causal arguments can provide explanations of broader political outcomes. Such a genealogical approach calls for an understanding of some of the fruitful connections between Focaultian and Weberian approaches to the social sciences. For a discussion of these possibilities see Rudolph 1995.

57. This rejection has missed philosophical and theoretical debates that have moved beyond polarized dichotomies between categories such as structure/discourse; culture/economy; epistemology/ontology.

58. While scholarship using such an approach has grown in political science it has not tended to shape the field of political economy.

59. Postcolonial approaches to South Asian studies that reject such discussions as a "functionalist" or "modular" social science approach to culture foreclose our theoretical and empirical understanding of how inequality works. See also McCall 2005 on the tensions between interdisciplinary feminist research and feminist social science scholarship on inequality.

60. This research was conducted over three periods: preliminary research in 1996, an extensive research period in 1998–99, and a shorter period updating the research in 2003. Mumbai provides an important site for analysis as it is a critical center of media and public cultural activity and is also located in Maharashtra, a state that has been both at the forefront in the implementation of national policies of economic liberalization and has also been characterized by a large and expanding services sector—the key sector of new-economy job growth.

61. See also, for example, renewed interest in contemporary city-based studies formalized in intellectual work such as the Mumbai Studies project and Sarai 2002. In my view, the globalization-based approach to cities tends to underestimate the significance of the nation-state in understanding developmental politics. For example, Saskia Sassen, whose work on global cities (1991) has shaped the research agendas on cities and globalization, has argued for more precise analyses that take into account the role of the state and the "embeddedness of much of globalization in national territory" (Sassen 2002, 91).

62. For example resistances from Hindi-speaking middle classes challenge the cultural-political primacy of the new middle class. See Hasan 1998 (136) for discussions on such dynamics in the northern Indian state of Uttar Pradesh. Despite the lack of explicit research on the middle class, the secondary source literature is ripe with data on the Indian middle class. Literature on colonial history, the nationalist movement, Hindu nationalism, and democratic politics also provide analyses and data on the middle class.

63. In keeping with standard ethnographic practice all individuals are kept anonymous or given pseudonyms throughout the book.

1. The Historical Roots of the New Middle Class

1. In keeping with its usage in cultural theory, I use the term "liminal" to denote the sense of the middle class being located in a shifting and indeterminate sociocultural space that lies between elite and subaltern groups.

2. Thomas Macauley was a colonial administrator who served on the Supreme Council of India from 1835–38. He advocated English-only education in India. The quote is taken from his well-known *Minute on Indian Education* (1835). See H. Sharp, *Selections from the Educational Records, pt I, 1781–1839*, p. 116, cited in Misra 1961, 11.

3. See Misra 1961 for a detailed discussion of various segments of the middle class (which he classifies as industrial, commercial, landed, and educational).

4. The Bombay, Madras, and Bengal Presidencies were colonial administrative units that the British developed from the East India Company's trading posts.

5. For discussions of education and Indian elites during the colonial period see Lelyveld 1978 and Srivastava 1998.

6. For an in-depth discussion of the production of English as a category see Sangari 2001.

7. The Indian Civil Service was the bureaucratic/administrative arm of the British colonial state.

8. There is a long history in Britain that resulted in the linkage between conceptions of respectability and class formation. See Skeggs 1997.

9. Note also that the urban colonial middle class was also often tied to rural relations of landownership. For instance, Misra (1961) has analyzed the growth of middle class landed interests in light of the Permanent Settlement (133). Furthermore, as Sangari (2001) has noted, the class of landed rentiers included less-affluent groups such as small traders, clerks, teachers, and artisans (101), the lower tiers of the colonial middle class.

10. In colonial Lucknow, Joshi (2001) notes that the middle classes were comprised of Ashrafs, Kayasthas, Brahmins, Kathris, and Banias (7). ICS recruits were mainly from Brahmin and Kayasth backgrounds (see Potter 1996, 118).

11. Elphinstone school was the first significant English school (founded in 1825) and the first college classes were organized in 1827 as Elphinstone College (see Dobbin 1972, 27).

12. However, as she notes, an exception to this pattern is in the Northwest Province, Awadh and Delhi Zone (193). For an overview see also Hardy 1972; Hasan 1997; Robinson 1974.

13. See also the growing religious polarization of the middle class in terms of the Hindu–Urdu question in the early twentieth century. Language

was a primary resource for the middle class, particularly in government service. See Joshi 2001, 137.

14. As I noted in the Introduction, this structural dimension of identity and group formation has been elided in postcolonial theories and studies of South Asia. In contrast to postcolonial assumptions that discussions of structure are inevitably unitary, teleological, or deterministic, there is a vast interdisciplinary research on intersectionality and on reconceptions of materiality and critical realism.

15. For a useful discussion of Macauley see Sangari 2001, 146–47.

16. See also Chatterjee 1993, chapter 3.

17. For a contrasting view see Chatterjee 1993, where he argues that the specificities of colonial rule prevented the emergence of a bourgeois public sphere as the bourgeoisie was unable to establish itself within civil society.

18. For a discussion on secular universalism and cultural differentiation see Sangari 2001, 134.

19. There is of course a vast literature on gender and the social reform debates of the nineteenth century. For instance, gendered roles became a primary site in the well-studied public social reform debates on women's education, dowry, widow remarriage, and sati (see Mani 1998; Oldenberg 2002; Sangari 2001).

20. For example, women's education was designed to improve their domestic roles thus preserving their location within the household rather than providing entry to activities in the public sphere. Note, however, that women were nevertheless able to subvert such expectation and assert their own agency (see Sarkar 2001).

21. See Chatterjee 1993 and Sarkar 2001.

22. See Chatterjee 1993, chapter 3.

23. For an alternative view see Chatterjee 1990.

24. Thus, Haynes notes that by the second half of the nineteenth century, urban centers had become increasingly important for the financial interests of the colonial state. This interest led to the rise of local municipalities that could develop civic services in urban areas (Haynes 1991, 111–15). See also Haynes 1991, chapter 8, for an extensive discussion of the political consolidation of the English-educated elite in Surat.

25. See Gooptu 2001 for a discussion on town planning in northern India.

26. See Kaviraj 1997; see Chakrabarty 1991 on public space and middle class reformism.

27. See Gooptu 2001; see also Haynes 1991 on the spatialized politics of cities in colonial India.

28. An extensive discussion of the nationalist movement is beyond the scope of this chapter.

29. See Gooptu 2001 and Jaffrelot 2005 on Ambedkar's critiques of Gandhi's approach to caste.

30. For a discussion of the distinctive subaltern appropriations and subversions of Gandhian nationalism see Amin 1995.

31. This was linked to Nehru's nostalgic image of the rural "masses" in India. Thus Nehru goes on to say, "I found in India's countryfolk something difficult to define, which attracted me. That something I had missed in our own middle classes" (1998 [1946], 57).

32. See also the important discussions of how Indian secularism becomes defined through the intersections of religious and gender identity in Menon and Bhasin 1998.

33. See Deshpande 2003 on the middle class and state-led development.

34. For instance, Vivek Chibber (2003) has argued that Indian industrialization was shaped primarily by a relationship between the state and domestic capitalists. Kohli (2004), on the other hand, has argued that the tensions and fissures associated with India's multiclass fragmented state shaped the direction of state-led development in India.

35. See for example Pranab Bardhan's (1998) discussion of professional and white-collar workers as one of the role of dominant propriety classes, which has had a relationship with state networks of patronage and subsidies.

36. On Nehruvian visions of India see Kaviraj 1991; Khilnani 1997.

37. This process was certainly contested by different visions of the Indian nation (for instance by Gandhians and communist parties, as well as by an array of social movements and protest politics). My point here is not to suggest a sense of historical inevitability but to provide an overview of the role of the middle class in the model of development that did become hegemonic.

38. See Kapur and Mehta 2004 for a discussion of trends leading to a proportional decline in education funding. I return to this point and a discussion of more recent trends in chapter 3.

39. Note that state governments are responsible for education and played a central role in this process.

40. As David Potter notes, there was significant opposition to maintaining this structure as many Congress leaders viewed the ICS as an embodiment of colonial domination. However, Vallabhai Patel's strong support of the ICS was successful in overcoming this opposition; see Potter 1996, 125, 148.

41. As Potter (1996) notes, until the 1970s, English was the only language used for IAS examinations. The decline from 94 percent to 71 percent indicates there was a shift in the social composition. The state did make some efforts in this regard through reservations for scheduled castes and tribes. However, the upper-tier English-educated middle classes continued to dominate in recruitment (232).

42. See also Kohli 2004, 266–68 for a discussion of bureaucratic and state-led development in India. As Kohli notes in his discussion of the steel industry, this process of politicization was exacerbated in later years under Indira Gandhi's regime as the IAS became increasingly politicized and IAS generalist bureaucrats intervened in economic and technocratic decision-making processes.

43. This has been missed in scholarship that has tended to focus mainly on questions of subsidies and welfare to poorer or more marginalized social groups. Potter (1996) notes that by 1983, 13 percent of IAS recruits were working in the public sector of the economy (214).

44. For discussions of the continuation of this relationship even within the context of current policies of liberalization see Bardhan 2001; Sridharan 1999.

45. Such processes often led to alliances with segments of organized labor in ways that would shape broader political outcomes. For example, Ranajit Dasgupta (n.d.) argues that one significant factor in understanding the strength of the Left political parties in West Bengal in contrast to Maharashtra lies in the production of a sociopolitical context in West Bengal which emphasized the connection of interests between the middle and working classes. He notes that, "The large scale entry of the Bengali white collar workers such as bank and insurance employees, government servants and even teachers coming from the *bhadralok* or upper-caste educated middle class background in the 1950s contributed to the widening and deepening of this impact. Relevantly, it needs to be noted that the Left including the Communists have generally functioned on the basis of some sort of similarity of interests between the urban middle class and white collar and at times even blue collar workers, particularly the Bengali component of the working class, and around common issues and demands. The numerous struggles around the issues of unionisation, job security and retrenchment, bonus and so on in the mills and factories, banks and mercantile offices reflected this commonality of interests, and often struck a sympathetic chord among broad sections of the urban Bengali middle class" (6).

This articulation of a commonality of interests was reinforced by a politics of ethnicity. The fact that the major owners of capital were from non-Bengali (primarily Marwari) communities meant, as Dasgupta suggests, that "in many of the conflicts between employers and labour, sympathy of the Bengali urban middle class lay with the labour" (5).

46. For a discussion of some of the uneven economic consequences for different segments of state employees see Rudolph 1987, 264.

47. See Migdal 2001 for a useful theoretical conceptualization of the state as simultaneously an autonomous entity and a set of practices within civil society.

48. Maharashtrians were underrepresented in a large cross-section of industries but the proportion of Gujaratis was higher than South Indians, the group targeted by the Shiv Sena. For historical background see Lele 1981.

49. See Katzenstein 1979, chapter 6.

50. Note that the casting of this demand in terms of a language-based identity (Marathi speakers) demonstrates the ways in which class identity is constructed through cultural identities such as caste, religion, ethnicity, and language.

51. See Gupta 1982 and Hansen 2001 on this point.

52. Hansen (2001) notes that the Shiv Sena has been careful not to alienate the middle class on such issues even as it has expanded its base among the poor and working class communities. I return to these issues in greater depth in chapters 4 and 5.

53. Note for example the importance of local municipal issues and municipal elections in the Shiv Sena's rise to power.

54. Such patterns are not peculiar to India but can also be seen in comparative contexts; e.g., Goheen 2003; Ryan 1998.

55. For discussion of this period see Tarlo 2003 and Visvanathan and Sethi 1998.

2. Framing the Liberalizing Middle Class

1. Interview with author, September 17, 1998.

2. Examples of shifts in cinematic representations include the fact that new genres often do not present outdoor street scenes of public spaces (the terrain of action is the domestic space of the middle class household, place of employment and space of travel), or include images of poor and working class individuals. A classic example is the hit film *Dilwale Dulhania Le Jayenge*. On popular culture and the middle classes in India see Dwyer 2000.

3. For a theoretical critique of cartesian models of identity see Barad 2001.

4. I distinguish between symbolic and material realms for the purpose of analytical clarity; my objective, however, is to demonstrate the interaction between these realms and to move away from the treatment of symbolic realms as epiphenomenal.

5. For example, there are often vernacular resistances to this model of new middle class identity expressed through *swadeshi* (the manufacture and consumption of goods that are made in India, first popularized by Gandhi during the colonial period) movements, middle class moralism, and progressive secular critiques by NGOs. Van Wessel (2004) has an interesting discussion on middle class discourses in Gujarat that express a moral ambivalence to modern consumption and materialism. However, her analysis misses the theoretical distinction between dominant constructions of new

middle class identity and local responses and expressions of middle class identity that contest this dominant identity. Thus, she mistakenly assumes vernacular expressions and contestations are evidence of the irrelevance of dominant discourses.

6. See for example Partha Chatterjee's (1990) discussion of middle class identity and its negotiation between an inner spiritual-cultural national identity and the external material identity of the West during the colonial period. See also Sumit Sarkar's (1992) in-depth discussion of middle class religiosity in the making of middle class identity and Tanika Sarkar's (2001) discussion of lower middle class and vernacular realms that contest these dominant constructions in the colonial period. See my discussion in chapter 1 for an analysis of historical parallels.

7. See for example Anne Norton's discussion of culture and politics (2004).

8. There is a rich scholarship in this field. See for example Abu-Lughod 1993, 2005; McClintock 1995; and Williamson 1994, among many others. On the intellectual differences between the study of political culture in political science and the study of culture in political anthropology see Aronoff and Kubik, forthcoming.

9. On languages of class see Scott 1988; Sewell 1980; Stedman Jones 1984.

10. Cited in Ninan 1985. Gandhi's vision for village development was influenced by this middle class orientation toward high technology, encapsulated in the slogan "A computer for every village."

11. Thus, my discussion of the Nehruvian state-managed middle class does not seek to set up a polarized contrast between pre- and postliberalization state–class relationship. Rather, my point is to outline such historical patterns in order to delineate the way in which the relationship between state and middle classes has been restructured. To prefigure my later arguments, the loosening of consumer controls represents a set of state policies that has opened up a new set of benefits for sections of the middle class. This is distinctive from the assumption that the state has merely been replaced by a market-oriented middle class.

12. "The New Maharajahs," *Sunday,* April 17–23, 1988, cited in Rudolph 1989, 2, footnote 1. See Rudolph 1989 for a useful discussion of the growing middle class disillusionment with Rajiv Gandhi in the midst of corruption scandals and domestic political turmoil.

13. My argument is not, of course, that the middle class did not hold significant political power both during the nationalist movement and during the early decades of independence. Rather, such changes are emblematic of a shift in the dominant model of national development (and the corresponding change in the relationship between this model and the role of the middle class). For an interesting discussion of representations of the Indian economy in postage stamps in the Nehruvian era see Wyatt 2005, 7.

14. The newness of this stems from the fact that this represented a change from an earlier dependence of the middle classes on the state, for example for employment (see chapter 1).

15. Ninan 1990, 44; see also Kohli's (1989) argument that this could serve as mass basis for support of reforms.

16. Thus there are frequent profiles of new entrepreneurs and successful businessmen in the media. See for example various issues of *India Today,* and Maakan and Jetley 1998.

17. See Iyengar 1999; Rudolph and Rudolph 2001.

18. On the role of state governments in promoting economic reforms see Sinha 2004.

19. This image would also be continually contrasted with satirical disdain for "rustic" figures such as Laloo Prasad Yadav, Bihar's most visible political figure and former chief minister, who for the urban middle class is a classic emblem of cultural and economic backwardness and of the politics of votebanks (the term in Indian politics for special interests that serve as electoral bases for political parties) for lower/backward caste groups.

20. Such visual signs of wealth represent the new symbols of national progress in India.

21. Interview with author, January 16, 1999.

22. By technologies of vision I am referring to visual media forms such as cable and satellite television, advertising images, and film. In state-owned television (Doordarshan) in 1992 four out of the top five advertisers were multinational corporations (accounting for 21 percent of total advertising revenue). However, the expenditure share of the advertising industry was still highest in the print media (67 percent for print media and 20 percent for television in 1992). See Bhatt 1994. In the decade since Rajiv Gandhi's early policies of liberalization, the number of television sets grew from 3.63 million in 1984 to 27.8 million at the end of 1990 (see Dubey 1992).

23. *Times of India,* January 6, 1998. While growth rates decreased to 8–9 percent by the late 1990s, the vice president of one leading advertising firm argued that such decreases should have been expected, as it was unreasonable to assume the industry could remain at levels of 40 percent growth (interview with author, September 2, 1998).

24. My aim is not to provide an intensive deconstruction of signification processes in each image and in relationship to consuming subjects (see Mazzarella 2003; Rajagopal 2001b for such an approach) but to point to the broad symbolic patterns that begin to constitute the visual terrain of national political culture in contemporary India.

25. Interview with author, September 2, 1998. See also Mazzarella 2003 for an in-depth discussion of Coca-Cola marketing strategies. Mazazarella provides an analysis of the professional requirements and industry practices that went into such marketing strategies. My concern in this analysis is to

speak to the broader patterns of national narratives produced through such strategies.

26. The use of Orientalist imagery depicts a wider pattern in cultural representation. See Juluri 2003.

27. For a discussion of the relationship between the media and the Hindutva movement see Rajagopal 2001a.

28. For a discussion of how such representations also intersect with religious nationalism see Rajagopal 2001b.

29. Such concerns are also reflected in a study sponsored by the Indian advertising industry in order to assess (and disprove) the potential negative effects of advertising. See National Council of Applied Economic Research, Indian Society of Advertisers, 1992.

30. Interview with author, August 29, 1998.

31. For an analysis of postnationalism see Appadurai 1996.

32. Note also that the Ambassador is a symbol of early protectionist economic policies as it was historically the main domestically produced automobile. Rajiv Gandhi's early liberalization policies enabled the production of a new multinational production of the Maruti automobile. The Maruti continues to serve as a cultural signifier of urban upper middle class consumer culture.

33. See also Mazzarella 2003 on the aestheticization of citizenship that occurs through such processes (99).

34. For a critique of assumptions that globalization leads to cultural homogeneity see Appadurai 1996.

35. Interview with author, September 17, 1998.

36. There is by now a vast literature that has sought to move beyond a conception of "tradition" and "modernity" as oppositional or dichotomous terms. See Prakash 1999; Rudolph and Rudolph 1967. Note also that such processes are not peculiar to the Indian case. Similar dynamics around the politics of race, ethnicity, and religion are characteristic of the politics of globalization in comparative contexts (see Gonzalez et al. 2003).

37. *Times of India* 1999.

38. Interview with author, October 1, 1998.

39. Interview with author, October 6, 1998.

40. Interview with author, September 3, 1998.

41. India is estimated to have 21 million cable TV connections a figure that does not take into account community-owned televisions, which are common in working class and rural areas.

42. Note also that Indian channels have been more successful than satellite channels that air mainly English language programs. The music channel V, which airs mainly Hindi songs has been more successful than MTV, leading MTV to Indianize (Agarwal 1996). Star TV has also shifted from primarily English programs to popular Hindi films.

43. Hybridity in this context does not transcend but is intricately connected to processes of capital formation within the boundaries of the modern nation-state. The presumed subversive potential of hybridity rests on the assumption that hybrid cultural forms are subversive because they disrupt territorial national boundaries (Bhabha 1994). Such an assumption does not interrogate the ideological and material conditions that constitute the production of hybridity. On the contrary, hybridity in contemporary urban India is inextricably linked to an exclusionary class-based cosmopolitanism of the urban middle class.

44. See also Raval and Thapa 1999.

45. This is not to imply that there are no indigenous linguistic terms for "middle class" (for example *maddho-britto* in Bengali or *madhyam-varga* in Hindi). Or for example, since the colonial period the term *bhadralok* in Bengal has operated with connotations of a sociocultural elite similar to the kind of new middle class identity I am discussing. However, the term is marked by an upper class connotation that is distinctive from middle class, which purports to symbolize a horizontal "representative" social group. To take another kind of example, in the case of Maharashtra, the Shiv Sena has also deployed language politics to articulate class identity in exclusionary ethnic-linguistic terms (for example by coding middle class identity through Marathi and constructing English-speaking South Indians as a threat to the Maharashtrian middle class). I am grateful to Sumit Guha for comments on this question of linguistic identity.

46. For example, there are strong differences between the English and vernacular public spheres. For a discussion of English and class formation see Ahmad 1994. For a discussion of vernacular versus English public spheres see Rajagopal 2001a.

47. See also Rajagopal 2001b, 79.

48. Advertisers also began to consciously focus on small towns, as they have proved to be easier to open up than rural markets (interview with advertising executive, September 3, 1998). For a humorous look at the effects in small towns see Mishra 1995. See also Traub 2001 and Vinayak 2002 for a discussion of Aurangabad.

49. This is also true of some upwardly mobile sections of the working class. See Mankekar 1999 for ethnographic examples of such overextension.

50. Note also the parallels with World Exhibits held during the colonial period. See Mitchell 1991b, 31.

51. See Rodrigues 1998 and Thakkar 1998. According to one estimate, by 2003, the Indian food sector was over Rs 40,000 crore (growing an average of 25 percent per year from 1998–2003) and 11 percent of discretionary spending of Indians went to eating out (Shastri 2003). Data are based on figures from the market research company KSA Technopak.

52. Shastri 2003.

53. See for example Baria 1999; Gupta 1998; and Khan 1998.

54. See Bidwai 2003. See also the BJP finance minister's argument that, "consumerism is the greatest 'evil' released by liberalisation," quoted in *Economic Times* 1998c.

55. In this study the income groups were classified as follows (annual income in rupees): low income < Rs 12,500; lower middle income Rs. 12,500–25000; middle and upper middle income Rs 25,000–56,000. See Rao 1994, 10.

56. The survey was based on interviews of 5,122 Indians over the age of eighteen years and involved in-depth interviews in 144 villages and eighty-four towns and cities. A separate study of the major metropolitan cities (Mumbai, Delhi, Madras, Calcutta, and Bangalore) was also conducted as part of this survey.

57. See Appadurai's (1993) discussion of enumeration and the census. For an alternative analysis see Guha 2003.

58. See Waldman 2003.

59. One report states, "Even for the super rich households in the country, buying a 29-inch TV that costs over Rs 1 lakh or drinking scotch remains a distant dream" (Gupta 1998).

60. Interview with author, October 6, 1998.

61. According to an ORG-MARG survey cited in Rao 2000, 3570.

62. Interview with author, September 11, 1998.

63. For an overview of problems with existing data see Deshpande 2003; for an analysis that attempts a quantitative measurement of the middle class based on occupation and income see E. Sridharan 2004.

64. There are of course regional, state, and rural-urban variations. For comprehensive data see NCAER 2002. My purpose at this stage is to provide an outline of the parameters of all-India measures of income and occupation for the middle class.

65. Thus, by the late 1990s the credit card business was growing at a rate of 25 to 30 percent a year (see Ray 1998). Generational differences in attitudes to money are also significant. See also Aiyar 1999 who estimated that there were more than 3.5 million card holders whose billing was in excess on Rs 9,000 crore.

66. For example a boom in consumption in 2002 was linked to falling prices, the expansion of service sector jobs (especially in relation to the outsourcing boom), consumer financing, and low interest rates (see Goyal 2003).

67. Interview with author, September 2, 1998.

68. Thanks to Peter De Souza for providing these political cartoons.

3. Social Capital, Labor Market Restructuring, and India's New Economy

1. See Chandrasekhar 2003, 128. For a general analysis of India's knowledge economy see Richter and Banerjee 2003. On the Indian software industry see D'Costa and Sridharan 2004. On Bangalore's "Silicon Valley" see Saxenian 2002.

2. See Aiyar 2003, 23. Note however that manufacturing has recently benefited from a boom in foreign investment (Jayakar 2005).

3. There has also been a shift in the social composition of the Indian Civil Service with an increase in rural and small town, middle class individuals joining the cadres. See Jung Thapa 2001.

4. See in a parallel shift the changing composition of the Indian civil service with declining urban and increasing rural composition described in Jung Thapa 2001.

5. Interview with author, October 15, 1998.

6. In this sense, the invention of the new Indian middle class corresponds to the older construction of the new middle class in advanced industrialized countries.

7. Such studies, as noted in the Introduction, tend to view the middle classes as beneficiaries of liberalization and as a homogeneous elite usually defined by consumption.

8. An exception to this is Sridharan 2004.

9. Even pro-reform institutions such as the World Bank have begun to address the negative socioeconomic effects of liberalization, and support social programs that can serve as a "safety net." On employment and liberalization see Dev 2000.

10. Ibid.

11. See also the rise of Indian executives in multinationals, the highest end of the corporate structure (David and Rohatgi 2003).

12. See for example Joshi and Chowdhury 1999.

13. In the late 1990s, starting salaries for MBAs ranged from Rs 6,000–8000 for an MBA graduate from an average institute but rose as high as Rs 10,000–15,000 for MBAs from highly ranked institutions such as Bajaj or the Indian Institute for Management (IIM). However, such scales fluctuated widely depending on the sector and type of company in question. Salaries have continued to rise since then, with one 2006 estimate that the country has had a record salary increase of 13.9 percent (Srivastava 2006). A corporate salary guide estimates that lower-level white-collar salaries range from Rs 10,000–25,000 per month, while managerial salaries range from Rs 40,000–100,000 per month (Kelly Services 2006).

14. Interview with author, September 28, 1998.

15. This sharp rise in such institutions has also prompted fears of illegal operations and false advertising. The All India Council for Technical Education, for instance, has advertised warnings to "MBA aspirants not to fall prey to fly-by-night B-schools which claim their diploma in management is equivalent to an MBA" (*Economic Times* 1999b).

16. Author's observation, August 23, 1998.

17. Interview with author, September 28, 1998.

18. See for example Wadhwa 2003, 56. For an analysis of higher education and reforms see Kapur and Mehta 2004.

19. Interview with author, August 24, 1998.

20. See Chatterjee 1998 and Kunwar 1998.

21. Interview with author, September 28, 1998.

22. For a comparative discussion of gender and restructuring see Bakker 1994.

23. Interview with author, September 28, 1998.

24. Systematic data on women's employment is difficult to obtain particularly for recent trends in the service and private sector. Deshpande and Deshpande (1992) argue that urban women were increasingly moving into self-employment and regular salaried work in the 1980s. Banerjee (2002, 58) notes that while overall patterns of women's employment have not changed significantly, sections of middle class women have been able to take advantage of education and training to gain access to employment in the professions, public services, and business. For a discussion of state policy and women's employment in Maharashtra see Gothoskar, Gandhi, and Shah 1994.

25. Interview with author, October 6, 1998.

26. Note that one of the few attempts to measure income levels of the Indian middle class was a 1994–95 NCAER study. According to published reports this study defined the "consuming class" as being in an annual income range of Rs 45,000—215,000 and estimated it at 28.6 million households (see Sen Gupta 1998). Note that this conceptualization corresponds to the boundaries of the new middle class I have examined. This monthly income range spans from Rs 3,750–17,916. Radha's income of Rs 30,000 per month would place her in the "new rich" category (Robison and Goodman 1996), or according to NCAER, the "very rich category" (with an annual income over Rs 215,000). However, the NCAER study is an all-India study of market demographics and does not qualify the boundaries of the "consuming class" in relation to specific cost of living factors such as the real estate market in metropolitan cities like Mumbai.

27. The fact that the high costs of merely renting an apartment is out of the reach of most single women employed in such positions begins to demonstrate the significant limitations to the idealized images of the new

middle class which I have described. As one woman who was employed as a secretary in a small private Indian firm and who was residing in a working women's hostel put it, "I want a house. More than being married first I want a house. In Bombay that's the main thing to have. I told you even if I save my whole lifetime I won't be able to afford a house." See chapter 4 for a discussion of this quote.

28. Thus the urban background (defined by the place of parents' residence) of entrants in the civil services declined from 32.2 percent in 1990 to 25 percent in 1997 (Jung Thapa 2001, 37). Myron Weiner (2001) has argued that the political rise of groups such as the backward castes has helped promote middle class segments through strategies such as civil service appointments but has not changed broader policies regarding health and education that would benefit the lower castes in general.

29. Sheth (1999a) argues that caste has moved away from a ritually based hierarchy to a "classisized" concept; i.e., a social distinction intersecting in unique ways with class inequalities and identities. For a critical response to Sheth see Natraj 1999.

30. Interview with vice president, All India Bank Employees Association, August 21, 1998. I interviewed union officials in the banking and insurance sectors—two of the major public-sector industries with strong white-collar unions facing economic restructuring.

31. Interview with author, August 21, 1998.

32. For other reports see also Jetley 1997 and *Times of India* 1998a.

33. Interview with author, October 10, 1998.

34. The financial sector was a key area that experienced an initial boom in white-collar salaries (see Somakhar 1995).

35. Interview with author, October 2, 1998.

36. Ibid.

37. Ibid.

38. Ibid.

39. Ibid.

40. Interview with author, September 28, 1998.

41. Note that this pattern has also characterized the urban middle class job market when there has been a boom in hiring. See for example trends in the 2005 job market described in Goyal 2005.

42. See Goyal 2004b.

43. Source of data is NASSCOM 2000 and Ministry of Finance cited in Saxenian 2002.

44. Consider the following description: "The bureaucracy's grip on the service sector is less stifling. . . . No wonder there is hope that services will breed a new class of entrepreneurs in India. A class that will be more competitive, more innovative and more global in outlook than some of the established industrialists" (Saran 2001, 34).

45. According to *Dataquest,* an information technology industry journal, cited in Chandrasekhar 2003.

46. According to one estimate, the outsourcing industry currently employed 200,000 people in 2004 (see Doshi and Ravindran 2004, 38). McMillin (2006) has noted new investment in the industry reached $800 million by the end of 2002 and the outsourcing market in India is expected to reach $20 billion by 2008, with the number of jobs estimated at 1.1 million (236).

47. See Rai 2003. Meanwhile, employment patterns of the call center industry also reflect the gendered and caste-based dynamics of the formations of the new middle class. Estimates suggest close to 50 percent of call center workers are women (Doshi and Ravindran 2004; McMillin 2006).

48. See Padmanabhan 2004a, 2004b.

49. See for example Bhaumik 2004. See also well-known pro-globalization economist Bhagwati 2004b.

50. Quoted in BBC News 2003.

51. This is of course in contrast to the unionized white-collar workers in the public sector.

52. Interview with author, January 25, 1999.

53. Interview with author, September 25, 1998.

54. Interview with author, January 25, 1999.

55. There are some instances of more organized activity. For instance, officer associations have been on the rise in the pharmaceutical company Bayer India. This association has mobilized junior managers and supervisors to gain better wage deals and bonuses, but has not engaged in anti-reform activities similar to those in public-sector unions. See *Economic Times* 1998a and 1998b.

56. Interview with author, January 23, 1999.

57. The extent of the appeal of such informal strategies is marked by the Indian government's decision to monitor the activities of direct marketing companies such as Amway (*Economic Times* 1999a).

58. This is not unique to the Indian context. See for example Wilson 2004 for a discussion of Amway in Thailand.

59. In contrast, migration to advanced industrialized countries tends to be a longer-term strategy that often requires a higher investment of personal or family resources.

60. Such disparities include regional, rural–urban, and socioeconomic (such as income) differences.

61. Kapur and Mehta (2004) estimate that there are about 110,000 Indian students studying abroad (75,000 in the United States, about 14,000 each in the United Kingdom and Australia, and 5,000 in Canada and New Zealand) (8).

62. For an interesting discussion of changing gendered and household strategies of middle class families in Calcutta see Donner 2005.

63. See for example 1998 estimates that for high school admissions such "donations" ranged from Rs 5,000–25,000 and for elementary school from Rs 3,500—5,000 (Pawar 1998); for similar estimates see also Deshmukh 1998b.

64. This would suggest that caste would also be a significant factor in shaping such networks. While I was not able to find systematic data on caste and access to health care, my research suggests the need for further examination of such relations.

4. State Power, Urban Space, and Civic Life

1. Such uncertainties represent a broader trend that characterized the Asian middle classes, particularly in the period after the Asian economic crisis (see Beng-Huat 2000).

2. Space in this context is not merely an empty physical container but a material-discursive embodiment of social relations. There is a vast literature that has theorized this sociality of space; e.g., de Certeau 2002; Harvey 2001; Lefebvre 1991; Massey 1994.

3. Such dynamics can also be seen in advanced industrialized countries. For historical examples, see Goheen 2003 and Ryan 1998.

4. This entails a move away from an analysis that juxtaposes the generalized claims and rights of citizenship with "ascriptive" social and cultural identities. See Smith 1997 for a view that adheres to such a juxtaposition.

5. In contrast to approaches that assume that policies of economic liberalization are associated with a retreat of the state, I point instead to an approach that focuses on the restructuring of the state. Thus, while India's policies of economic liberalization have led to the retreat of the state in some areas of the economy, the state continues to play an important role in the management of liberalization.

6. See for example Chhibber and Eldersveld 2000; Przeworski 1996; Stokes 1996. On the significance of organizational mechanisms see Haggard and Kaufman 1995. For a discussion of individual cognitive-psychological factors see Weyland 2003.

7. Note such an analysis does not treat "culture" in functionalist terms or as an epiphenomenal reflection of structure. Rather my aim is to demonstrate that cultural practices (such as those coded as "lifestyle" are systematically related to processes of economic restructuring. The significance of this systematic relationship is underplayed in approaches that view cultural practices as purely subjective processes or as solely shaped by the contingencies of daily life. See chapter 5 for a further discussion of such theoretical questions. A postcolonial studies approach or narrowly culturalist approach that engages in an unreflective rejection of structural analysis as necessarily

modular or functionalist fundamentally missed the political significance of the linkages, tensions, and interactions between cultural practices and processes of restructuring. As I note in chapter 5, fields such as postcolonial studies have not benefited (and in many cases have not been open to) the insights of social science paradigms that have sought in nuanced ways to theorize structure—a theoretical project that is crucial in analyzing the reproduction of socioeconomic inequalities.

8. Thus, analysts noted that in the midst of an economic recession in 1998, the leisure and entertainment industry continued to demonstrate strong growth (see Jetley 1998).

9. One only has to follow the lifestyle section of the news magazine *India Today* to gain a glimpse of the social construction of elite lifestyle practices. The magazine has covered activities as varying as bar cultures, horseback riding, cosmetic surgery, diet and weight loss, fashion, and tourism.

10. See Conlon 1995 for a historical perspective on the emergence of restaurant culture in Mumbai.

11. Metal plates that have culturally specific associations compared to Westernized dinner plates.

12. Interview with author, September 3, 1998.

13. Anthropological research has tended to neglect the structural dimensions of such changes, partly because of the narrow culturalist readings of Bourdieu's original work on the production of lifestyle, distinction, and taste. Bourdieu's work has consistently bridged both the symbolic and structural realms of analysis. For a more accurate reading of Bourdieu see Wacquant 1991.

14. The western side of the suburbs (for instance Andheri west or Santa Cruz east) tend to be considered the upscale side while the eastern side tend to house working and lower middle class neighborhoods (for instance Andheri east or Santa Cruz east).

15. See Seabrook 1996 for a discussion of urban space and poverty in the developing world.

16. See for example Evans 2002 for empirical examples in Asia and Latin America.

17. *Bombay Times* 1999.

18. *Bombay Times* 1998a and *Times of India* 1998b. In this context, the spatial manifestation of cultural purity is not simply a class-based project aimed at cleansing the public of its poor and homeless, but also one that reproduces strict gendered ideologies with the objective of purging the public sphere of state defined elements of "sexual deviance."

19. See *Bombay Times* 1998a.

20. For comparative discussions on civil society see Bermeo and Nord 2000.

21. The Bombay Hawkers Union is estimated to represent 120,000 hawkers (Dixit 1998). Bal Thackeray opposed the BMC's plan and some Shiv Sena leaders were said to have been concerned that the anti-hawker drive would produce Sena losses in local assembly elections (*Times of India* 1998c).

22. See Harriss 2005 for a discussion of the ways in which associational life in Delhi has been dominated by middle class activism.

23. See Heitzman 1999. For a broader discussion of civic life in Bangalore see Srinivas 2001.

24. Scholars have debated the impact of West Bengal's rural reforms. While some scholars have pointed to its benefits (Kohli 1989) others have argued that it consolidated the CPM's political base (the middle peasantry) and failed to help landless and most marginalized groups (Mallick 1993).

25. See Roy 2003 for a detailed and insightful analysis of the Left Front government and urban development.

26. See Jayal 2001 for an analysis of different visions of the state that emerged in 1990s political discourses. See also Sengupta's (2001) discussion of the ways in which the rhetoric of liberalization coexists with but has not displaced models of state-aided development in Orissa.

27. For an analysis on the decline of the state see Strange 1996. Feminist scholarship has also tended to reproduce this thesis of the declining state by focusing exclusively on the decline of government supports for welfare (see Bakker 1994). On the significance of understanding the role of the state in shaping development paths see Kohli 2004. Despite the proliferation of studies that have drawn on a global city approach and treated as autonomous units of analysis that are not constrained by the nation-state, Sassen (2002) argues for an understanding of a broader set of kinds of state participation, rather than a thesis that posits the decline of the state (96.)

28. This is both a legal and a sociocultural category. NRIs get specific financial and legal benefits designed to attract investment. The term also has broader sociocultural implications—provoking responses as varied as satirical derision of wealthy NRIs to long-distance nationalist forms of identification of the Indian diaspora.

29. Devidayal 1998a. Note that these patterns are replicated in comparative contexts in Asia (see Bhowmick 2005).

30. There is a long history to such practices extending back to some of India's oldest industries, such as the jute industry. Industrialists have generally used factory lockouts and large casual labor forces to conduct retrenchment.

31. On such internal contradictions within the modern state see Migdal 2001.

32. These processes have broader comparative implications. Timothy Mitchell (2002) has analyzed similar overlapping zones between the state and private sector in Egypt (233). See also Kirin Aziz Chaudhry's (1994) argument that the state ultimately determines reform outcomes.

33. I draw here on a large feminist scholarship on the intersectional nature of identity, e.g., Crenshaw 1994.

34. Such gendered effects are not of course unitary. New television shows, for instance, also produce middle class spaces for the discussion of issues of gender and sexuality. My point here is to analyze the ways in which a politics of purity is serving a critical site for the management of the disjunctures of globalization.

35. Note that the law only applied to the service industry. The Maharashtra Bar and Restaurant Ladies' Employees' Union organized the march. According to one estimate, 500 bars in the Mumbai area employed over 30,000 waitresses (see Akthar 1995). The restrictions were eventually withdrawn.

36. The Shiv Sena represents a Maharashtrian party that has been known for its conservative regional nativism and has been a long-standing political ally of the BJP in national and state-level politics. For a discussion of the Shiv Sena see Lele 1995.

37. The shows include women dancing to the latest popular Hindi film songs but do not, in general, involve any form of public nudity.

38. In addition, the morality drive required restaurants to close at 12:30 PM. Note, however, that five-star hotels catering to transnational businessmen were exempted from this legislation.

39. The election results failed to produce a clear parliamentary victory for the leading national political parties and the president asked the Bharatiya Janata Party, the single largest party in parliament to form a government and prove its majority in parliament within two weeks. The BJP led government failed to gain enough allies to prove a majority and the government only lasted twelve days. However, the next national election returned the BJP to power as the leading party of a new coalition government. Limits of space prevent a full discussion of the role of communalism and Hindutva. For a discussion of the relationship between the media and the Hindutva movement see Rajagopal, 2001a.

40. This has also characterized the new BJP-led government. While the BJP continues to espouse a policy of *swadeshi,* the government has also made assurances that foreign investors will not be affected. Note also that the Hindutva movement in general and the BJP party are not a homogeneous unit and are comprised of both pro- and anti-economic reform wings.

41. See Kapur and Cossman 1996, 253, for an analysis of the legal ramifications of this trend.

42. See Oza 2001 for an analysis of these dynamics.

43. Note in contrast, the Shiv Sena sponsored a highly publicized Michael Jackson concert. A "Western" cultural event that did not threaten hegemonic gender codes was clearly acceptable to the Shiv Sena's code of "cultural" and "national purity."

44. Similar discourses operate in relation to women employed in factories (Fernandes 1997).

45. Thus, for instance, during the course of my fieldwork much public attention was focused on the rising price of vegetables, in particular of onions, a
staple for both working and middle class families. Note also that pressures of
higher consumption expectations have also affected dowry standards as
dowry demands on middle class families now include newly available consumer goods such as washing machines or color televisions (see Kumar 1993).

46. See Chopra and Raval 2000.

47. A majority of middle class women rely on domestic workers to facili-
tate their own dual forms of labor. Thus, the employment of middle class
women and relative privilege of the middle class becomes structurally determined by the class and gender inequalities of primarily female domestic
workers. The gendered boundaries of middle class women's patterns of work
and family life are thus produced through a politics of class inequality structured through this relationship with working class women.

48. Interview with author, August 26, 1998.

49. While there have been changes in such gendered codes in larger metropolitan cities, such prejudices still affect working women.

50. Interview with author, November 14, 1998.

51. Interview with author, October 5, 1998.

52. See Poggendorf-Kakar 2001.

53. For a more general discussion of the Hindu nationalist use of spatial
strategies see Deshpande 1998.

54. The Shiv Sena's originally focused, when it emerged in the 1960s, on a
nativist agenda that campaigned for the exclusion of migrants, particularly
South Indians from Mumbai. It later shifted toward an anti-Muslim Hindu
nationalist agenda. The current attacks on Bangladeshi immigrants bring together both forms of exclusion as it is based on both ethnicity and religion.
Note that while the Shiv Sena lost power in the state government it dominates
the BMC and also wields considerable power in local communities through
grassroots political networks as well as through the use of coercive methods.

5. Liberalization, Democracy, and Middle Class Politics

1. At one level, this has occurred through an extension of late-twentieth-
century patterns of middle class protest politics that have been based on
caste and religion. The political impetus of such claims rests on a slippage
between the new middle class on the one hand and generalized discourses
on the middle classes and the national public interest on the other. This slippage rests on the exclusion of marginalized social groups.

2. The 1980 Mandal Commission report documented systemic caste-based
social discrimination and recommended governmental caste-based reserva-

tions for other backward castes (OBC). The report recommended the reservation of 27 percent of educational seats and government jobs for this group. The recommendations became a major national political issue when Prime Minister V. P. Singh indicated that he intended to implement the recommendations in 1990. The result was a strong upper-caste, middle class backlash. See Corbridge and Harriss 2000; Hansen 1999; Hasan 1998; Jaffrelot 2000; and Jeffry and Basu 1997. Note that the question of caste reservations has once again become a significant political issue (see Yadav and Deshpande 2006).

3. See, for example, Corbridge and Harriss 2000; Hansen 1999; Hasan 1998; Jaffrelot 1996.

4. On caste-based politics see K. Chandra 2004 and Hasan 1998.

5. See Hansen 1999 and Jaffrelot 2000.

6. An elderly Muslim woman, Shah Bano, sued her former husband for financial support. She pursued the case through the court system and was finally successful when the Supreme Court ruled in her favor. Rajiv Gandhi overruled the Court's decision in order to assuage conservative Muslim women.

7. For a discussion of the Shah Bano case see Hasan 1998. For a general discussion of gender and citizenship in India see Rajan 2003.

8. Mandir (temple) here refers to the well-known Hindu nationalist mobilization aimed at building a temple in the place of a mosque (the Babri Masjid); the mosque was eventually destroyed by militant Hindu nationalist activists but the conflict has not been resolved.

9. Interview with author, September 10, 1998.

10. The notion of votebank politics is used in contemporary Indian political discourse (in the English public sphere) to imply that political parties and the state have been captured by particular social groups (generally subaltern groups such as Muslims, backward castes, and the poor).

11. According to Jaffrelot (2000), voting levels are higher for those who are very poor, scheduled castes, and villagers. Voting levels are lower than average for upper castes, urban dwellers, and those with higher education (378) (data is based on CSDS survey research).

12. For discussions of civil society see Bermeo and Nord 2000.

13. The NDA refers to the BJP-led coalition of parties and Sonia Shining refers to Sonia Gandhi, leader of the Congress party.

14. Interview with Nirvik Singh, CEO, Grey Worldwide, on Indiantelevision.com, by Sonali Krishna, July 20, 2004.

15. The ad was aired 9,472 times (B. Chandra 2004).

16. Ibid.

17. Interview with Singh by Sonali Krishna (2004, p8)

18. Kumar and Bhattacharya 2004. Estimates for the campaign have ranged from 100–150 crores. The campaign ads were later banned by the Election Commission (*The Telegraph* 2004).

19. See also Harriss 2005 for a discussion of the ways in which associational activity has represented a primary arena for middle class activism in New Delhi; see Mawdsley 2004 for an overview of middle class attitudes toward environmentalism.

20. Such processes provide important implications for debates on the relationship between democratic and economic transitions. While most scholarship has sought to assess this relationship based on electoral considerations (that is, whether voters will reject reforms in democratic polities), my analysis suggests that nonelectoral democratic politics and mechanisms of accessing state power are equally important in shaping this relationship. As we have seen, the new middle class has been able to engage in a reshaping of the terms of democracy and in the production of a political culture in support of liberalization through a range of nonelectoral practices. The significance of these processes is underlined by ways in which they may successfully produce a more lasting distinction between the realms of electoral politics and policy formation.

21. For a cogent critique of the myth of middle class capture in higher education see Kapur and Mehta 2004.

22. Movements that target migrants from other states within India and press for rights that favor "native inhabitants"; that is, people born in and of the same ethnic origin of inhabitants of particular states.

23. In some areas in cities such as Delhi and Chandigarh, prices were reported to have reached as high as Rs 60–65 per kg.

24. Deb 1998a, 56. According to one report, as late as November 1998 in Delhi imports outstripped demand yet hoarding kept prices high at Rs 40–50 per kg (Purie 1998). See also Rekhi and Singh 1998.

25. For an analysis of this movement see Gandhi 1996.

26. Interview with author, November 18, 1998.

27. Some speeches at the rally also interpreted the rising prices as a direct effect of liberalization; as one speaker put it, "the problem is that they are sending onions out of the country—to foreign countries—so nothing is left for us here" (Author's observation, November 12, 1998).

28. The estimate is based on exit polling by the "C-Voter" exit poll (*Times of India* 1998d).

29. This is not to say that there are no cross-class alliances or attempts of middle class organizations that produce a different vision of democratic citizenship. See for example a long history of women's activism and the rise of NGOs. In this work I am outlining dominant trends. Furthermore, NGOs often fit within—rather than contest—the trend toward the privatization of state responsibilities (see chapter 4).

30. Interview with author, September 19, 1998.

Conclusion

1. See Barad's theory of agential realism (1996) for an approach that effectively moves beyond presumed oppositions between social constructivism on the one hand and theories of agency and materiality on the other.

2. There have been wide-ranging theoretical debates on the paradigm of globalization. For an overview of such debates see Held and McGraw 2002.

3. Note that the identity and interests that are claimed in this way correspond to the dominant construction of the new middle class. Thus middle class organizations that assert agency in this way also conflate new middle class interests with the middle class as a whole.

4. For research that does address the middle classes see Bardhan 1998; Davis 2004; and Rueschemeyer, Stephens, and Stephens 1992. The comparative politics literature on economic reforms in political science has in general tended to pay less attention to the category of class.

5. Bardhan 1998. The two other dominant proprietary classes that Bardhan discusses are industrial capitalists and rich farmers.

6. For a critique of the ways in which survey research misses both the dynamism and power relations of class practices see Bourdieu 1984, 245.

7. See the Introduction for an overview of this literature.

8. See for example Haggard and Kaufman 1995. On the relationship between class and democracy see Rueschemeyer, Stephens, and Stephens 1992.

9. See for example Heller and Safran 1985; Koo 1991; Lett 1998; Sen and Stevens 1998.

10. There is a tendency for postcolonial approaches to the study of South Asia to characterize structuralist approaches as a return to a deterministic, teleological, or modular form of analysis. Such characterizations mistakenly assume that theoretical innovation requires a complete break from older categories of analysis. The tendency of interdisciplinary postcolonial studies to rest on binary distinctions between old and new epistemological practices has meant that the field of postcolonial studies has not benefited from the insights of social science disciplines such as sociology and political science. Such tendencies also exist in other interdisciplinary fields. For an interesting critical discussion of women's studies see McCall 2005.

11. See Chakrabarty 1989 and Ong 1988. For an overview of the subaltern studies approach to South Asia see Ludden 2002.

12. For example, similar patterns can be discerned in relationship to the construction of class through the politics of gender, ethnicity, and religion in Southeast Asia or the politics of race and gender in Latin America or the United States.

Glossary of Acronyms and Indian Terms

———— ✳ ————

AIBEA	All India Bank Employees Association
BEST	Brihanmumbai Electric Supply and Transportation
bhadralok	gentlemen; Bengali elite social category with caste- and class-based connotations
BJP	Bharatiya Janata Party
BMC	Brihanmumbai Municipal Corporation
Citispace	Citizens Forum for Protection of Public Space
CPM	Communist Party of India-Marxist
crore	one hundred million
dalit	"untouchable" caste
Doordarshan	Indian state television
IAS	Indian Administrative Service
ICS	Indian Civil Service
lakh	one hundred thousand
Mandal Commission	Indian governmental commission that investigated caste-based discrimination
MNC	multinational corporation
NCAER	National Council of Applied Economic Research
NES	National Election Study
NGO	nongovernmental organization
NRI	nonresident Indian (person of Indian citizenship living abroad)

OBC	other backward caste
sati	widow self-immolation
swadeshi	production and consumption of Indian goods
votebank	special interests that serve as electoral bases for political parties
VRS	voluntary retirement scheme

Works Cited

---*---

Abu-Lughod, Lila. 1991. Writing Against Culture. In *Recapturing Anthropology: Working in the Present,* ed. Richard Fox, 137–62. Santa Fe, N. Mex.: School of American Research Press.

———. 1993. Finding a Place for Islam: Egyptian Television Serials and the National Interest. *Public Culture* 5, 3: 493–513.

———. 2005. *Dramas of Nationhood: The Politics of Television in Egypt.* Chicago: University of Chicago Press.

Adams, John. 1990. Breaking Away: India's Economic Vault into the 1990s. In *India Briefing,* eds. Marshall Bouton and Philip Oldernberg, 77–100. Boulder, Colo.: Westview Press.

Agarwal, A. 1996. MTV Starting from Scratch: The Channel Seeks to Indianise yet Retain Its Global Appeal. *India Today* (March 15): 160–1.

Ahmad, Aijaz. 1994. *In Theory: Classes, Nations, Literatures.* New York: Verso.

Ahmad, Imtiaz, and Helmut Reifeld. 2001. *Middle Class Values in India and Western Europe.* New Delhi: Social Science Press.

Aiyar, V. Shankar. 1997. Snip Snip Snip. *India Today* (September 8): 40–45.

———. 1999. Shoppers' Bonanza. *India Today International* (November 1).

———. 2003. The Ticking Time Bomb *India Today International* (December 15): 22–24.

Akthar, Shameem, 1995. Barred Maids. *Indian Express.* May 14.

Alexander, Jacqui. 1994. Not Just Any(Body) Can Be a Citizen: The Politics of Law, Sexuality and Citizenship in Trinidad and Tobago and the Bahamas. *Feminist Review* 48 (Autumn): 5–23.

Amin, Shahid. 1995. *Event, Metaphor and Memory: Chauri Chaura 1922–1992.* Berkeley: University of California Press.

Anderson, Benedict. 1983. *Imagined Communities: Reflections on the Origin and Spread of Nationalism.* New York: Verso.

———. 1990. *Language and Power: Exploring Political Cultures in Indonesia.* Ithaca: Cornell University Press.

Appadurai, A. 1993. Number in the Colonial Imagination. In *Orientalism and the Postcolonial Predicament,* eds. Carol Breckenridge and Peter van der Veer, 314–39. Philadelphia: University of Pennsylvania Press.

———. 1996. *Modernity at Large: Cultural Dimensions of Globalization.* Minneapolis: University of Minnesota Press.

Appadurai, Arjun, and Carol Breckenridge. 1995. Public Modernity in India. In Breckenridge 1995, 1–22.

Aronoff, Myron, and Jan Kubik. Forthcoming. *Anthropology and Political Science: Power, Culture and Identity.* New York: Berghan Books.

Asian Age. 2001. Civic Body to Employ Private Guards for Evictions. October 1.

Bakker, Isabella, ed. 1994. *The Strategic Silence: Gender and Economic Policy.* Atlantic Highlands, N. J.: Zed Books.

Balakrishnan, S. 1998. Tied up in Red Tape, Imported Onions Raise a Stink. *Times of India.* October 27.

———. 2001. Rokade Was Shunted out by Hawkers' Lobby. *Times of India.* October 1.

Banerjee, Nirmala. 2002. Between the Devil and the Deep Sea: Shrinking Options for Women in Contemporary India. In *The Violence of Development: The Politics of Identity, Gender and Social Inequalities in India,* ed. Karin Kapadia. New York: Zed Books.

Barad, Karen. 1996. Meeting the Universe Halfway: Realism and Social Constructivism without Contradiction. In *Feminism, Science and the Philosophy of Science,* eds. L. H. Nelson and J. Nelson, 161–94. Boston: Kluwer Academic Publishers.

———. 2001. Re(con)figuring Space, Time and Matter. In *Feminist Locations: Global and Local, Theory and Practice,* ed. Marianne de Koven, 75–109. New Brunswick, N.J.: Rutgers University Press.

Bardhan, Pranab. 1993. The "Intermediate Regime": Any Sign of Graduation? In *Development and Change: Essays in Honour of K.N. Raj,* eds. Pranab Bardhan, Mrinal Datta-Chaudhuri, and T.N. Krishnan, 214–24. Bombay: Oxford University Press.

———. 1998. *The Political Economy of Development in India.* London: Oxford University Press.

———. 1999. *The Political Economy of Reform in India.* New Delhi: National Council of Applied Economic Research.

———. 2001. Sharing the Spoils: Group Equity, Development and Democracy. In *The Success of India's Democracy,* ed. Atul Kohli, 226–41. Cambridge: Cambridge University Press.

Baria, Farah. 1999. Lil' Lords Live it Big. *India Today International* (August 30): 44–45.

———. 2000. The New Threat. *India Today International* (November 27): 34–39.

Baruah, A. K. 1991. *Social Tensions in Assam: Middle Class Politics.* Purbanchal Prakash: Guwahati.

Baruah, Sanjib. 1999. *India Against Itself: Assam and the Politics of Nationality*. Philadelphia: University of Pennsylvania Press.

Barucha, Nauzer, and Anil Singh. 1998. The Man Who Turns Mumbai Topsy-Turvey at the Drop of a Hat. *The Sunday Times of India*. October 11.

Baumgartner, Frank, and Beth Leech. 1998. *Basic Interests*. Princeton: Princeton University Press.

BBC News. 2003. *Call Centres: Bad for India*. December 11.

Beng-Huat, Chua, ed. 2000. *Consumption in Asia: Lifestyles and Identities*. New York: Routledge.

Bermeo, Nancy, and Philip Nord, eds., 2000. *Civil Society Before Democracy: Lessons from Nineteenth Century Europe*. New York: Rowman and Littlefield.

Beteille, Andre. 2001. The Social Character of the Indian Middle Class. In *Middle Class Values in India and Western Europe*, eds. Imtiaz Ahmad and Helmut Reifeld, 73–85. New Delhi: Social Science Press.

Bhabha, H. 1994. *The Location of Culture*. New York: Routledge.

Bhagwati, Jagdish. 2004a. *In Defense of Globalization*. New York: Oxford University Press.

———. 2004b. Why Your Job Isn't Moving to Bangalore. *The New York Times*. February 25.

Bhatia, B. M. 1994. *India's Middle Class: Role in Nation Building*. New Delhi: Konark Publishers.

Bhatia, Gauri. 2001. Getting Rogered. *Outlook* (November 5): 80–81.

Bhatt, S. C. 1994. *Satellite Invasion of India*. New Delhi: Gyan Publishing House.

Bhaumik, T. K. 2004. Outsourcing Outcry: West Should Compete, not Whine. *Times of India* (April 26).

Bhowmick, Sharit. 2002a. Mumbai: 'Citizens' Versus the Urban Poor. *One India One People Magazine* (October).

———. 2002b. *Hawkers and the Urban Informal Sector: A Study of Street Vending in Seven Cities*. Report prepared for National Alliance of Street Vendors in India.

———. 2005. Street Vendors in Asia: A Review. *Economic and Political Weekly* (May 28–June 4): 2256–64.

Bidwai, Praful. 2003. Indian Elite in Mammon's Grip: The Greed Creed's High Cost. *The Praful Bidwai Column* (November 3).

Bishop, Ryan, and Lillian Robinson. 1998. *Night Market: Sexual Cultures and the Thai Economic Miracle*. New York: Routledge.

Bombay Times. 1998a. BMC gets Serious about Clean Mumbai. September 18.

———. 1998b. Mumbaites Are Held to Ransom. October 7.

———. 1999. Beautification Is All the Rage Now. January 8.

Bose, Ashish. 2003. Consumer Demographics: People's Assets in Census 2001. *Economic and Political Weekly* (September 27): 4085–87.

Bourdieu, Pierre. 1984. *Distinction: A Social Critique of the Judgment of Taste.* Trans. Richard Nice. Cambridge, Mass.: Harvard University Press.

Breckenridge, Carol, ed. 1995. *Consuming Modernity: Public Culture in a South Asian World.* Minneapolis: University of Minnesota Press.

Brown, Wendy. 1995. *States of Injury.* Princeton: Princeton University Press.

Bunsha, Dionne. 2002. Targetting Hawkers. *Frontline* (February 1): 94–95.

Burawoy Michael, and Katherine Verdery, eds. 1999. *Uncertain Transition: Ethnographies of Change in the Post-Socialist World.* New York: Rowman and Littlefield.

Burke, Timothy. 1996. *Lifebuoy Men, Lux Women: Commodification, Consumption and Cleanliness in Modern Zimbabwe.* Durham, N.C.: Duke University Press.

Callahan, William. 2005. Social Capital and Corruption: Vote Buying and the Politics of Reform in Thailand. *Perspectives on Politics* 3, 3: 495–508.

Camp, Roderic Ai. 2002. *Mexico's Mandarins: Crafting a Power Elite for the Twenty-First Century.* Berkeley: University of California Press.

Castells, Manuel. 1996. *The Rise of the Network Society.* Oxford: Blackwell Publishing.

Chakrabarty, Dipesh. 1989. *Rethinking Working Class History: Bengal 1890–1940.* New Delhi: Oxford University Press.

———. 1991. Open Space/Public Place: Garbage, Modernity and India. *South Asia* 14, 1: 15–31.

———. 2000. *Provincializing Europe.* Princeton: Princeton University Press.

Chakravarty, Sayantan. 1998. Not Knowing Their Onions. *India Today* (October 19): 21–22.

Chakravarty, S. 2003. The Immigrants: Banglo-Indians. *India Today International.* February 17.

Chandra, A., and A. Agarwal. 1996. Cellular Phones: Upwardly Mobile. *India Today.* January 31.

Chandra, Bipan. 2004. India Shining amongst Biggest Ad Campaigns, February 24, www.rediff.com.

Chandra, Kanchan. 2004. *Why Ethnic Parties Succeed: Patronage and Ethnic Head Counts in India.* New York: Cambridge University Press.

Chandrasekhar, C. P. 2003. Ites and Hard Facts. *Frontline:*127–29.

Chang, Grace. 2000. *Disposable Domestics: Immigrant Women Workers in the Global Economy.* Boston: South End Press.

Chatterjee, Partha. 1986. *Nationalist Thought and the Colonial World: A Derivative Discourse.* Minneapolis: University of Minnesota Press.

———. 1990. The Nationalist Resolution of the Women's Question. In *Recasting Women: Essays in Indian Colonial History,* eds. K. Sangari and S. Vaid, 233–53. New Brunswick: Rutgers University Press.

————. 1992. A Religion of Urban Domesticity: Sri Ramakrishna and the Calcutta Middle Class. In *Subaltern Studies VII*, eds. Partha Chatterjee and Gyanendra Pandey, 40–68. New Delhi: Oxford University Press.

————. 1993. *The Nation and Its Fragments: Colonial and Postcolonial Histories*. Princeton: Princeton University Press.

————. 2004. *The Politics of the Governed: Reflections on Popular Politics in Most of the World*. New York: Columbia University Press.

Chatterjee, Promothesh. 1998. No Place in the Sun. *Economic Times* (October 26).

Chatterji, Rakahari. 1980. *Unions, Politics and the State: A Study of Labour Politics*. New Delhi: South Asian Publishers.

Chaudhry, Kirin Aziz. 1994. Economic Liberalization and the Lineages of the Rentier State. *Comparative Politics* 27, 1: 1–26.

Chaudhry, Lina. 1999. Clubs Mushroom in Middle Class Suburbs. *Times of India*. January 12.

Chengappa, R. 2003. A Neighbourhood of Trouble. *India Today International*. February 17.

Chhibber, Pradeep, and Samuel Eldersveld. 2000. Local Elites and Popular Support for Economic Reform in China and India. *Comparative Political Studies* 33, 3: 350–73.

Chibber, Vivek. 2003. *Locked in Place: State-Building and Late Industrialization in India*. Princeton: Princeton University Press.

Chibber, Yash Pal. 1968. *From Caste to Class: A Study of the Indian Middle Classes*. New Delhi: Associated Publishing House.

Chopra, Anupama, and Sheela Raval. 2000. Work Hard. Play Harder. *India Today International*. August 14.

Conlon, Frank.1995. Dining Out in Mumbai. In *Consuming Modernity: Public Culture in a South Asian World*, ed. Carol Breckenridge, 90–127. Minneapolis: University of Minnesota Press.

Corbridge, Stuart, and John Harriss. 2000. *Reinventing India: Liberalization, Hindu Nationalism and Popular Democracy*. Cambridge: Polity Press.

Crenshaw, Kimberle. 1994. Mapping the Margins. In *In the Public Nature of Private Violence*, eds. Martha Fineman and Roxanne Mykitiuk, 93–120. New York: Routledge.

Crompton, Rosemary, and Gareth Jones. 1986. *Gender and Stratification*. Cambridge: Polity Press.

Das, Gurucharan. 2000. *India Unbound: The Social and Economic Revolution from Independence to the Global Information Age*. New York: Anchor Books.

Das, P. K. 2003. Slums: The Continuing Struggle for Housing. In *Bombay and Mumbai: The City in Transition*, eds. Sujata Patel and Jim Masselos, 207–34. New Delhi: Oxford University Press.

Das, Veena. 1996. Sexual Violence, Discursive Formations and the State. *Economic and Political Weekly* (September): 2411–23.

Dasgupta, Ranajit. n.d. *Comparisons and Contrasts in Working Class Politics and Organisation: Bombay Cotton Textile Labour Force and Calcutta Jute Textile Labour Force with Focus on Post-Independence Period*. Unpublished paper: 1–14.

David, Stephen, and Shilpa Rohatgi. 2003. Sweeping the Board. *India Today International* (December 22): 26–30.

Davis, Diane. 2004. *Discipline and Development: Middle Classes and Prosperity in East Asia and Latin America*. New York: Cambridge University Press.

Davis, Mike. 1992. *City of Quartz*. London: Vintage Books.

D'Costa, Anthony, and E. Sridharan. 2004. *India in the Global Software Industry: Innovation, Firm Strategies and Development*. Hampshire: Palgrave Macmillan.

De Certeau, Michel. 2002. *The Practice of Everyday Life*. Trans. Steven Rendall. Berkeley: University of California Press.

Deb, Sandipan. 1998a. Forgetting One's Onions. *Outlook* (October 19): 56.

———. 1998b. Vegetable Soup. *Outlook* (November 9): 59.

———. 1998c. Countdown Has Begun: India's First Ever Survey on How Three Generations of Indians Look at Money. *Intelligent Investor* (August 26): 8–27.

Deshmukh, Smita. 1998a. "Aquarium Project Gets the Green Signal," *Bombay Times* (September 11).

———. 1998b. Schools Continue to Demand Donations. *Times of India*. April 14.

———. 1998c. Strikes—We've Had Enough. *Times of India*. October 12.

Deshpande, Satish. 1998. Hegemonic Spatial Strategies: The Nation-Space and Hindu Communalism in Twentieth Century India. *Public Culture* 10, 2: 249–84.

———. 2003. *Contemporary India: A Sociological View*. New Delhi: Penguin Books.

Deshpande, Sudha, and L. K. Deshpande. 1992. New Economic Policy and Female Employment. *Economic and Political Weekly* (October 10): 2248–52.

Dev, Mahendra. 2000. Economic Liberalisation and Employment in South Asia. *Economic and Political Weekly* (January 8): 40–51.

Devidayal, Namita. 1998a. From Handloom to Hafta. *Times of India* (September 26).

———. 1998b. BMC Outlines before HC [High Court] its Plan to Regulate Hawking. *Times of India*. November 12.

Dixit, Rekha. 1998. BMC's Anti-Hawker Drive Hinges on New Agreement. *Times of India*. August 24.

D'Monte, Darryl. 2002. *Ripping the Fabric: The Decline of Mumbai and its Mills*. New Delhi: Oxford University Press.

Dobbin, Christine. 1972. *Urban Leadership in Western India: Politics and Communities in Bombay City 1840–1885*. New York: Oxford University Press.

Donner, Henrike. 2004. Labour, Privatisation and Class: Middle-Class Women's Experience of Changing Hospital Births in Calcutta. In *Reproductive Agency and the State: Cultural Transformations of Childbearing*, ed. Maya Unnithan-Kumar, 113–35. Oxford: Berghahn.

———. 2005. "Children Are Capital, Grandchildren Are Interest": Changing Educational Strategies and Parenting in Calcutta's Middle Class Families. In *Globalizing India: Perspectives from Below*, eds. Jackie Assayag and C. J. Fuller, 119–39. London: Anthem Press.

Doshi, Anjali, and Nirmala Ravindran. 2004. The Other Side of Midnight. *India Today International* (April 12): 38–40.

Dubey, Suman. 1992. The Middle Class. In *India Briefing 1992*, ed. Philip Oldenberg, 137–64. Boulder, Colo.: Westview Press.

Dwyer, Rachel. 2000. *All You Want is Money, All You Need Is Love*. New York: Cassell.

Economic Times. 1997. The Mirage of the Middle Class. August 20.

———. 1998a. Executives in Union Strike for Better Deals. February 28.

———. 1998b. Executives Don Trade Union Robes. February 28.

———. 1999a. Government Puts MNCs in Direct Marketing Under Watch. April 3.

———. 1999b. Fly By Night Business Schools. August 30.

Embong, Abdul Rahman. 2002. *State-Led Modernization and the New Middle Class in Malaysia*. New York: Palgrave.

Escobar, Arturo. 1994. *Encountering Development: The Making and Unmaking of the Third World*. Princeton: Princeton University Press.

Evans, Peter. 1995. *Embedded Autonomy: States and Industrial Transformation*. Princeton: Princeton University Press.

Evans, Peter, ed. 2002. *Liveable Cities? Urban Struggles for Livelihood and Sustainability*. Berkeley: University of California Press.

Favero, Paolo. 2005. *India Dreams: Cultural Identity among Young Middle Class Men in New Delhi*. Stockholm: Almqvist and Wiksell International (Stockholm Studies in Social Anthropology).

Fernandes, Leela. 1997. *Producing Workers: The Politics of Gender, Class and Culture in the Calcutta Jute Mills*. Philadelphia: University of Pennsylvania Press.

Fernandes, Naresh. 1996. Urban Fabric. *The India Magazine of Her People and Culture*. July.

Frankel, Francine. 1991. Middle Classes and Castes in India's Politics: Prospects for Accommodation. In *India's Democracy: An Analysis of*

Changing State-Society Relations, ed. Atul Kohli, 225–61. Princeton: Princeton University Press.

Frankel, Francine, Zoya Hasan, Rajeev Bhargava, and Balveer Arora, eds. 2000. *Transforming India: Social and Political Dynamics of Democracy.* New Delhi: Oxford University Press.

Friedman, Thomas. 2005. *The World Is Flat: A Brief History of the Twenty-first Century.* New York: Farrar, Straus and Giroux.

Gallup Organization. 2000. *Indian Survey Consumer Report.* Princeton, N.J.: Author.

Gandhi, Nandita. 1996. *When the Rolling Pins Hit the Streets: Women in the Anti-Price Rise Movement in Maharashtra.* New Delhi: Kali for Women.

Gerke, Solvay. 2000. Global Lifestyles Under Local Conditions: The New Indonesian Middle Class. In *Consumption in Asia: Lifestyles and Identities,* ed. Chua Beng-Huat, 135–58. New York: Routledge.

Ghosh, Jayati. 1994. Gender Concerns in Macro-Economic Policy. *Economic and Political Weekly* (April 30): WS2–WS18.

Gills, Dong-Sook, and Nicole Piper, eds. 2002. *Women and Work in Globalising Asia.* London: Routledge.

Glenn, Evelyn Nakano. 2002. *Unequal Freedom: How Race and Gender Shaped American Citizenship and Labor.* Cambridge, Mass.: Harvard University Press.

Godement, Francois. 1999. *The Downsizing of Asia.* New York: Routledge Press.

Goheen, Peter. 2003. The Assertion of Middle-Class Claims to Public Space in Late Victorian Toronto. *Journal of Historical Geography* 29, 1: 73–92.

Gonzalez, Gilbert, Raul Fernandez, Vivian Price, David Smith, and Linda Vo, eds. 2004. *Labor Versus Empire: Race, Gender and Migration.* New York: Routledge.

Gooptu, Nandini. 2001. *The Politics of the Urban Poor in Early Twentieth Century India.* Cambridge: Cambridge University Press.

Gothoskar, Sujata, Nandita Gandhi, and Nandita Shah. 1994. Maharashtra's Policy for Women. *Economic and Political Weekly* (November 26): 3019–22.

Government of India. 2001. Tables on Housing, Household Amenities and Assets (H Series Tables). *Census of India 2001.* New Delhi: Office of the Registrar General.

Goyal, Malini. 2003. Urge to Splurge. *India Today International* 9: 28–37.

———. 2004a. The I & Me Consumer. *India Today International.* July 12.

———. 2004b. Jobs in Installments. *India Today International* (February 16): 22–24.

———. 2005. Hot Jobs. *India Today International* (March 7): 10–19.

Guha, Sumit. 2003. The Politics of Identity and Enumeration in India 1600–1990. *Comparative Studies in Society and History* 45, 2: 148–67.

Gupta, Dipankar. 1982. *Nativism in a Metropolis: Shiv Sena in Bombay*. New Delhi: South Asia Books.

———. 1998. Elitist Middle Class: No Consciousness Beyond Consumption. *Times of India*. June 3.

———. 2000. *Mistaken Modernity: India Between Worlds*. New Delhi: Harper Collins.

Haggard, Stephen, and Robert Kaufman. 1995. *The Political Economy of Democratic Transitions*. Princeton: Princeton University Press.

Hansen, Thomas Blom. 1999. *The Saffron Wave: Democracy and Hindu Nationalism in Modern India*. Princeton: Princeton University Press.

———. 2001. *Wages of Violence: Naming and Identity in Postcolonial Bombay*. Princeton: Princeton University Press.

Hardy, Peter. 1972. *The Muslims of British India*. Cambridge: Cambridge University Press.

Harriss, John. 2005. *Middle-Class Activism and Poor People's Politics: Citizen-State Relations in Delhi and the Role of Civil and Political Organisations*. Unpublished paper.

Harvey, David. 2001. *Spaces of Capital: Towards a Critical Geography*. New York: Routledge.

Hasan, Mushirul. 1997. *Legacy of a Divided Nation: India's Muslims Since Independence*. Boulder, Colo.: Westview Press.

Hasan, Zoya. 1998. *Quest for Power: Oppositional Movements and Post-Congress Politics in Uttar Pradesh*. New Delhi: Oxford University Press.

Haug, W. F. 1986. *Critique of Commodity Aesthetics: Appearance, Sexuality and Advertising in Capitalist Society*. Minneapolis: University of Minnesota Press.

Haynes, Douglass. 1991. *Rhetoric and Ritual in Colonial India: the Shaping of a Public Culture in Surat City, 1852–1928*. Berkeley: University of California Press.

Held, David, and Anthony McGrew, eds, 2002. *The Global Transformations Reader*. Malden, Mass.: Blackwell.

Heller, Mark, and Nadav Safran. 1985. *The New Middle Class and Regime Stability in Saudi Arabia*. Harvard Middle East Papers No. 3. Cambridge, Mass.: Center for Middle Eastern Studies, Harvard University.

Heitzman, James. 1999. Corporate Strategy and Planning in the Science City: Bangalore as "Silicon Valley." *Economic and Political Weekly* (January 30): PE2–11.

Heuze, Gerard. 1996. Cultural Populism: The Appeal of the Shiv Sena in Bombay. In *Bombay Metaphor for a Modern India*, eds. Sujata Patel and Alice Thorner, 213–47. Bombay: Oxford University Press.

———. 2000. Populism, Religion and Nation in Contemporary India: The Evolution of the Shiv Sena in Maharashtra. *Comparative Studies of South Asia Africa and the Middle East* XX, 1 &2: 3–43.

Hsiao, Hsin-Huang Michael, ed. 1999. *East Asian Middle Classes in Comparative Perspective.* Taipei: Academia Sinica.

Irani, Madhavi, and Priyanka Singh. 1996. Reading the Market Wrong. *Economic Times.* April 3.

Islam, Shahnawaz. 2002. Employees Hang Up on Call Centers. *Times of India.* May 2.

Iyengar, Pushpa. 1999. How Chandrababu Naidu Lives in the Future. *Times of India.* March 28.

Jaffrelot, Christophe. 1996. *The Hindu Nationalist Movement in India.* New York: Columbia University Press.

———. 2000. Hindu Nationalism and Democracy. In *Transforming India: Social and Political Dynamics of Democracy,* ed. Francine Frankel, Zoya Hasan, Rajeev Bhargava, and Balveer Arora, 353–78. New Delhi: Oxford University Press.

———. 2005. *Dr. Ambedkar and Untouchability: Analyzing and Fighting Caste.* London: Hurst.

Jayakar, Roshni. 2005. The Next Great Wave *India Today International* (May 2): 18–21.

Jayal, Niraja Gopal. 2001. Reinventing the State: The Emergence of Alternative Models of Governance in India in the 1990s. In *Democratic Governance in India: Challenges of Poverty, Development and Identity,* Niraga Gopal Jayal and Sudha Pai, eds., 132–50. New Delhi: Sage.

Jeffrey, Patricia, and Amrita Basu, eds. 1997. *Appropriating Gender: Women's Activism and Politicized Religion in South Asia.* New York: Routledge.

Jenkins, Rob. 1999. *Democratic Politics and Economic Reform in India.* Cambridge: Cambridge University Press.

Jenson, Jane, Elisabeth Hagen, and Ceallaigh Reddy. 1988. *Feminization of the Labor Force: Paradoxes and Promises.* New York: Oxford University Press.

Jetley, Neera. 1997. Blood, Sweat and Downsizing. *Outlook.* April 23.

Jetley, Neerja Pawha. 1998. e=entertainment[2]. *Outlook* (November 16): 52–56.

Jones, David Martin. 1998. Democratization, Civil Society and Illiberal Middle Class Culture in Pacific Asia. *Comparative Politics* 30, 2: 147–70.

Joshi, Namrata, and Nandita Chowdhury. 1999. On the Fast Track. *India Today International* (August 2): 38–45.

Joshi, Sanjay. 2001. *Fractured Modernity: Making of a Middle Class in Colonial North India.* New York: Oxford University Press.

Juluri, Vamsee. 2003. *Becoming a Global Audience: Longing and Belonging in Indian Music Television.* New York: Lang.

Jung Thapa, Vijay. 2001. Enter the New Babu. *India Today International* (January 1): 36–40.

Kakodkar, Priyanka. 2003. Landslide Logistics *Outlook* (June 23): 32–33.

Kapur, Devesh, and Pratap Mehta. 2004. *Indian Higher Education Reform: From Half Baked Socialism to Half Baked Capitalism.* Center for International Development Harvard University, Working Paper No. 108 (September): 1–49.

Kapur, Devesh, and Ravi Ramamurti. In press. Privatization in India: The Imperatives and Consequences of Gradualism. In *India After a Decade of Economic Reforms: Retrospect and Prospects,* ed. T. N. Srinivasan, forthcoming. Stanford: Stanford University Press.

Kapur, Ratna, and Brenda Cossman. 1996. *Subversive Sites: Feminist Engagements with Law in India.* New Delhi: Sage.

Karkaria, Urvakesh. 1997. Dadar Residents See Red in BMC's "Concrete" Plans for Shivaji Park. *Times of India* (April 8).

Katzenstein, Mary. 1979. *Ethnicity and Equality: The Shiv Sena Party and Preferential Policies in Bombay.* Ithaca: Cornell University Press.

Katzenstein, Mary, Uday Singh Mehta, and Usha Thakkar. 1997. The Rebirth of Shiv Sena: The Symbiosis of Discursive and Organizational Power. *Journal of Asian Studies*: 371–90.

Katznelson, Ira. 1983. *City Trenches: Urban Politics and the Patterning of Class in the United States.* New York: Pantheon Books.

———. 1986. Introduction. In *Working Class Formation: Nineteenth Century Patterns in Western Europe and the United States,* ed. Ira Katznelson and Aristide Zolberg. Princeton: Princeton University Press.

Kaviraj, Sudipta. 1991. On State, Society and Discourse in India. In *Rethinking Third World Politics,* ed. James Manor, 72–99. London: Longman.

———. 1997. Filth and the Public Sphere: Concepts and Practices about Space in Calcutta. *Public Culture* 10, 1: 83–113.

Kelly Services. 2006. *India Salary Guide 2006.* www.kellyservices.co.in. Accessed July 25, 2006.

Khan, Sameera. 1990. For Workout Buffs, Gyms Are the Newfound Shrines. *Times of India.* August 2.

Khilnani, Sunil. 1997. *The Idea of India.* New York: Farrar, Straus and Giroux.

Kohli, Atul. 1989. The Politics of Liberalisation in India. *World Development* 17, 3: 305–28.

Kohli, Atul, ed. 2001. *The Success of India's Democracy.* Cambridge: Cambridge University Press.

———. 2004. *State-Directed Development: Political Power and Industrialization in the Global Periphery.* Cambridge: Cambridge University Press.

Koo, Hagen. n.d. "Globalization and the Asian Middle Classes: A Tentative Research Agenda." Unpublished paper.

———. 1991. Middle Classes, Democratization and Class Formation. *Theory and Society,* 20:485–509.

Kothari, Rajni. 1993. *Growing Amnesia: An Essay on Poverty and Human Consciousness.* New Delhi: Viking.

Krishna, Sonali. 2004. Interview with Grey Worldwide Chairman South Asia Nirvik Singh. www.Indiantelevision.com (July 20): 1–10.

Krugman, Paul. 2002. The End of Middle-Class America. *The New York Times Magazine* (October 20): 62.

Kumar, Navika, and Santwana Bhattacharya. 2004. Government Does Account Juggling for India Shining. *Indian Express.* February 12.

Kumar, Radha. 1993. *The History of Doing: An Illustrated Account of Movements for Women's Rights and Feminism 1800–1990.* New York: Verso.

Kumar, Sanjay. 2004. Impact of Economic Reforms on Indian Electorate. *Economic and Political Weekly* (April 17): 1621–30.

Kunwar, Manish. 1998. Name of the Ranking Game. *Economic Times.* August 17.

Lakha, Salim. 1999. The State Globalisation and Indian Middle Class Identity. In *Culture and Privilege in Capitalist Asia,* ed. Michael Pinches, 251–74. New York: Routledge.

Lamont, Michele. 1992. *Money, Morals and Manners: The Culture of the French and American Upper Middle Class.* Chicago: University of Chicago Press.

Lefebvre, Henri. 1991. *The Production of Space.* London: Blackwell.

Lele, Jayant. 1981. *Elite Pluralism and Class Rule: Political Development in Maharashtra, India.* Toronto: University of Toronto Press.

———. 1995. Saffronisation of Shiv Sena: Political Economy of City, State and Nation. *Economic and Political Weekly* (June 24): 1520–28.

Lelyveld, David. 1978. *Aligarh's First Generation: Muslim Solidarity in British India.* Princeton: Princeton University Press.

Lett, Denise Potrzeba. 1998. *In Pursuit of Status: The Making of South Korea's "New" Urban Middle Class.* Cambridge, Mass.: Harvard University Asia Center.

Liechty, Mark. 2003. *Suitably Modern: Making Middle Class Culture in a New Consumer Society.* Princeton: Princeton University Press.

Lipset, Seymour Martin. 1963. *Political Man: The Social Bases of Politics.* New York: Anchor.

Ludden, David. 2002. Introduction: A Brief History of Subalternity. In *Reading Subaltern Studies: Critical History, Contested Meaning and the Globalization of South Asia,* ed. David Ludden, 1–42. London: Anthem Press.

Maakan, Anupama, and Neerja Pawha Jetley. 1998. The World in my Pocket. *Intelligent Investor.* December 16.

Majumdar, Alok. 2001. The Golden Handshake. *Business India.* June 11–24.

Mallick, Ross. 1993. *Development Policy of a Communist Government: West Bengal since 1977.* Cambridge: Cambridge University Press.

Mankekar, Purnima. 1999. *Screening Culture, Viewing Politics: An Ethnography of Television, Womanhood and Nation in Postcolonial India.* Durham, N.C.: Duke University Press.

Mani, Lata. 1998. *Contentious Traditions: The Debate on Sati in Colonial India.* Berkeley: University of California Press.

Massey, Doreen. 1994. *Space, Place and Gender.* Minneapolis: University of Minnesota Press.

Mawdsley, Emma. 2004. India's Middle Classes and the Environment. *Development and Change*: 79–103.

Mazzarella, William. 2003. *Shovelling Smoke: Advertising and Globalization in Contemporary India.* Durham, N.C.: Duke University Press.

McCall, Leslie. 2005. The Complexity of Intersectionality. *Signs: A Journal of Women, Culture and Society* 30, 3 (Spring): 1771–1800.

McClintock, Anne. 1995. *Imperial Leather: Race, Gender and Sexuality in the Colonial Contest.* New York: Routledge.

McMillin, Divya. 2006. Outsourcing Identities: Call Centres and Cultural Transformation in India. *Economic and Political Weekly* (January 21): 235–41.

Menon, Ritu, and Kamla Bhasin. 1998. *Borders and Boundaries: Women in India's Partition.* New Brunswick, N.J.: Rutgers University Press.

Migdal, Joel. 2001. *State in Society: Studying How States and Societies Transform and Constitute One Another.* Cambridge: Cambridge University Press.

Mills, C. Wright. 2002 (1951). *White Collar: The American Middle Classes.* New York: Oxford University Press.

Mishra, Pankaj. 1995. *Butter Chicken in Ludhiana: Travels in Small Town India.* New Delhi: Penguin Books.

Misra, B. B. 1961. *The Indian Middle Classes: Their Growth in Modern Times.* New Delhi: Oxford University Press.

Mitchell, Timothy. 1991a. The Limits of the State: Beyond Statist Approaches and their Critics. *American Political Science Review* 85(1): 77–96.

———. 1991b. *Colonizing Egypt.* Berkeley: University of California Press.

———. 2002. *Rule of Experts: Egypt, Techno-Politics, Modernity.* Berkeley: University of California Press.

Mitra, Subrata. 1991. Room to Manoevre in the Middle: Local Elites, Political Action and the State in India. *World Politics* 43, 3: 490–513.

———. 2001. Making Local Government Work: Local Elites, *Panchayati Raj* and Governance in India. In *The Success of India's Democracy*, ed. Atul Kohli, 103–26. Cambridge: Cambridge University Press.

Mukherjee, Sourav. 1998. Pink Slips Haunt the Envied Pinstripes at Foreign Banks. *Economic Times.* December 11.

National Council of Applied Economic Research, Indian Society of Advertisers. 1992. *Socio-economic Effects of Advertising.* New Delhi: National Council of Applied Economic Research.

National Council of Applied Economic Research (NCAER). 2002. *India Market Demographics Report.* New Delhi: Author.

Natraj, V. K. 1999. Caste and the New Middle Class. *Economic and Political Weekly* (November 27): 1–3.

Nehru, Jawaharlal. 1998 (1946). *The Discovery of India.* New Delhi: Oxford University Press.

Nijman, Jan. 2000. Mumbai's Real Estate Market in 1990s: Deregulation, Global Money and Casino Capitalism. *Economic and Political Weekly* (February 12): 575–82.

Ninan, T. N. 1985. Rise of the Middle Class. *India Today* (December 3): 71.

———. 1990. Business and Economy: Reaching Out and Upward. In *India Briefing 1989,* eds. Marshall Bouton and Philip Oldenburg, 35–59. Boulder, Colo.: Westview Press.

Norton, Anne. 2004. *95 Theses on Politics, Culture and Method.* New Haven: Yale University Press.

O'Dougherty, Maureen. 2002. *Consumption Intensified: The Politics of Middle Class Daily Life in Brazil.* Durham, N.C.: Duke University Press.

Oldenburg, Veena. 2002. *Dowry Murder: The Imperial Origins of a Cultural Crime.* New York: Oxford University Press.

Ong, Aihwa. 1988. *Spirits of Resistance and Capitalist Discipline: Factory Women in Malaysia.* Albany: State University of New York Press.

Ong, Aihwa, and Donald Nonini. 1997. *Ungrounded Empires: The Cultural Politics of Modern Chinese Transnationalism.* New York: Routledge.

Owensby, Brian. 1999. *Intimate Ironies: Modernity and the Making of Middle Class Lives in Brazil.* Stanford: Stanford University Press.

Oza, Rupal. 2001. Showcasing India: Gender, Geography and Globalization. *Signs: A Journal of Women, Culture and Society* 26, 4: 1067–95.

Padmanabhan, Anil. 2003. Don't Lose Sleep. *India Today International* (June 23): 20–21.

———. 2004a. One for the Ballot. *India Today International* (February 9): 39–40.

———. 2004b. Call to Notice. *India Today International* (March 22): 24–26.

Palshikar, Suhas. 2001. Politics of India's Middle Classes. In *Middle Class Values in India and Western Europe,* eds. Imtiaz Ahmad and Helmut Reifeld, 171–93. New Delhi: Social Science Press.

Parrenas, Rhacel. 2001. *Servants of Globalization: Women, Migration and Domestic Work.* Stanford: Stanford University Press.

Pawar, Yogesh. 1998. Schools Cash in on Admission Frenzy. *Indian Express* (June 12).

Pempel, T. J , ed. 1999. *The Politics of the Asian Economic Crisis.* Ithaca: Cornell University Press.

Perry, Alex. 2004. Subcontinental Divide. *Timeasia.* February 23.

Pinches, Michael, ed. 1999. *Culture and Privilege in Capitalist Asia*. New York: Routledge.

Poggendorf-Kakar, Katharina. 2001. Middle-Class Formation and the Cultural Construction of Gender in Urban India. In *Middle Class Values in India and Western Europe*, eds. Imtiaz Ahmad and Helmut Reifeld, 125–51. New Delhi: Social Science Press.

Potter, David C. 1996. *India's Political Administrators: From ICS to IAS*. New Delhi: Oxford University Press.

Prakash, Gyan. 1999. *Another Reason: Science and the Imagination of Modern India*. Princeton: Princeton University Press.

———. 2002. The Urban Turn. *Sarai Reader 2002: The Cities of Everyday Life*: 2–7.

Prasannan, R. 1995. Great Indian Middle Class. *The Week* (June 25): 51–65.

Przeworski, Adam. 1992. *Democracy and the Market: Political and Economic Reforms in Eastern Europe and Latin America*. New York: Cambridge University Press.

———. 1996. Public Support for Economic Reforms in Poland. *Comparative Political Studies* 29, 5: 520–43.

Puliyenthuruthal, Josey. 2002. IT-enabled, People-disabled. *Business Standard* (July 3).

Purie, Aroon. 1998. From the Editor in Chief. *India Today* (November 9): 1.

Putnam, Robert. 1993. *Making Democracy Work: Civic Traditions in Modern Italy*. Princeton: Princeton University Press.

———. 2000. *Bowling Alone: The Collapse and Revival of American Community*. New York: Simon and Schuster.

Ragunath, P. 2003. Sena Steps Up Campaign Against Mumbai Migrants. *Gulf News*. May 6.

Rai, S. 1997. Middle Class . . . But Millionaires. *India Today*, July 7.

Rai, Saritha. 2003. Indian Companies Are Adding Western Flavor. *New York Times* (August 19).

Raj, Yashwant. 1998. Onions Will Be Major Poll Issue in Three States. *Times of India*. October 9.

Rajagopal, Arvind. 2001a. *Politics After Television: Religious Nationalism and the Making of a Hindu Public*. Cambridge: Cambridge University Press.

———. 2001b. Thinking about the New Middle Class: Gender, Advertising and Politics in an Age of Globalisation. In *Signposts: Gender Issues in Post-Independence India*, ed. Rajeswari Sunder Rajan, 57–99. New Brunswick: Rutgers University Press.

Rajan, R. 1993. *Real and Imagined Women: Gender, Culture and Postcolonialism*. New York: Routledge.

———. 2003. *The Scandal of the State: Women, Law and Citizenship in Postcolonial India*. Durham, N.C.: Duke University Press.

Ram, Nandu. 1988. *The Mobile Scheduled Castes: Rise of a New Middle Class.* New Delhi: Hindustan Publishing Corporation.

Ramachandran, Sujata. 2002. Operation Pushback: The Sangh Parivar, State, Slums and Surreptitious Bangladeshis in New Delhi. *Singapore Journal of Tropical Geography* 23, 3: 311–32.

Rao, S. L. 1994. *Consumer Market Demographics in India.* New Delhi: NCAER.

———. 2000. India's Rapidly Changing Consumer Markets. *Economic and Political Weekly* (Sept. 30): 3570–72.

Raval, Sheela. 2000. Mills and Boom. *India Today International* (May 8): 37–40.

———. 2002. Urban Heroes. *India Today International* (May 13): 38–40.

Raval, Sheela, and Vijay Thapa. 1999. Hey Kya Bolti Tu? *India Today International* (March 22): 44–47.

Ray, Shantanu Guha. 1998. Boom-Time Shuffle. *Outlook*: 46–48.

Rayani, Bhagranji. 1998. Advocate and President of FFIE to Get Standard 1 Admissions. *Times of India.* July 17.

Reddy, C. Rammanohar. 1997. What Happened to the 200 Million Consumers? *The Hindu* (May 26).

Rekhi, Shefali, and Kumar Sanjoya Singh. 1998. The Great Onions Disaster. *India Today* (November 9): 20–26

Richter, Frank-Jurgen, and Parthasarathi Banerjee, eds. 2003. *The Knowledge Economy in India.* New York: Palgrave Macmillan.

Robinson, Francis. 1974. *Separatism among Indian Muslims: The Politics of the United Provinces, 1883–1923.* Cambridge: Cambridge University Press.

Robison, Richard, and David Goodman, eds. 1996. *The New Rich in Asia: Mobile Phones, McDonalds and Middle-Class Revolution.* New York: Routledge.

Rodrigues, Pradip. 1998. Head for the Pub Straight from Work. *Bombay Times* (August 31).

Rohde, David. 2003. Sleepy City Has High Hopes, Dreaming of High Tech. *New York Times.* November 20.

Roy, Ananya. 2003. *City Requiem, Calcutta: Gender and the Politics of Poverty.* Minneapolis: University of Minnesota Press.

Rudolph, Lloyd, 1989. The Faltering Novitiate: Rajiv at Home and Abroad. In *India Briefing 1988,* eds. Marshall Bouton and Philip Oldenberg, 1–33. Boulder, Colo.: Westview Press.

Rudolph, Lloyd, and Susanne Rudolph. 1967. *The Modernity of Tradition.* Chicago: University of Chicago Press.

———. 1987. *In Pursuit of Lakshmi: The Political Economy of the Indian State.* Chicago: University of Chicago Press.

————. 2001. The Iconization of Chandrababu: Sharing Sovereignty in India's Federal Market Economy. *Economic and Political Weekly* XXXVI (May 5–11): 1154–551.

Rudolph, Susanne. 1995. The Role of Theory in Comparative Politics: A Symposium, (From Weber to Weber via Foucault). *World Politics* 48, 1 (October): 12–15.

Rudra, Ashok. 1989. Emergence of the Intelligentsia as a Ruling Class in India. *Economic and Political Weekly* XXIV, 3 (January 21): 142–50.

Rueschemeyer, Dietrich, Evelyn Huber Stephens, and John Stephens. 1992. *Capitalist Development and Democracy*. Chicago: University of Chicago Press.

Rutten, Mario, and Carol Upadhya, eds. 1997. *Small Business Entrepreneurs in Asia and Europe: Towards a Comparative Perspective*. New Delhi: Sage.

Ryan, Mary. 1998. *Civic Wars: Democracy and Public Life in the American City During the Nineteenth Century*. Berkeley: University of California Press.

Sahgal, Priya. 1998. Understanding the Middle Class. *Sunday* (February 8–14): 12–23.

Sangari, Kumkum. 2001. *Politics of the Possible: Essays on Gender, History, Narratives, Colonial English*. London: Anthem Press.

Sarai, The New Media Initiative. 2002. *Sarai Reader: The Cities of Everyday Life*. New Delhi: Center for the Study of Developing Societies.

Saran, Rohin. 2000. Dressed to Kill. *India Today International.* September 11.

Saran, Rohit. 2001. Growth Engine. *India Today International.* February 19.

Sarkar, Sumit. 1992. Kaliyug, Chakri and Bhakti: Ramakrishna and His Times. *Economic and Political Weekly* (July 18): 1543–66.

Sarkar, Tanika. 2001. *Hindu Wife, Hindu Nation: Community, Religion, and Cultural Nationalism*. London: Hurst.

Sassen, Saskia. 1991. *The Global City: New York, London, Tokyo*. Princeton: Princeton University Press.

————. 2002. The State and Globalization, In *The Emergence of Private Authority in Global Governance*, eds. Rodney Bruce Hall and Thomas Biersteker, 91–114. New York: Cambridge University Press.

Savage, Mike, P. Dickens, and A. J. Fielding. 1992. *Property, Bureaucracy and Culture: Middle Class Formation in Contemporary Britain*. London: Routledge.

Saxenian, Annalee. 2002. Bangalore: The Silicon Valley of Asia? In *Economic Policy Reforms and the Indian Economy*, ed. Anne Krueger, 169–210. Chicago: University of Chicago Press.

Scott, James. 1985. *Weapons of the Weak: Everyday Forms of Peasant Resistance.* New Haven: Yale University Press.

————. 1999. *Seeing Like a State: How Certain Schemes to Improve the Human Condition Have Failed*. New Haven: Yale University Press.

Scott, Joan. 1988. *Gender and the Politics of History*. New York: Columbia University Press.

Seabrook, Jeremy. 1996. *In the Cities of the South*. New York: Verso.

Sen, Krishna, and Maila Stevens, eds. 1998. *Gender and Power in Affluent Asia*. New York: Routledge Press.

Sen Gupta, Nandini. 1998. Consumer India on a Highway to Prosperity. *Economic Times* (June 14).

Sengupta, Jayanta. 2001. State, Market and Democracy in the 1990s: Liberalization and the Politics of Oriya Identity. In *Democratic Governance in India: Challenges of Poverty, Development and Identity*, Niraga Gopal Jayal and Sudha Pai, eds., 179–200. New Delhi: Sage.

Seshu, Geeta. 1998. Mammon Versus Merit. *Sunday Observer*. July 5.

Sewell, William. 1980. *The Language of Labor: From the Old Regime to 1848*. New York: Cambridge University Press.

Shaloff, Rebecca. n.d. *Insourcing: An Examination of Women Workers in Mumbai's International Call Centres*. Unpublished paper: 1–55.

Sharan, Awadhendra. 2002. Claims on Cleanliness: Environment and Justice in Contemporary Delhi. *Sarai Reader*: 31–38.

Sharma, Anirudh. 1998. Clean and Beautiful That's Chowpatty. *Bombay Times*. October 1.

Shastri. 2003. Finger Lickin' Good. *Outlook* (June 9): 46–52.

Sheth, D. L. 1999a. Secularisation of Caste and Making of New Middle Class, *Economic and Political Weekly* (August 21–28): 2502–10.

———. 1999b. Caste and Class: Social Reality and Political Representations. In Contemporary India, ed. V. A. Pai Panandiker and Ashis Nandy, 337–63. New Delhi: Tata McGraw Hill.

Sibley, David. 1995. *Geographies of Exclusion*. New York: Routledge.

Sinha, Aseema. 2004. *The Regional Roots of Developmental Politics in India: A Divided Leviathan*. Bloomington: Indiana University Press.

Skeggs, Beverly. 1997. *Formations of Class and Gender: Becoming Respectable*. London: Sage.

Smith, Neil. 1996. *The New Urban Frontier: Gentrification and the Revanchist City*. New York: Routledge.

Smith, Rogers. 1997. *Civic Ideals: Conflicting Visions of Citizenship in U.S. History*. New Haven: Yale University Press.

Somakar, S. 1995. A Lakh Is not Enough. *Times of India* (February 12).

Sridharan, E. 1999. Role of the State and the Market in the Indian Economy. In *Contemporary India*, ed. V. A. Pai Panandiker and Ashis Nandy, 107–36. New Delhi: Tata McGraw Hill.

———. 2004. The Growth and Sectoral Composition of India's Middle Classes: Its Impact on the Politics of Liberalization in India. *India Review* 1, 4: 405–28.

Srinivas, Smriti. 2001. *Landscapes of Urban Memory: The Sacred and the Civic in India's High Tech City*. Minneapolis: University of Minnesota Press.

Srivastava, Sanjay. 1998. *Constructing Post-Colonial India: National Character and the Doon School*. New York: Routledge.

Srivastava, Siddharth. 2006. Bright Outlook for India's IT Industry. *Asia-Times*. July 26.

Stedman Jones, Gareth. 1984. *Languages of Class: Studies in English Working Class History 1832–1982*. Cambridge: Cambridge University Press.

Steijn, Bram, Jan Berting, and Mart-Jan de Jong, eds. 1998. *Economic Restructuring and the Growing Uncertainty of the Middle Class*. Boston: Kluwer Academic Publishers.

Stivens, Maila. 1998. Sex, Gender and the Making of the New Malay Middle Classes. In *Gender and Power in Affluent Asia*, eds. Krishna Sen and Maila Stivens, 87–126. New York: Routledge.

Stokes, Susan. 1996a. Public Opinion and Market Reforms: The Limits of Economic Voting. *Comparative Political Studies* 29, 5: 499–519.

———. 1996b. Economic Reform and Public Opinion in Peru, 1990–1995. *Comparative Political Studies* 29, 5: 544–65.

Strange, Susan. 1996. *The Retreat of the State: The Diffusion of Power in the World Economy*. Cambridge: Cambridge University Press.

Tarlo, Emma. 2003. *Unsettling Memories: Narratives of the Emergency in India*. Berkeley: University of California Press.

The Telegraph. 2004. Scanner on Government Shining Funds. March 3.

Thakkar, Dharmesh. 1998. Dance Those Nights Away. *Asian Age* (August 17).

Thakraney, Anil. 1998. Interview with Pradeep Guha. The Advertising Brief (November 5): 22–25.

Times of India. 1997. Middle Class Myths: Overestimating Upmarket Trends. June 11.

———. 1998a. Job Security: A Shattered Myth. *Your Money* (August).

———. 1998b. Public to Be Banned from Chowpatty at Night. September 11.

———. 1998c. Bal Thackerey Opposes BMC Plan for Hawkers. September 24.

———. 1998d. Upset by Price Rise, Delhi Women Vote for Congress. November 26.

———. 1999. New Horizons Opening up for the Print Media. July 4.

Thompson, E. P. 1966. *The Making of the English Working Class*. New York: Vintage Books.

Traub, James. 2001. Keeping up with the Shindayes, *The New York Times Magazine* (April 15): 32–37.

Urry, John. 1971. Towards a Structural Theory of the Middle Class. *Acta Sociologica* 18, 3: 175–88.

Van Wessel, Margrit. 2001. *Modernity and Identity: An Ethnography of Moral Ambiguity and Negotiations in an Indian Middle Class.* Unpublished PhD thesis, University of Amsterdam.

———. 2004. Talking about Consumption: How an Indian Middle Class Dissociates from Middle Class Life. *Cultural Dynamics* 16, 1 (July): 93–116.

Varma, Pavan. 1998. *The Great Indian Middle Class.* New Delhi: Viking.

Varshney, Ashutosh. 2003. *Ethnic Conflict and Civic Life: Hindus and Muslims in India.* New Haven: Yale University Press.

Vasavi, A. R. 1996. Co-opting Culture: Managerialism in Age of Consumer Capitalism. *Economic and Political Weekly* (May 25): M-22–M-25.

Vasudev, Shefalee. 2003. Groom Showroom. *India Today International* (June 9): 34–37.

Vinayak, Ramesh. 2002. Punjab Club Class. *India Today International*: 48–50.

Visvanathan, Shiv, and Harsh Sethi. 1998. *Foul Play: Chronicles of Corruption.* New Delhi: Banyan Books.

Wacquant, Loic. 1991. Making Class: The Middle Class(es) in Social Theory and Social Structure. In *Bringing Class Back in: Contemporary and Historical Perspectives,* eds. Scott McNall, Rhonda Levine, and Rick Fantasia, 39–64. Boulder, Colo.: Westview Press.

Wadhwa, Soma. 2003. Riding the Riverdale High. *Outlook* (April 28): 49–56.

Waldman, Amy. 2003. Sizzling Economy Revitalizes India: Despite Widespread Poverty a Consumer Class Emerges. *The New York Times.* October 20.

Watt, Carey A. 2005. *Serving the Nation: Cultures of Service, Association and Citizenship in Colonial India.* New Delhi: Oxford University Press.

Weiner, Myron. 1987. Rajiv Gandhi: A Midterm Assessment. In *India Briefing 1987,* ed. Marshall Bouton, 1–23. Boulder, Colo.: Westview Press.

———. 2001. The Struggle for Equality: Caste in India Politics. In *The Success of India's Democracy,* ed. Atul Kohli, 193–225. Cambridge: Cambridge University Press.

Weiner, Myron, and Mary Katzenstein, with K. V. Narayana Rao. 1981. *India's Preferential Policies: Migrants the Middle Classes and Ethnic Equality.* Chicago: University of Chicago Press.

West, Michael. 2002. *The Rise of an African Middle Class: Colonial Zimbabwe, 1898–1965.* Bloomington: Indiana University Press.

Weyland, Kurt. 2003. *The Politics of Market Reform in Fragile Democracies.* Princeton: Princeton University Press.

Williamson, Judith. 1994 (1978). *Decoding Advertisements: Ideology and Meaning in Advertisements.* London: Calder and Boyars.

Wilson, Ara. 2004. *The Intimate Economies of Bangkok: Tomboys, Tycoons and Avon Ladies in the Global City.* Berkeley: University of California.

Wright, Erik Olin. 1978. *Class, Crisis and the State*. New York: Verso.

———. 1997 (1985). *Classes*. New York: Verso.

Wyatt, Andrew. 2005. (Re)Imagining the Indian (Inter)National Economy. *New Political Economy* 10, 2: 1–17.

Wynne, Derek. 1998. *Leisure, Lifestyle and the New Middle Class*. London: Routledge.

Yadav, Yogendra. 1999. The BJP's New Social Bloc: Analysis by CSDS Based on the Electoral Outcome and Findings of a Nationwide Post-election Survey. *Frontline*. November 19.

———. 2004. The Elusive Mandate of 2004. *Economic and Political Weekly* (December 18): 5383–95.

Yadav, Yogendra, and Satish Deshpande. 2006. Wrong Route, Right Direction. *Times of India*. May 31.

Index

---- ❋ ----

Leela Fernandes is associate professor of political science at Rutgers University in New Brunswick, New Jersey. She is the author of *Producing Workers: The Politics of Gender, Class, and Culture in the Calcutta Jute Mills* and *Transforming Feminist Practice: Non-Violence, Social Justice, and the Possibilities of a Spiritualized Feminism.* Her research interests lie at the intersection of the study of culture, gender, and political economy, and she has published on labor, gender, cultural politics, nationalism, human rights, and globalization.